D1474117

Time and Anthony Powell

Time and Anthony Powell

A Critical Study

Robert L. Selig

Rutherford ● Madison ● Teaneck
Fairleigh Dickinson University Press
London and Toronto: Associated University Presses

Associated University Presses
440 Forsgate Drive
Cranbury, NJ 08512

Associated University Presses
25 Sicilian Avenue
London WC1A 2QH, England

Associated University Presses
P.O. Box 39, Clarkson Pstl. Stn.
Mississauga, Ontario
Canada L5J 3X9

The paper used in this publication meets the requirements
of the American National Standard for Permanence of Paper
for Printed Materials Z39.48-1984.

Library of Congress Cataloging-in-Publication Data

Selig, Robert L.
    Time and Anthony Powell: a critical study / Robert L. Selig.
        p.   cm.
    Includes bibliographical references and index.
    ISBN 0-8386-3405-2 (alk. paper)
    1. Powell, Anthony, 1905–   Dance to the music of time.   2. Time
in literature.   I. Title.
PR6031.074D33365   1991
823'.912—dc20   89-46409
                                                           CIP

PRINTED IN THE UNITED STATES OF AMERICA

Contents

Preface

THIS book has one main purpose: to explore Anthony Powell's complex use of time in his masterwork entitled *A Dance to the Music of Time*, or put slightly differently, to investigate the ways that his vast and intricate novel works on the reader's time sense. Although Powell is a great twentieth-century writer, he has yet to receive the detailed critical scrutiny accorded to other major figures of our era. In addition, one basic characteristic has kept *A Dance* from reaching many potential readers who might well enjoy its fascinating breadth: its volumes have their own separate plots and follow one another in sequence, yet each one resists a self-enclosed reading. Newcomers to *A Dance* cannot begin any random volume with ease. Although some of the twelve have highly dramatic plots—*Books Do Furnish a Room*, for example, or *Temporary Kings*—they also form part of a much larger structure. Readers who start this great *roman-fleuve* at a less-than-spectacular place may think it formless and merely anecdotal through a lack of full perspective. This present study may help to ease these problems of sequence by providing detailed discussions of the overall temporal patterns as well as the patterns of each distinct volume. With these in mind, readers may choose any volume that appeals to them as a good point of entry before moving on to the others. Even for those who read *A Dance* straight through or have, in fact, already read it, a study such as this can help them to grasp its almost one million words with a broader sense of the richly ordered whole.

Problems of time and sequence apply to critical studies as well as to works of fiction, to *Time and Anthony Powell* as well as to *A Dance to the Music of Time*. For example, this study's first section consists of a survey of Powell's life and writings, but it skips across *A Dance* itself, reserving full discussion of this twelve-volume work for the subsequent seven chapters—a departure from chronology prompted, of course, by an emphasis on *A Dance* as Powell's supreme masterpiece. Part II takes a systematic and cross-volume look at *A Dance*'s temporal singularities: the subtle and important interplay between the time of the story line and the time of the narrating act, the tendency to merge separate events in a vast web of analogies, and the complex use of time shifts as a means of narrative enrichment. Readers impatient for comment on specific volumes of *A Dance* may conduct their own flash-forward by skipping to Part III—a volume-by-volume discussion of *A*

Dance—before shifting back to the generalized view. Although this study's overall sequence has its own inner logic, readers may freely use it in their own preferred order.

Within Powell's masterpiece itself, time and sequence relate to one another in a paradoxical way. Even if we read his volumes chronologically, we must also reread them or at least rethink them later—this time with a consciousness that cuts across the whole. The ideal reader of *A Dance* should have an ideal memory. To read time's enigmas in *A Dance*'s separate volumes, we need a double vision of events: those that at first look random and then distant interconnections that give retroactive meaning to what once seemed aimless.

Acknowledgments

I wish to thank Purdue University Calumet for making this study possible by the generous granting of one half-sabbatical leave and two Scholarly Research awards.

I am indebted to Anthony Powell for his gracious permission to quote from his letter to me.

I gratefully acknowledge that quotations from the following books by Anthony Powell have been reprinted by permission of William Heinemann Ltd: *A Question of Upbringing* (London: William Heinemann Ltd, 1951; © Anthony Powell, 1951); *The Acceptance World* (London: William Heinemann Ltd, 1955; © Anthony Powell, 1955); *Casanova's Chinese Restaurant* (London: William Heinemann Ltd, 1960; © Anthony Powell, 1960); *The Valley of Bones* (London: William Heinemann Ltd, 1964; © Anthony Powell, 1964); *The Military Philosophers* (London: William Heinemann Ltd, 1968; © Anthony Powell, 1968); *Temporary Kings* (London: William Heinemann Ltd, 1973; © Anthony Powell, 1973); *Hearing Secret Harmonies* (London: William Heinemann Ltd, 1975; © Anthony Powell, 1975).

I wish to express my gratitude to the Center for Research Libraries, Chicago, for the use of their newspaper collection and for their help in tracking down Anthony Powell's book reviews in the *Daily Telegraph*.

Finally, I should like to thank my former student at Purdue University Calumet, Judith Lebryk, for having first aroused my interest in Anthony Powell's novels.

List of Abbreviations of Anthony Powell's Books Cited in This Study

AM   *Afternoon Men* (London: Heinemann, 1952)

AP   *Agents and Patients* (London: Heinemann, 1955)

AW   *The Acceptance World: A Novel* (London: Heinemann, 1955)

BDFR   *Books Do Furnish a Room: A Novel* (London: Heinemann, 1971)

BM   *A Buyer's Market: A Novel* (London: Heinemann, 1952)

CCR   *Casanova's Chinese Restaurant: A Novel* (London: Heinemann, 1960)

FK   *The Fisher King: A Novel* (New York: W. W. Norton, 1986)

FMT   *Faces in My Time*, Vol. 3 of *To Keep the Ball Rolling: The Memoirs of Anthony Powell* (London: Heinemann, 1980)

FVD   *From a View to a Death* (London: Heinemann, 1945)

HSH   *Hearing Secret Harmonies: A Novel* (London: Heinemann, 1975)

HWB   *O, How the Wheel Becomes It!: A Novel* (London: Heinemann, 1983)

IS   *Infants of the Spring*, Vol. 1 of *To Keep the Ball Rolling: The Memoirs of Anthony Powell* (London: Heinemann, 1976)

KO   *The Kindly Ones: A Novel* (London: Heinemann, 1962)

LM   *At Lady Molly's: A Novel* (London: Heinemann, 1957)

MD   *Messengers of Day*, Vol. 2 of *To Keep the Ball Rolling: The Memoirs of Anthony Powell* (London: Heinemann, 1978)

MP   *The Military Philosophers: A Novel* (London: Heinemann, 1968)

QU   *A Question of Upbringing: A Novel* (London: Heinemann, 1951)

SA   *The Soldier's Art: A Novel* (London: Heinemann, 1966)

SAAG   *The Strangers All Are Gone*, Vol 4 of *To Keep the Ball Rolling: The Memoirs of Anthony Powell* (London: Heinemann, 1982)

TK   *Temporary Kings: A Novel* (London: Heinemann, 1973)

LIST OF ABBREVIATIONS

V   *Venusberg* (London: Heinemann, 1955)
VB   *The Valley of Bones: A Novel* (London: Heinemann, 1964)
WBW   *What's Become of Waring* (London: William Heinemann,
           1953)

Part I
Introductory Survey

1

An Introduction to Anthony Powell

NUMEROUS reviewers and critics have recognized Anthony Powell as a major British novelist of the twentieth century, but many literate readers have never discovered him, not even his very finest achievement—*A Dance to the Music of Time*. This twelve-volume sequence traces a colorful group of English acquaintances across a span of many years from 1914 to 1971. The slowly developing narrative centers around life's poignant encounters between friends and lovers who later drift apart and yet keep reencountering each other over numerous unfolding decades as they move through the vicissitudes of marriage, work, aging, and ultimately death. Until the three last volumes, the standard excitements of old-fashioned plots (What will happen next? Will *x* marry *y*? Will *y* murder *z*?) seem far less important than time's slow reshuffling of friends, acquaintances, and lovers in intricate human arabesques. But if long duration is essential to *A Dance*'s basic method, we must allow the work a very long span of reading time to make its pattern clear in an accumulative manner. Those in a hurry will miss the special pleasures achieved by Powell's vast work: a sad yet comic retrospective view of time's surprising changes. In the end, *A Dance* richly rewards a reader's long patience and persistence. By the close of its more than one million words, the work has revealed itself as a worthy successor to the modernist complexities of Conrad and James as well as to Proust's intricate games with time itself.

Because *A Dance* takes the form of a fictional memoir that draws upon details from the author's own experience even while transforming them, some knowledge of Anthony Powell's life can help put the work in context. He has revealed much about himself in a four-volume reminiscence: *To Keep the Ball Rolling: The Memoirs of Anthony Powell* (London: Heinemann, 1976, 1978, 1980, 1982). Anthony Dymoke Powell (pronounced to rhyme with *Lowell*, as in James Russell Lowell) was born in Edwardian London in 1905 to a somewhat nomadic military family. At the time, his father served as army lieutenant; eventually his less than brilliant career took him to the rank of lieutenant colonel. Anthony Powell's mother—the second daughter of a nonpracticing attorney-at-law and former army man—served as a devoted military wife who moved from place to place because of her husband's frequent reassignments. Although the Powells could trace their line back to Welsh kings and princes of the twelfth and thirteenth centuries, the family had gradually declined to a more-or-less land-pinched kind of respectability. On Anthony Powell's maternal side, the Wells-Dymokes of Lincolnshire had no exalted kings or princes in their history but instead had parsons and squires. Like the Powells, however, the Wells-Dymokes lived in rather respectable circumstances, if not in exuberant wealth (IS, 1–40; MD, 28–29). Although, generally speaking, young Powell might qualify by birth as one of the so-called privileged classes, he began pretty much on the fringes. His parents did send him to the rather exclusive Eton, but his father complained frequently about his son's public-school bills. In any case, as a student there, Powell made friends with such literary schoolmates as Henry Yorke (pen name: Henry Green) and Cyril Connolly—early connections to the world of letters (IS, 72–73, 105–7, 119–22). With a certain amount of difficulty, Powell convinced his unenthusiastic father to let him go on to Balliol College, Oxford—another expensive and fairly exclusive place. Once there, he met more of the literary elite—Peter Quennell, Maurice Bowra, and Evelyn Waugh—but Powell himself took a disappointing Third in his history degree (Fourth being the lowest), hardly a brilliant start for a would-be man of letters (IS, 146–47, 158, 160–62, 178–90, 166–68, 196–97).

Through the influence of his father's former staff-captain, now a publisher's director at Duckworth's, Powell became an apprentice of the firm and began to learn the trade. When Lieutenant Colonel Powell declined to buy his son a partnership there, young Powell had to settle for a mere subordinate editorship at rather meager pay. But he sold his first novel to the firm itself, *Afternoon Men* (1931), and also his subsequent one, *Venusberg* (1932). At the height of the depression in 1932, he took a salary cut along with shorter working hours—an involuntary change that allowed more time for writing. During this period he composed more novels that Duckworth also published: *A View to a Death* (1933) and *Agents and Patients* (1936) (IS, 59; MD, 1–14, 22–37, 75–76, 155, 182–87; FMT, 1–2). He married Violet Pakenham at the close of 1934 and resigned his low-paying Duckworth job in 1936 to write scripts at a much higher salary for the so-called "quota quickies"—low-grade motion pictures churned out in Great Britain to fulfill the percentage of British-made films required by protectionism. When his studio allowed his contract to lapse, he sailed to Hollywood with a rather vague lead about movie work there, but no one took him on. At last, back in England, he turned to book reviews—regular assignments for London's *Daily Telegraph* and intermittent ones for *The Spectator*—a common means of day-to-day support among twentieth-century British writers. Amid the distractions of approaching world conflict, Powell's last prewar work of fiction, *What's Become of Waring* (Cassell 1939), sold less well than his earlier books, all moderately successful (FMT, 11–13, 17–18, 34–43, 47, 49–50, 54, 61, 70, 73–75).

World War II opened up a chasm in Powell's career as a writer. From 1939 to 1945, he composed absolutely nothing. Wholly absorbed by the war, he talked his way into the army, first as second lieutenant of a Welsh battalion in training and eventually as liaison officer for allied attachés in London. In spite of his early efforts to plunge into combat, this middle-aged writer remained, in effect, a desk-side warrior (FMT, 92–95, 130–33, 136, 143–44, 145–46, 156–59, 160–70, 176–79). Yet the four-and-a-half-year break in his literary life deepened his prose fiction by increasing an awareness of the transitory nature of all that he had known before the war. His one supreme novel about time's relentless changes still lay ahead.

The demobilized writer began a purely scholarly task for which he had done some reading since 1939 as a mild relief from war: *John Aubrey and His Friends* (1948)—an antiquarian detour that led to the further one of editing Aubrey's *Brief Lives and Other Selected Writings* (1949). Meanwhile Powell increased his literary earnings by book reviews here and there, and in 1947 became chief review-editor for the *Times Literary Supplement* (FMT, 88–89, 193–95, 196, 200–4, 206–8). Near the end of this decade, he came to the most crucial decision in his career as a writer: to return to fiction with a multivolume novel that would take many years to complete. When Heinemann published *A Dance*'s opening volume in 1951, it marked Powell's first prose fiction in twelve full years. A 1953 appointment by Malcom Muggeridge as *Punch*'s literary editor gave Powell further security for his huge novelistic task. But in 1959, after Muggeridge left *Punch*, the magazine dismissed Powell as one of the old regime. With a certain relief at losing this time-consuming position, he returned to book reviewing for the *Daily Telegraph* to supplement his steady (though not best-selling) earnings from the ongoing *Dance* itself. Finally, at the age of sixty-nine, he finished *A Dance* (1975). Still in command of his full creative powers, he has gone on writing since then: a four-volume memoir (1976–82); an amusing light novella, *O, How the Wheel Becomes It!* (1983); and an important one-volume novel, *The Fisher King* (1986). This master of narrative time seems somehow to have extracted from Father Time himself an extension clause for writing.

A knowledge of Powell's other books before and after *A Dance* can give one a sense of his development, especially in his games with time. The writer's first novel, *Afternoon Men* (1931), published at twenty-four, has surprising comic poise, yet its temporal patterns differ from all his later work and particularly from *A Dance* itself. In contrast to that masterpiece of leisurely style, which meanders back and forth in fictional time, the present-obsessed first novel shoots out choppy sentences and succinct bits of dialogue as if from a literary Bren gun. Its brevity resembles Hemingway's famous staccato style yet also seems tinged with Ronald Firbank's witty nonchalance and mocking deadpan terseness:

> They passed two or three cottages and the church. The Goat stood a little way back from the road and had a strip of grass in front of it. Pringle pushed the door open and Harriet and Sophy went in first. The bar was large and fairly crowded. Darts and shove-halfpenny were being played.
> " 'Arlots," said a voice from the other end of the bar as they sat down.
> "Oh no, we're not," said Harriet. "We're nothing of the sort, so just you keep quiet." (AM, 156)

In this chopped-up discourse without any dramatized "I," each sentence breaks off connection with events before and after. This dot-dot-dot narrative disrupts the momentum of accumulated meanings. These discrete, brief segments of narrative suggest a series of temporal pinpoints, of virtually separate instants. In *Afternoon Men* as a whole, even longer sentences tend to split apart into very simple units connected mainly by *ands*—a style analogous to the story line itself. A young man named Atwater cannot seduce an elusive young woman who attracts him, but he sleeps instead with others who do not. When his best friend's mistress gets caught having sex with another man, Atwater then seduces her in secret at the very same moment that his jealous friend resolves to drown himself. But once in the water, the friend quickly changes his mind and decides to go on living after all. These unthinking characters exist just from instant to instant, unlike *A Dance*'s acutely time-conscious beings.

In the wistful yet ironic *Venusberg* (1932), young Powell begins to employ techniques of discourse that reach beyond the moment. In a number of poignant passages, the undramatized narrating voice without any "I" reflects on the past and the future, e.g.: "That night in his bath he had begun to realise that he was going away and would never see her again" (V, 155). As if to accommodate complexities of time, the sentence length and structure assume greater variety than in the first novel. On the level of the story line, too, cross-temporal complications tend to dominate. At the start, the hero, Lushington, loves Lucy, who loves another man who does not love her. On a visit to a musical-comedy-like North European country, Lushington has an affair with an ardent married woman, young Ortrud Mavrin, who fuses past and present by reminding him of Lucy. When stray assassins' bullets kill Ortrud as well as the man adored by Lucy herself, the surviving hero and the languishing English girl are left with one another, but they miss their vanished loves. Even in this youthful novel, one detects early glimmers of time's inexorable changes.

From a View to a Death (1933) pits a man without a past worth mentioning, the fortune-hunting painter, Arthur Zouch (FVD, 24), against respectable country families with no true distinction except in their past (FVD, 8, 14). In this almost Meredithian comedy of manners, Zouch tries to resist all time but the present by blotting out his personal history. He feels moral outrage when the sister of his prey happens to know of an old love affair of his with a somewhat disreputable woman. Soon he succeeds in banishing "from his mind the cavalcade of" models seduced by him. And his "brain" reels in disgusted disbelief when bohemian friends from his past suddenly appear in a nearby country field. As he proposes marriage to the family's younger daughter, he tries to forget his seduction, just the night before, of a young woman staying with the family (FVD, 30–33, 77, 135–36, 138, 142). For the past-enveloped townspeople, activities center around a costume-dress pageant about Charles II, who once chanced to visit this out-of-the-way place (FVD, 55, 135–37). At the novel's climax a time-honored fox hunt kills the man without a past (FVD, 196–201, 204–5, 206). In his case suppression of times gone by becomes absolutely fatal.

Powell's amusing *Agents and Patients* (1936) foreshadows *A Dance*'s use of haphazard meetings and fortuitous reencounters. But unlike *A Dance*'s very broad time span, Powell's fourth novel deals with just a few months, so that its chance encounters and reencounters arise through a continual rushing about of characters from one place to the next—a comic perpetual motion. The plot hinges on the merely chance meeting of Chipchase and Maltravers, two London confidence men, with naive Blore-Smith, a shy young man of sufficient wealth to make a good victim. The three almost converge on a crowded London corner when they all stop to watch an absurd street performer. Only moments later, Chipchase sees young Blore-Smith make a fool of himself in a nearby art gallery by paying lots of money for a very bad painting. Yet even then neither character addresses the other. Shortly afterwards, a full introduction at last takes place, literally by accident: Blore-Smith is struck by Maltravers's car. Maltravers soon persuades the unhurt young man to underwrite a so-called documentary film, and not long after, Blore-Smith begins to pay as well for so-called psychoanalysis by fast-talking Chipchase (AP, 15–16, 18, 21, 23–24, 29–30, 48–51, 66–67). The rest of the plot unfolds through more chance encounters: a meeting on a Paris street with a crazy French marquis, a meeting in Berlin with an eccentric British colonel who had turned up before at the London art gallery and also in a Paris night-club, and the art-gallery owner's airplane descent on the English estate where Maltravers is shooting his fraudulent film (AP, 76–78, 83, 141, 207).

The bustling movement of these human collisions reminds one of films from the 1930s: to take a classic example, the random street encounters in Chaplin's *City Lights* (1931). The novel even gives a self-reflexive wink at its own cinematic methods when Maltravers explains his plan for creating a motion picture: ". . . Once a good situation between a group of suitable people has been discovered"—people who meet by chance—"we collect them together in the same house and await developments, shooting when we think best" (AP, 54). Indeed, he actually films the climax of *Agents and Patients* itself—a movielike scene framed within a fictional motion picture (AP, 204–7). In Powell's twelve-volume masterpiece, however, cinematic movement gives way instead to a very slow pattern of fortuitous encounters and reencounters extending more in time than in space.

Of Powell's prewar novels, the last is the least. *What's Become of Waring* (1936) is a lightweight farce whose exceedingly busy plot overwhelms this author's usual evocativeness and subtlety. Yet this story of a mysterious travel-writer who has plagiarized all his books foreshadows the postwar *Dance* in one brief section. Here we have a beginning exploration of the intricacies of *iterative* tellings—fused single accounts, by a voice with an "I," of often-repeated happenings: "We used to breakfast at about ten. . . ," "We used to go to Sablettes most days," "Now and then droves of sailors loafed along. . . ," "Sometimes a door would open and a being like a decayed housemaid in a brown bathing-dress would look out for a moment. . . ," " 'It gets me down,' Eustace used to say, 'having to tramp past these cat-houses. . . ,' " "We usually drank a white burgundy. . . ," "He reported always that he was making good progress," "He used always to read in bed before going to sleep" (WBW, 149, 150, 151, 152, 154). Later, this bemused fascination with time's repetitions assumes enormous importance in the overall scheme of *A Dance*.

After his quarter century of work on *A Dance* itself, Powell's later books have continued his exploration of time's complex patterns. In a rather playful way, the temporal structure of his four-volume memoir, *To Keep the Ball Rolling* (1976, 1978, 1980, 1982), recalls *A Dance's* own memoirlike form: flashbacks and flash-forwards about friends and acquaintances, strung onto a chronological thread of autobiography or pseudoautobiography. If life imitates art, Powell's four-volume real-life autobiography imitates his twelve-volume fictional one. But the differences remain even more important than these surface similarities. The actual memoir is very loosely structured. As it moves back and forth across the years, its separate little anecdotes lack the vast interactions of *A Dance*'s convoluted text. To give a very obvious example of this contrast, *A Dance* begins and ends by alluding to Poussin's great painting from which the novel draws its title (QU, 2; HSH, 272), but the memoir starts with the author's genealogy and ends with speculations about Shakespeare's sexual life (IS, 1–40; SAAG, 196–200)—two entirely unconnected things. The novel provides the reader with subtle and intricate patterns over a long duration, but the memoir ambles through numerous years with a loosely anecdotal insouciance.

Although Powell's first fiction after *A Dance* was a rather light novella titled *O, How the Wheel Becomes It!* (1983), it continued to work with complexities of time's interactions. This comic tale hinges upon a single minor incident from the distant 1920s in the life of the literary critic, Shadbold, now an elderly man of letters in the early 1970s. On a walk with a secretly resented old friend—Cedric Winterwade—Shadbold encounters a fashion-model beauty, Isolde Upjohn, who had rebuffed his "hopeless" love. This event reemerges almost half a century later with a twist of new disclosure from Winterwade's diary: Isolde and Winterwade had concealed their preacquaintance and slipped off soon to Paris for a sexual liaison. In an effort to suppress this old erotic defeat, Shadbold keeps an editor from publishing the diary. Yet the past erupts anyway, like a disobliging jack-in-the-box. In a television taping of an interview with Shadbold and also Isolde, the old events burst out again. A month or so later, they finally reappear in a most humiliating way: a maliciously edited tape exposes Shadbold's jealousy in a very unflattering light to an army of viewers (HWB, 17–19, 31–35, 98, 103–5, 123–24). In this tale of distant yet intersecting years, the past will not stay buried.

Finally, Powell's impressive *The Fisher King* (1986) is a sad yet comic novel with complexities of time and of telling in a game of narrative absence and presence that recalls *A Dance* itself. In the nature of things, fictional presence always remains an illusion evoked by language, but *The Fisher King* goes out of its way to complicate and distance our sense of this presence. The story of how the crippled and impotent Saul Henchman, a famous photographer, loses his beautiful companion and helper—Miss Barberina Rookwood, a former ballet star—emerges from a tangle of recountings within recountings, intri-

cate webs of telling distanced from events by elusive gaps in time as
well as by repeated retellings of the original actions. The main narrating source, one Valentine Beals, sailed on the cruise ship where the
story unfolded. He has described it ever since to many different
listeners, developing and rethinking his account along the way. But he
does not tell it to us directly, for we receive the tale from an undramatized voice without any "I"—a self-effacing narrator who fuses
into a single whole Beals's oft-repeated tellings. Specific frequency
markers keep reminding us throughout of the many times that Beals
has recounted these events: "Beals tended to ruminate a moment on
that question," ". . . Beals was always at pains to insist. . . ," "He
used to mull it over," "Beals often reiterated. . . ," ". . . Beals used to
say. . . ," "In the end Beals always returned to his original conten-
tion," "Beals used to employ a whole series of metaphors. . . ,"
"Beals used to say . . ." (FK, 31, 52, 103, 104, 108, 111, 188, 233).

Although the story line unfolds in only a few days during 1979 or
later, the narrating chain stretches over an indeterminate span of at
least two years.[1] At each subsequent recounting, the story's events slip
further and further from the present. Yet some of Beals's telling takes
place on the cruise itself, as voices of fellow passengers occasionally
break in with comments, on shipboard or even later, often to protest
Beals's fanciful linkage of Henchman with the Fisher King of
Arthurian romance and *The Waste Land*. Although the voice that
speaks to us quotes at times directly from Beals's own speeches, we are
usually distanced from events by second-, third-, or even fourth-hand
tellings. In spite of these folds within narrating folds, the novel's
splendid climax—Barberina Rookwood's return to ballet, which she
had renounced for Henchman (FK, 208–13)—bursts vividly forth
with a strong sense of presence, like a pea revealed in an old fictional
shell game, now you see it, now you don't: the very same mastery of
absence and presence that Powell revealed in *A Dance* itself. Having
completed our survey of Powell's life and work, we can now begin to
explore in full the fascinating complexities of *A Dance to the Music of
Time*—his one supreme masterpiece.

Part II
The Narrative Uses of Time

2

Narrative Open-Endedness and Closure

Instance of Narrating and Time of the Story Line

On the very first page of *A Dance to the Music of Time*, a first-person voice speaks to us from unknown period and describes street workmen in an also unknown period as they move around their coke-bucket fire with weather-chilled gestures—gestures that remind the narrator of Poussin's great painting with the very same name as the novel that we have just begun to read. When we finally have finished this vast twelve-volume work, we still remain unsure of the temporal position of the opening scene or of the voice that has described it to us. One or two hasty critics have asserted that the closing pages of *A Dance* return us to the first scene of the workmen around their fire—now supposedly dated as 1971, some fifty years after most of the events of volume one. Thus, according to these critics, all of Powell's novel except the beginning and the end stands as one huge flashback of some three thousand pages.[1] But these critics have overlooked textual details that nullify their theory of a million-word flashback. Time in *A Dance* works differently than in their account, as a single complex sequence will illustrate.

If the opening of volume one links up with the final pages of volume twelve, the start of volume two—*A Buyer's Market*—also connects itself with the close of the final volume. The narrator lays down a strand of this string in the second volume's opening sentence: "The last time I saw any examples of Mr. Deacon's work was at a sale, held obscurely in the neighborhood of Euston Road, many years after his death" (BM, 1). Putting aside until later the significance of Deacon's paintings within the entire novel, we find toward the end of volume twelve—*Hearing Secret Harmonies*—that the narrator-character Nicholas Jenkins sees "examples of Mr. Deacon's work" at a much later period than in volume two. We can date the first Deacon sale as approximately 1945 because in *Hearing Secret Harmonies* the narrator recalls it as having taken place "just after the second war" (HSH, 246). This postwar event occurs at a humble auction hall. Mr. Deacon's four canvases stand "grouped" around a washstand—one upside down—amid a jumble of rolled linoleum, a battered old typewriter, used luggage cases, and other scattered merchandise. In an era when Deacon's representational art on Greek and Roman subjects seems little more than a pseudo-pre-Raphaelite anachronism, the narrator naturally expects never to see any more of the dead man's paintings (BM, 1–3). Yet in volume twelve he describes at some length the surprising revival of this long-forgotten artist—the Deacon Centenary Exhibition—which we can date from internal references throughout this volume as autumn 1971 (HSH, 245–52). Could the very same narrator in the earlier *A Buyer's Market* have somehow forgotten the resurrection of Deacon's buried art—a highly vivid event? Volume twelve eliminates this unlikely possibility, for after its narrator remembers having "watched four Deacons knocked down for a few pounds in a shabby saleroom between Euston Road and Camden Town," he explicitly adds that "at the time, I had supposed those to be the last Deacons I should ever set eyes on" (HSH, 246). Only if the time of narrating at the start of volume two preceded the late autumn of 1971 and the Deacon exhibition, could the voice of this volume say that he never again saw any Deacon paintings. In short, the instance of narrating in the second volume must occur earlier than that in the twelfth.[2] This shift in narrating instances from a very early volume to the final one plays havoc with the assumption that the voice at the start of *A Dance* speaks from the same time as the voice at its conclusion.[3]

Let us consider the problem more directly: the times of the story line and the instances of narrating in the street worker episodes at the start and close of *A Dance*. First of all, we must reject the suggestion that these similar happenings are a mere single event recounted in two places (although many genuine examples do appear throughout *A Dance* of what Genette has labeled *repeating* narrative, as discussed in my third chapter). As we have already shown, the narrating instance at the start of volume two lies somewhere between approximately 1945 and late autumn 1971; and we can deduce, without the shadow of a doubt, that the instance of narrating in volume one's opening pages cannot occur later than the voice in the second volume. By an axiomatic rule of written narratives, when a single voice recounts a whole story line throughout an entire work (in *A Dance*'s case, Jenkins's first-person telling), any passage appearing on a previous line or page must have either an identical narrating instance or an earlier one. The identical instance has a paradoxical yet very common effect that Genette has described in lovely Proustian phrases as "a moment brief as a flash of lightening," "a minute freed from" time.[4] The earlier instance has a less common effect exemplified by Sterne's *Tristram*

Shandy and Ford's *The Good Soldier.* No indication of a narrating lag appears between the first page of *A Question of Upbringing* and page one of *A Buyer's Market,* so that we may, if we wish, consider them as parts of a seamless narrating unity—a unity in which time has become unmeasurable or perhaps merely beside the point, even though 231 pages separate the two. As we have seen, however, a narrating lag does exist in the telling between the first page of *A Buyer's Market* and the close of the final volume—a lag that may take in some forty odd years or maybe simply a week, a day, or only several hours. Although we cannot determine specifically just where this lag enters in any single volume running from two through twelve, in the voids between each volume, or even in spaces between the fifty odd chapters or the white blank lines between separated paragraphs, we can assert absolutely that the instance of narrating at the very start of *A Dance* (the street workmen episode) occurs before the narrating moment or instance of the street-repair incident in *A Dance*'s closing pages. What does this fact tell us about the story-line times of these two different episodes at the beginning and the end of Powell's huge novel?

By a further narrative axiom arising from the way that verbs work within the English language and in most other languages as well, a narrating instance in the past tense (or preterite) must occur after or in unison with the story line that it itself relates. With a first-person actor-narrator, used throughout *A Dance*, the past tense can suggest an interval that may vary from a few ticking seconds to countless vast aeons.[5] Thus the narrating instance of *A Dance*'s first passage takes place after the described events, and the narrating instance of *A Dance*'s final pages occurs after the happenings that it itself depicts. Consequently, the story-line time of street repair number one (before the exhibition) has to come earlier than the story-line time of street repair number two (during the exhibition) at the close of volume twelve: Q.E.D.

One can easily see how the critics might confuse the two events. Both involve strikingly similar details yet ones that remain common enough in a modern big city whose many square miles of roadways and walkways must often be repaired or conversely broken into for fixing pipes and drains:

> The men at work at the corner of the street had made a kind of camp for themselves, where, marked out by tripods hung with red hurricane-lamps, an abyss in the road led down to a network of subterranean drain-pipes. Gathered round the bucket of coke that burned in front of the shelter, several figures were swinging arms against bodies and rubbing hands together with large, pantomimic gestures: like comedians giving formal expression to the concept of extreme cold. One of them, a spare fellow in

blue overalls, taller than the rest, with a jocular demeanour and long, pointed nose like that of a Shakespearian clown, suddenly stepped forward, and, as if performing a rite, cast some substance—apparently the remains of two kippers, loosely wrapped in newspaper—on the bright coals of the fire, causing flames to leap fiercely upward, smoke curling about in eddies of the north-east wind. As the dark fumes floated above the houses, snow began to fall gently from a dull sky, each flake giving a small hiss as it reached the bucket. The flames died down again; and the men, as if required observances were for the moment at an end, all turned away from the fire, lowering themselves laboriously into the pit, or withdrawing to the shadows of their tarpaulin shelter. The grey, undecided flakes continued to come down, though not heavily, while a harsh odour, bitter and gaseous, penetrated the air. The day was drawing in. (QU, 1)

It was rather late in the afternoon when I finally reached the place, a newly painted exterior, the street in process of being rebuilt, the road up. . . . (HSH, 246)

It was getting dark outside, and much colder. A snowflake fell. At first that seemed a chance descent. Now others followed in a leisurely way. The men taking up the road in front of the gallery were preparing to knock off work. Some of them were gathering round their fire-bucket. (HSH, 271)

These passages from volumes one and twelve certainly have striking points in common: (1) In both we find repairmen working on a roadway: in *A Question of Upbringing*, to repair drain-pipes (some lower themselves into the pit to get at these pipes), though perhaps as part of a general road repair; in *Hearing Secret Harmonies*, explicitly to rebuild a whole street. (2) In subsequent actions within *A Question*'s opening paragraph, the men gather round a coke-bucket fire and gesture to warm themselves, and one of them throws kipper scraps and paper onto the coals, which burst into smoking flames; in *Harmonies*, some workmen merely begin to leave while others cluster around their glowing coke-bucket. (3) In volume one, as day ends, light snow flutters down; in volume twelve, it also gets dark as snow begins a leisurely fall. As for the location, however, the details provided do not necessarily match from one volume to the other: in *A Question*, "at the corner of the street"; in *Harmonies*, "in front of the gallery," with no indication at all that the gallery sits on a corner. Indeed, volume one's description as a whole offers far greater specificity than does that in volume twelve. If we did not know the time lag in the story line from the first episode to the second, we would say that the two had very close resemblances or were perhaps the same. But because of that lag, we can assert that the second episode returns us to the first only by analogy—not by repeating the identical event. As we shall see in our third chapter, numerous other analogous occurrences play central roles in *A Dance*'s vast textual network.

I have given much space to the story-line times and the narrating instances at the start and close of *A Dance* to establish a point of departure for the rest of our analysis. If the hundreds of thousands of words in this very long novel do not form a single flashback, what, then, do they form? What is its temporal structure? *A Dance* has, in fact, an open-ended time scheme, complicated and enriched by subtle interrelations of the instances of telling and the story-line times. Although this is essentially a novel of memory, the narrator cannot recall events that have yet to happen as the story keeps unrolling into the narrator's future. This intricate temporal pattern running throughout *A Dance* deserves close attention.

Author, Reader, and Sequence Novel

Let us venture briefly away from the novel itself and into the realms of time that lie beyond the text: time of the writer, time of the reader, and time of publication. We may enrich our understanding of *A Dance*'s overall method by some knowledge of its genesis: how Powell wrote it book by book and year by year, how Heinemann published it book by book and year by year, and how many readers in England and abroad went through it in this very same way—part by part from 1951 through its final volume in 1975. At some point before 1951, Powell began to work on this multisequence novel: as he himself put it, a project "of a fairly large number of volumes, just how many could not be decided at the outset" (FMT, 212). Quite early in the creation of the sequence, Powell's publisher declared that it would run to just six volumes—half its ultimate length.[6] And internal details suggest that Powell may have planned it only through World War II, instead of taking it, as he ultimately did, up to 1971. In any event, he hammered out the sequence of *A Dance* over a quarter of a century. It took him on average slightly over two years to complete each volume and see it into print, though the time could vary from as little as one to as many as four whole years. In any case, during its very long gestation, *A Dance* remained open-ended in the strictest sense of the term.

Both internal and external evidence suggests that Powell began *A Dance* with a flexible overall plan—one that allowed for mid-course changes and later inspirations. As he himself has explained in a note to the present writer, "one of the techniques necessary in a novel of this kind is to leave wide open a great many cards of reentry, which may or may not have to be used."[7] The card metaphor aptly conveys the kind of fictional game that Powell undertook in *A Dance*. Games always involve self-imposed limits. Because *A Dance* appeared from year to year, its author adhered to a fundamental rule about his creative options. If required by the plot or the pattern, he could modify the account of an incident already given in an earlier published volume only by returning to that incident within some later volume and by adding fresh details. He could not change an incident itself within a volume already in print: such events must remain frozen within the textual past.[8]

One small web of interconnecting plot will illustrate how Powell works within his special ground rules: open-endedness for the future volumes but closed-book permanence for the already published ones. On pages 226 and 227 of *A Buyer's Market* (volume two of *A Dance*), six- or seven-year-old Pamela Flitton falls "sick" at Stringham's wedding. According to the *Oxford English Dictionary, sick* in British means "having an inclination to vomit, or being actually in the condition of vomiting," in contrast to American English in which it simply means "ill"—itself a seventeenth-century British usage.[9] Yet, although she feels like vomiting, the scene in volume two fails to describe explicitly what happens as a result. Does she actually, as Americans would say, throw up, or does her church-service nausea harmlessly subside without active illness. It hardly seems surprising that *A Buyer's Market* omits these details, for at this point in *A Dance*, Pam remains an extremely minor character, having appeared only this once. In any event, on page 48 of *Books Do Furnish a Room* (volume ten), we read that little Pamela had actually vomited into the church's font. And on page 82 of *Books*, Pamela's history repeats itself with a comic variation when she is sick in the Tollands' five-foot-high oriental vessel—a joke extending over some quarter century of story-line time and some eighteen hundred pages. A reference in volume nine, however—*The Military Philosophers*—serves as a way station between these widely separated events:

> This was Stringham's niece. I remembered her holding the bride's train at his wedding. She must have been five or six years old then. At one stage of the service there had been a disturbance at the back of the church and someone afterwards said she had been sick in the font. Whoever had remarked that had found nothing surprising in unsatisfactory behaviour from her. Someone else had commented: "That child's a fiend." (MP, 58)

We cannot know directly the author's inner processes. Even the writer himself cannot tell us with any certainty, for much of creation takes place in the unconscious, and even some conscious acts may later slip back into an unconscious realm. Yet we can make some sagacious conjectures about Powell's procedures here. He appears to have introduced little Pamela into volume two without specific awareness that he later would employ her in volume ten's comic scene—her vomiting into the vase. We can deduce this creative sequence from the absence in volume two of any passage where Pamela is sick into the font—a childhood scene needed to prepare the reader for the greatly delayed comic variation. Subsequent at least to volume two's publication and perhaps much later, it appears to have occurred to Powell that Pam could fall sick first in a sacred basin and then long afterward in a purely secular vessel—a decorative object, made temporarily less aesthetic by Pamela's desperate remedy. In order to unify the two distant scenes, Powell in volumes nine and ten creates the illusion that he actually and specifically described her as vomiting into the church font towards the end of *A Buyer's Market*. (This particular reader had to reread the first passage in order to make sure that Powell had not provided any such description.) We might also note the artful vagueness in both volumes nine and ten: ". . . someone afterwards said . . ." (MP, 58); "Someone else had commented: 'That child's a fiend'" (MP, 58); ". . . so it was alleged, causing herself to be lifted in order to be sick into the font. 'That little girl's a fiend,' someone had remarked afterwards at the reception" (BDFR, 48). In *The Military Philosophers* an unidentified observer describes Pam's desecration of the font, and another unnamed person remarks about her fiendishness. In *Books* the explicit assertion that she wished to pollute the basin is related in the form of the mere passive voice, so that no one appears to do the asserting. The added details in volumes nine and ten are imprecise enough to blend with the reader's memory of the earlier volume's scene yet precise enough for him to insert them in memory's blank spaces.

We can make broader surmises about Powell's open-ended use of Pamela Flitton. In the later volumes she takes center stage as a gorgeous but angry femme fatale, an oxymoronic nymphomaniac suffering from frigidity, an explosive human bomb of feminine contradictions, resentments, and yearnings. Yet in her walk-on role within the second volume, Powell omits a description of her manner and appearance except for one adjective—"little" (BM, 226). If, at the time of writing volume two, he had already planned her later spectacular developments, he would have depicted her explicitly, one supposes, as a pretty little six- or seven-year-old with a devilish look in her eyes.

If we switch our perspective from the writer to the reader, we can trace in the Pamela sequence the peculiar way that we must read an open-ended and multivolumed text. We might note, first of all, a curious general distinction about the position in time of various readers of a work like *A Dance*. A person who read of Pamela in *A Buyer's*

Market (volume two) when it first appeared in print (1952) viewed the scene differently than someone who perused it after all of *A Dance* had appeared (1975). Although both readers had to consider the possibility that the sick child Pamela provided merely local color and might never appear again, the 1952 reader faced far more uncertainty: *A Dance* itself might never proceed beyond this second volume. The author could become uninterested in the sequence and turn to other novels, or he could die before completing any more volumes, eliminating, all at once, writer and future text.

From 1975 onward, the reader of *A Dance* still faces a certain open-endedness but one now bound within a completed sequence. This peruser of an already finished work can note the specifics of little Pamela's sickness as anticipating either something or nothing—alternatives to be definitely settled at some later point in the multivolumed novel. When he encounters the Pamela passage within volume two, this reader may consider it mere illustrative detail in support of the narrator's disenchanted generalization: "Weddings are notoriously depressing affairs" (BM, 226). When *The Military Philosophers* recalls and expands on Pamela's girlhood sickness, this very same reader may see it as a device simply for linking the beautiful woman with the child of volume two. When the reader encounters this anecdote again in *Books Do Furnish a Room*, he interprets it now in the context of a vastly expanded knowledge of her explosive temperament—a psychosomatic equivalent of spiritual retching, a desire to do dirt on the people around her. And at last in the same volume, when Pamela vomits gracefully into the huge upright vase, the reader gets a shock of comic recognition, for Pamela's history has repeated itself as a witty variation on an earlier event.

The process of reading this single Pamela sequence can go beyond this point. One can complete all twelve volumes, return to the beginning, and begin another perusal of *A Dance*. In the story of Pam's sickness, one can now read time backwards. In *A Buyer's Market* one can perceive her bridesmaid nausea in context of volumes nine and ten and can fill in blank details. One can now see volume two's vaguely described sickness as the little child's fiendish retching in the font and, even more importantly, as the comic counterpart of her subsequent misadventure with the great Tolland vase. On this second reading, one can do even more than observe time backwards: one can simultaneously also read it forwards. One can reenact a former ignorance of the network of later incidents. One can, in short, combine a godlike awareness of the fictional future with a human ability to read the tale sequentially, scene by scene and page by page.

Powell's method of building upon already published episodes has obvious affinities with the usual practice of Victorian novelists such as Dickens, George Eliot, and Thackeray. As is well known, Dickens published his novels in either monthly or weekly parts while he still worked on the whole, so that earlier episodes became fixed and frozen long before he had completed the story.[10] Dickens sometimes changed the plan of his story midway through publication in order to bolster sales or mollify his readers. Consider, for example, the case of *Martin Chuzzlewit,* when he sent his hero off to America to renew reader interest. In an era with a vastly different writer-reader relationship, Powell appears to have remained essentially unaffected by audience desires and whims. In addition, Dickens serialized on a much smaller scale than Powell and over a much shorter time span for the whole writing process. And while Dickens insisted on a melodramatic web of contrived interconnections, Powell's pattern takes a far subtler form— one lending itself better to second thoughts and subsequent reconsiderations.[11]

So-called "sequence novels" in general stand closer than Dickens to Powell's basic method.[12] We might note, however, that such a string of novels in its most common form tends to break up into independent units that we can read in any order or even in isolation. Trollope's Barchester novels, for example—*The Warden* (1855), *Barchester Towers* (1857), *Doctor Thorne* (1858), *Framley Parsonage* (1861), *The Small House at Allington* (1864), and *The Last Chronicle of Barset* (1867)— deal with a single geographical setting and reuse various characters from one book to the next; but each book in itself has an old-fashioned, well-plotted structure, and the sequence taken together can hardly be considered a single unified novel. To cite a variant example, the three volumes of Galsworthy's *The Forsyte Saga* (1906, 1920, 1921) all flow from Soames's "rape" of his wife in the very first volume. As a result, the whole sequence has a well-plotted structure far more old fashioned than that of *A Dance.* Ford Madox Ford's *Parade's End* (1924, 1925, 1926, 1928), centering on World War I, presents a closer analogy to Powell (especially his volumes on World War II), although Ford's work keeps to a much smaller scale than Powell's and also lacks its persistent and unifying pattern. The one "sequence novel" contemporary with Powell's to which it has been most often compared—C. P. Snow's *Strangers and Brothers* (1940, 1947, 1949, 1951, 1954, 1956, 1958,1960, 1964, 1968, 1970)—is actually a wholly different kind of fiction. Snow constructs his individual volumes in a foursquare way around traditional plot devices such as the outcome of a trial, but he does not achieve a pattern of significant interconnections from one book to the next. For a close analogue to *A Dance to the Music of Time,* one must look elsewhere than at C. P. Snow's unflowing *roman-fleuve.*

In the fictional handling of time throughout his vast twelve-volume narrative, Powell's master was, of course, Marcel Proust. Critics have noted, yet also minimized, the relationship of *A Dance* to *A la recherche du temps perdu*—a very important relationship in spite of cultural and temperamental differences between the two writers.[13] As Powell himself tells us, he read half of *A la recherche* at Oxford (1923–26) and frequently discussed it with his friend Henry Yorke (pen name: Henry Green). Powell finished Proust's masterpiece sometime after the appearance of its final volume in 1927 (MD, 115). In any case, volume nine of *A Dance*, *The Military Philosophers*, pays explicit homage to Proust. Jenkins reads *A la recherche* in wartime London (MP, 69); is greatly moved in liberated France by a visit to the model for Proustian Balbec, Cabourg (MP, 167–68); and, most surprisingly of all, reads a page-and-a-half imitation of *A la recherche* itself, concocted in English by Anthony Powell (MP, 119–21).

Powell seems to owe to Proust the curious technique of what Genette has called *pseudo-iterative* narrative—describing some event as happening habitually, although it has too much uniqueness to have happened more than once. We can illustrate this by choosing at random from hundreds of such passages throughout *A Dance*: " 'Coming to sit with the Regiment tonight, Captain Gwatkin,' Bithel would say when he joined us; then add in his muttered, confidential tone: 'Between you and me, they're not much of a crowd on this course. Pretty second-rate' " (VB, 199).[14] Even more importantly, Powell moves a step beyond a purely *iterative* narrative by presenting events that resemble one another but remain distinct and apart—a technique of analogy especially well suited to his open-ended method: developing variations on what has gone before but has already been frozen in print. The two street workmen episodes that we have previously examined are examples of such analogous events—a central structural principle of *A Dance*.

One fundamental difference exists between the genesis of *A Dance* and *A la recherche*. Proust created his novel in anything but an open-ended way. Instead he used a method reminiscent of that of Edgar Allan Poe, who set up the tricky puzzles of his stories by writing the endings first. Proust did not quite write his end before his beginning, but he did compose the concluding pages of his very last volume— with its quasi-mystical vision of time's recoverability—during the same period when he also was writing in *Du côte de chez Swann* (volume one) of his hero's frustrated search for the answer to time's riddle.[15] Powell, by contrast, in his note to me explicitly insists that "I was not writing a detective story. . . ." He adds that "obviously, as one progresses, an increasing amount of back material comes into play, which the author did not know was relevant, any more than it would have been known in real life. . . ."[16] In short, the steps of Powell's dance to time do gradually assume a unified pattern but one that he could not wholly foresee when he started to write his work.

Open-Endedness Versus Closure

What then are the overall effects of this tension in *A Dance* between its open-ended tendency and the pattern of closure that the completed work finally offers to the reader? The entire work represents the attempt by the narrator, Nicholas Jenkins, to find just such a pattern in the interweaving relations of his friends, lovers, and acquaintances over some fifty years. But, at least in the early volumes, the actor-character Jenkins cannot perceive clearly life's web of interconnections simply because he lacks adequate experience in his still brief span of years. At this point the narrator sees a great deal more than young Jenkins does.

With this gap between character and narrator, a continual tension develops in the text between open-endedness and closure. To start with an important strand from volume one, Jenkins's best friend, Stringham—a man with a witty and exuberant tongue—breaks a dinner appointment with Jenkins, but Nicholas can make out little more at the moment than that "this parting was one of those final things that happen recurrently, as time passes: until at last they may be recognised fairly easily as the close of a period. This was the last I should see of Stringham for a long time" (QU, 229). Indeed, the actor-character Jenkins at the end of volume one lacks the wisdom of the narrator at the start of this same volume, who applies to life itself and to life within the novel the dance metaphor from Poussin: ". . . partners disappear only to reappear again, once more giving pattern to the spectacle . . ." (QU, 2). In other words, young Jenkins sees his break with Stringham as the close of an era, but the older narrator perceives such human disengagements as part of a larger pattern of departures and reinsertions.

Like most of the other characters within *A Dance*, Stringham reappears in seemingly random encounters. In *A Buyer's Market* Jenkins runs into a strikingly older and more reserved Stringham in a London coffee stall and accompanies him to a rather wild party (BM, 92–148), meets him shortly afterward at Sir Magnus Donners's mansion (BM, 187), and a few months later attends Stringham's depressing wedding (BM, 224 26). In *The Acceptance World* some four or five years afterwards, Jenkins finds Stringham at a public school reunion, now fallen into chronic drunkenness, although still funny and even quite endearing (AW, 184–209). In *Casanova's Chinese Restaurant* about two years later, an intoxicated Stringham escapes temporarily from a self-appointed keeper and appears at a party given for Jenkins's best friend of the moment, the composer Hugh Moreland—also a witty conversationalist. Stringham delights Moreland with a humorous flow of speech, so that Jenkins feels surprised at the absolute triumph of one talker over the other. Nick speculates that the two would not remain friendly in any extended relationship, yet he finds them alike in spite of differing backgrounds and interests (CCR, 161–85). During the scene itself, however, Nick does not enunciate the specific characteristic that the two men have in common. Some twenty-three years later, though, in *Temporary Kings* after Jenkins's final meeting with the now dying Moreland (Stringham has died some fifteen years earlier), the narrator sums up Moreland's appeal for him and, by implicit analogy, that of Stringham: "It was . . . the last time I had, with anyone, the sort of talk we used to have together" (TK, 276). An amicable exuberance of humorous talk makes Moreland and Stringham both very delightful friends.

Yet a special sadness colors Nick's later relationship with Stringham. When Nicholas encounters his former friend in the wartime British army about five years after their volume five meeting, Jenkins is a second-lieutenant and ex-drunkard Stringham is a mere mess-hall waiter who shies away from resuming their old friendship because of a wish to stick to his own humble ranks (SA, 75–78). Although Stringham remains a beguiling human being, he goes to his wartime death without any renewing of his closeness to Jenkins (TK, 208–9). If Nick's relationship with Moreland, the rival great talker, also ends sadly with Moreland's later death, it serves nevertheless for much of *A Dance* as a consolation prize for the loss of Stringham. Toward the end of the novel, though, this consolation is vitiated by a very bitter twist. One of the few of Jenkins's schoolmates to survive till almost the end and to remain in touch with him is detestable Kenneth Widmerpool— a master of pomposity and boring human speech and the man responsible, at least indirectly, for Stringham's having died. This striking example of life's little ironies has caused many critics to see Widmerpool as *A Dance*'s central figure.[17] Powell's grotesque opportunist does, indeed, dominate a number of the volumes, including the very last, yet certainly not as a hero and perhaps not even as an out-and-out villain but rather as a human disaster. His obnoxious persistence throughout the long narrative well illustrates a dismaying social truism: worthwhile human beings whom we love and respect often drop out of our lives, but despicable persons can cling to us like leeches. In his role as a character in the story that he tells, Jenkins himself perceives at least part of this general rule as early as volume two:

> He [Widmerpool] was merely one single instance, among many, of the fact that certain acquaintances remain firmly fixed within this or that person's particular orbit; a law which seems to lead inexorably to the conclusion that the often repeated saying that people can "choose their friends" is true only in a most strictly limited degree. (BM, 126–27)

The youthful Jenkins cannot, however, perceive the positive side of the law. If people whom we love often vanish from our lives, the dance of time may restore them to us later or provide us with substitutes who share the very qualities that made us love the others. The Jenkins-Stringham-Moreland link can stand as a paradigm for the web of human connections running through the work from beginning to end. Although the narrator's opening evocation of Poussin's great painting, *A Dance to the Music of Time*, hints at the later pattern of recurring relationships, Jenkins, the actor-character, does not wholly comprehend it until the final volumes.

As always in fiction that uses an autobiographical "I," the actor-character is separated most sharply in the early parts of the novel from the narrator's wisdom, experience, and age. To take a random example from the very first volume, the narrator comments explicitly on his own greater wisdom compared to his younger self about social criteria for discarding old acquaintances: "Clearly some complicated process of sorting-out was in progress among those who surrounded me: though only years later did I become aware how such voluntary segregations begin to develop; and of how they continue through life" (QU, 69). In the final volume the narrator spells out the broad general principle that allows his aged self much fuller understanding than in his younger days:

> . . . A vantage point gained for acquiring embellishments to narratives that have been unfolding for years beside one's own, trimmings that can even appear to supply the conclusion of a given story, though finality is never certain, a dimension always possible to add. (HSH, 30)

In the *Bildungsroman* tradition to which *A Dance* belongs at least in its early volumes, the actor-character "I" will usually grow so wise by the end of his apprenticeship that he finally matches the narrator's awareness—an awareness present from the start.[18] At the close of *A Dance*, the insights of the character Jenkins have blended with those of the narrator. Yet, as that very same voice also reminds us in the passage quoted above, "finality is never certain," and "a dimension is always possible to add."

In terms of the overall pattern of this novel—one in which friends and lovers join, disjoin, regather by chance and then slip away one by one at last into final friendless death—death itself provides a "dimension" of uncertainty. The last volume's title, *Hearing Secret Harmonies*, serves as a mystical euphemism for death—a circumlocution used first in volume eleven by the psychic Myra Erdleigh:

> "Where, as again Vaughan writes, the liberated soul ascends, looking at the sunset towards the west wind, and hearing secret harmonies. He calls this world, where we are now, an outdoor theatre, in whose wings the Dead wait their cue for return to the stage. . . ." (TK, 246)[19]

In effect, Mrs. Erdleigh explains death away as a state where friends and lovers can finally perceive a magical web of human interconnectedness before undergoing a reincarnation back to the realm of time. Throughout *A Dance*, however, the narrator handles such occult propositions with a seriocomic blend of respect and ridicule. The question of whether the human personality vanishes with death remains open-ended—a point on which the character Jenkins and also the wise narrator lack final certainty even at the close.

3

Frequency, Analogy, and Eternal Recurrences

Iterative Narrative

POWELL often uses a Proustian device that plays odd tricks with time: a technique that Genette calls *iterative* narrative, of telling only once what has happened more than once, of merging repeated events into a single recounting.[1] More than two hundred pages throughout *A Dance* contain *iterative* passages. A striking example appears at the start of volume three, where the "I" describes in a single concrete narrative his frequent visits at the Ufford to his boring Uncle Giles. The opening sentence quantifies a recurring rhythm in these visits: "perhaps as often as every eighteen months" (AW, 1). Unlike the French language, whose imperfect tense can signify habitual action—a tense well suited to Proust's love affair with the *iterative*—English must make do with auxiliary verbs or adverbial forms to convey such repetitions.[2] Powell sprinkles the first five pages with these frequency markers: "often," "would," "from time to time," "usually," "on most of the occasions," "always," "permanently," "for ever" "eternally," "used invariably to remark," "periodical efforts," "intermittantly," and "sometimes." Although this rather extended *iterative* section cannot match such gargantuan ones as Proust's forty-six pages on the Guermantes' habitual wit,[3] Powell's stress on frequency seems unusual enough for a writer whose language lacks the French imperfect.

The section emphasizes not only the recurrence of the visits themselves but other regularities that inevitably go with them. Giles always sends Jenkins a postcard in rigidly tiny writing, always invites him for Sunday afternoon tea, and always takes it with him in the hotel lounge (AW, 1 and 3). No one else is ever in this lounge, and Giles always makes the identical remark about the lack of people:

> "I think we shall have this place to ourselves," Uncle Giles used invariably to remark, as if we had come there by chance on a specially lucky day, "so that we shall be able to talk over our business without disturbance. Nothing I hate more than having some damn'd fellow listening to every word I say." (AW, 4)

Giles comically ignores the fact that their solitary teas have a stupifying pattern of sameness, just as the Ufford itself seems frozen into
sameness. Its halls and public rooms remain absolutely deserted, and
at the reception desk, "letters in the green baize board criss-crossed
with tape remained yellowing, for ever unclaimed, unread, un-
changed" (AW, 2). Outside walls block the sky from the windows of
the lounge, so that even on sunny days no light breaks through in this
realm "of perpetual night" or "sky for ever dark" (AW, 3). The inner
doors to the lounge remain "permanently closed" (AW, 3), as if sealing
off the place hermetically from the world of time and change. One
small but striking detail underscores the lack of variation in all these
Ufford teas: the lounge clock "stood eternally at twenty minutes past
five" (AW, 4)—tea-time, of course—rather like the frozen six o'clock
time of the mad tea-party in *Alice in Wonderland*.[4] Although Jenkins
tells us that these teas occur about once very eighteen months, he does
not specify the years involved, so that we know the periodicity of these
boring occasions but not their total span. In a curious way, these
separate tea-parties have fused into one that stands beyond time. Even
at unusual moments with Giles at the Ufford when something finally
changes, it changes, in turn, to a new repetitive pattern. Because the
waitress Vera "often" infuriates Giles by trying to seat him elsewhere
than at his favorite table in the wholly empty lounge or because others
on the staff annoy him, he deserts the hotel "from time to time"
during his London stays. Yet, like an absurd human machine, he
returns "sooner or later" to resume his somnolent habits in this palace
of repetition (AW, 2). In a similar way, a brief flash-forward to more
than a decade later forms a humorous variation on the sameness of the
lounge. Nick tells us that he saw the inner doors opened during World
War II and amusingly speculates on a rule of regularity even in this
change: "like the doors of the Temple of Janus, . . . closed only in
time of Peace" (AW, 3). This particular Roman god may have double
relevance in a time-becalmed setting not only as the deity of entrances
but also of beginnings and units of time.

The sleepy *iterative* narrative at the start of volume three introduces
a contrastingly singular scene—one, however, with its own strange
connections to a pattern of repetition. On one "particular occasion" at
the Ufford, a third person—Myra Erdleigh—actually enters the
lounge at tea-time. Nick finds her presence there nearly as uncanny as
"a phantom, a being from another world" (AW, 5–6)—a world, we
might say, of singular events. Amid hints of a sexual relationship
between Giles and herself, she tells his fortune and then that of
Jenkins with a greasy pack of cards. Fortune-telling by cards implies
in itself a pattern of repetition for the whole human race—regularities

corresponding to limited combinations in a deck of fifty-two that are therefore predictable. Mrs. Erdleigh also mentions other recurrences. She "always" uses "the same dear cards," she laid them out for Giles "nearly six months" before (AW, 12), and she promises to encounter Jenkins once again "about a year from now" (AW, 17). And the narrator suggests a dimension of repetition over an endless span of time: "The rite had something solemn about it: something infinitely ancient, as if Mrs. Erdleigh had existed long before the gods we knew, even those belonging to the most distant past" (AW, 12). Even in this singular narrative event, frequency persists as a theme.

Still more oddly, this singular eruption in the Ufford's monotonous limbo repeats itself by analogy in later scenes spread out across *A Dance*. Within the same volume in about the predicted time, Mrs. Erdleigh reemerges as mistress of Jimmy Stripling, another elderly man. She enters in a way that "almost suggested that Stripling was propelling her in front of him like an automaton on castors" (AW, 81)—a whimsical mechanism for a timed reappearance. When she presides over fortune-telling with the use of a planchette, "the writing changed to a small, niggling hand, rather like that of Uncle Giles" (AW, 97)—a further link to the scene at the Ufford. In volume six she reappears at a seaside hotel rather like the Ufford, attends Uncle Giles's funeral, and inherits all his money (KO, 149, 152–53, 195–98, 202–3). Dr. Trelawney's description of her as a reincarnated priestess transcending "the puny fingers of Time" (KO, 196) echoes the narrator's whimsical hint about her preexistence in a long repetitive span. If she shows up in volume nine without an elderly admirer or even a pack of cards, she proceeds during an air raid to tell Pamela Flitton's fortune and also that of Odo Stevens (MP, 129–38)—a recall of her Ufford rites. In her final appearance toward the end of volume eleven, she once again has old Jimmy Stripling in tow, and she again tells fortunes (TK, 241–46, 259–61), as in the Ufford scene. In effect, this chain of analogous events involving Myra Erdleigh emerges from the *iterative* section about monotonous visits to the Ufford.

Other *iterative* passages in *A Dance* have a similar strategy: that is, to describe something as repeating itself over a stretch of time before an eruptive change, a sudden alteration that leads nevertheless to analogous scenes in a new repetitive pattern. In a single *iterative* narrative, for example, volume two describes the repeated frustrations of Jenkins's puppy love for young Barbara Goring. Many frequency markers serve to merge together a span of almost a year: "used to," "as a rule," "often," "always," "fond of remarking," "fairly often," "sometimes," "once in a way," "rare occasions," and "frequently" itself (BM, 21–23). Yet this repetition leads to a very striking occurrence, as Barbara, in the presence of Jenkins and another male suitor, pours sugar over the head of Widmerpool, a third frustrated rival (BM, 21–23). This singular happening resembles, nevertheless, other humiliations undergone by Widmerpool: an overripe banana that strikes him in the face (QU, 10–12), his automobile collision with his employer's outside urn (BM, 216–18), the student assault on him with a pot of red paint and then later with a stink bomb (HSH, 41, 43–46, 112–13), and a string of complex sexual embarrassments. Here, as in the Ufford passage, sameness leads to uniqueness, which in turn leads back to the sameness of repeated similar scenes.

The same pattern emerges from a slightly different form of repeating phenomena toward the close of volume three. This passage presents a single occurrence of Le Bas's Old Boy or school reunion speech as a virtual copy of all his other ones, including a quoted poem. ". . . His accustomed speech . . . varied hardly at all year by year" (AW, 187). "Here Le Bas, as usual, paused . . ." (AW, 188). "This comment always caused a certain amount of mild laughter and applause" (AW, 189). Then an unheard-of event breaks in upon the sameness. A former student despised by Le Bas, the self-important Widmerpool, begins a long and incomprehensible oration without being asked and so discomforts or enrages Le Bas that he has a mild stroke as the whole reunion disperses in disorder (AW, 190–97). Yet what seems to stunned observers just a onetime fiasco recurs by analogy in A Dance's closing volume. At the Magnus Donners Prize dinner, Widmerpool delivers an uninvited speech condemning Donners's capitalism, proclaiming himself as the cuckold described in the Donners Prize biography, and scorning all the decencies. Instead of Le Bas's stroke, a stink bomb attack concludes this second harangue of Widmerpool's (HSH, 107–14). As often in A Dance, the narrator himself comments on the pattern of reoccurrence: "The moment inevitably recalled that when, at a reunion dinner of Le Bas's Old Boys, Widmerpool had risen to give his views on the current financial situation" (HSH, 108). Again we find the same distinctive configuration: a description of a monotonous routine, shifting to an apparently unique occurrence that later repeats itself, though here in a single spectacular analogue.

Volume six contains a more complex example of the way that the narrative moves from habitual events to singular ones, which later assume a place in a network of repetitions. Within the first chapter, three separate *iterative* narratives merge into a climax on one unique afternoon of 1914. A soldier-servant in the Jenkins household, Bracey, has "periodic" days of near-psychotic depression described in a passage with many frequency markers (KO, 12–14). Three later *iterative* pages depict the entanglement of Billson, the housemaid, in a comic love-triangle: she adores the cook, who despises her, and she despises Bracey, who loves her (KO, 15–17). A third, short *iterative* passage describes the ritual joggings of Dr. Trelawney's long-haired mystical cult (KO, 29). These repetitive small lunacies all come together on a day of worldwide insanity. During this calamitous Sunday, Billson sees the mansion's ghost in the very early morning, Bracey suffers from depression, the cook gives his notice in order to marry another woman, the love-sick maid goes crazy and appears stark naked among drawing-room guests, Trelawney's cult comes jogging past the still-disturbed household, and Uncle Giles reports the Sarajevo assassination that leads to World War I (KO, 42–46, 49–50, 57–62, 63–66, 68, 69–70). Yet this clearly unique day has subtle interconnections with later analogous happenings. As World War II approaches, the jealous Betty Templer has a nervous breakdown very much like Billson's (KO, 118–22, 132–33), and Dr. Trelawney turns up again just before war's new outbreak (KO, 183–98). Billson's crazy nakedness repeats itself when the naked Pamela Flitton stalks Professor Gwinnett (TK, 192–95). And the association of lunacy and jogging reoccurs with the ritual naked run of Murtlock's hippie cult, accompanied by the half-crazed Widmerpool (HSH, 210–11, 265–69). Again and again in *A Dance*, the sameness of *iteration* breaks off into apparent uniqueness, but the broad time span of the full twelve volumes reveals similarities with other apparently unique events.

By contrast, a few other *iterative* sections in *A Dance* describe unchanging repetitions without breaking off into sudden uniqueness. In the second volume, for example, two paragraphs tell of elegant Archie Gilbert's perpetual attendance at debutante dances: "never been known to be late," "as usual," "as always," "it always turned out," and "he always gave the impression" (BM, 26–27). When Jenkins reencounters Gilbert nearly two decades later in volume nine, this ghost of dances past discusses former debutantes and calls attention to the marriage notice of one in his unfolded newspaper (MP, 244). Just as in the *iterative* passage on Gilbert, this later description of him shows a person adhering to a single life role in spite of time and change.

Three noteworthy sections in *A Dance* take a subtly different form from any that we have analyzed so far. These variant sections describe events that happened only once but have been told many times. Yet the narrator synthesizes their multiple recountings into his own single discourse. Volume six, for example, presents at some length the often-repeated family tale of the crazy Billson's naked self-display (KO, 55–62). The narrator blends together his own once-for-ever telling with composite direct quotations from his mother's habitual version and even a single sentence from his less-than-eloquent father: " 'She was stark,' he used to say, *'absolutely stark'* " (KO, 60). With a similar technique, the eleventh volume relates the oft-told tale of Trapnel's last stand at the Hero pub, of his buying drinks for everybody, and of his final collapse outside just before his death. The narrator combines his own descriptions of these events with composite direct quotations from the story's habitual teller, the poet Malcolm Crowding, and even composite responses by those who have listened to him over a span of years (TK, 29–35). Something quite similar happens, within the eleventh volume, in the description of how Pamela reveals her husband's shameful secrets. The narrative combines Moreland's frequent retellings with Stevens's apparently single one. Differences in their versions force the narrator to act half like a storyteller and half like a judge, blending his own evaluation with directly quoted speeches, some composite and some singular (TK, 252–66). One striking temporal oddity emerges in these three widely separated *repeating* passages. In each case the original event occurs just once, but the acts of telling become themselves events within the story line—events that keep recurring—and the "I" tries to unite these recurring events into his own singular telling. Here we have a movement from singularity to repetition and back again to singularity—temporal wheels within wheels.

Pseudo-Iterative Narrative

Even more paradoxical than these singularized accounts of oft-told tales is Powell's use of what Genette has labeled *pseudo-iterative* narrative.[5] In its English form this strange aspect of narrative conveys repeated occurrences by such markers as *would, used to,* and *always,* but it presents these events with such rich specifications that no sane reader can believe that they really might recur without notable changes in detail. Although the *pseudo-iterative* passages running throughout *A Dance* lack the lengthy expansion of many in *A la recherche,* Powell employs them strikingly for his own special ends, almost always in connection with dialogue. In volume seven, for instance, the following long flashback blends uniqueness and repetition in an anomalous way:

I tried to feel objective about the whole matter by recalling one of Moreland's favorite themes, the attraction exercised over women by men to whom they can safely feel complete superiority.
"Are you hideous, stunted, mentally arrested, sexually maladjusted,

marked with warts, gross in manner, with a cleft palate and an evil smell?"
Moreland used to say. "Then, oh boy, there's a treat ahead of you. You're
all set for a promising career as a lover. There's an absolutely ravishing girl
round the corner who'll find you irresistible. In fact her knickers are
bursting into flame at this very moment at the mere thought of you."

"But your description does not fit in with most of the lady-killers one
knows. I should have thought they tended to be decidedly good-looking, as
often as not, together with a lot of other useful qualities as well."

"What about Henri Quatre?"

"What about him?"

"He was impotent and he stank. It's in the histories. Yet he is remembered as one of the great lovers of all time."

"He was a king—and a good talker at that. Besides, we don't know him
personally, so it's hard to argue about him."

"Think of some of the ones we do know."

"But it would be an awful world if no one but an Adonis, who was also
an intellectual paragon and an international athlete, had a chance. It always
seems to me, on the contrary, that women's often expressed statement, that
male good looks don't interest them, is quite untrue. All things being
equal, the man who looks like a tailor's dummy stands a better chance than
the man who doesn't."

"All things never are equal," said Moreland, always impossible to shake
in his theories, "though I agree that to be no intellectual strain is an
advantage where the opposite sex is concerned. But you look into the
matter. The Bard knew." (VB, 127–28)

The "used to say" marks the whole passage as *iterative*. Yet it would
take a professional actor to memorize all of this well-phrased whimsy
and recite it on cue at every appropriate instance. Furthermore, the
"used to" applies to Jenkins's responses as well as to Moreland's
amusing improvisations. It indicates not only that Moreland always
spoke the same words but that Jenkins always answered them with his
own identical ones over a very long period. The frequency marker
even implies that, on every occasion when Moreland cited Henri
Quatre as a Bottom-like lover, the straight man, Jenkins, failed to see
the point. Such a literal reading, of course, creates all kinds of problems, so that we might instead interpret the "used to" as a more or less
traditional figure of rhetoric: in Genette's words, one implying that
very often "something of this kind happened, of which this is one
realization among others."[6] But *pseudo-iteration* throughout *A Dance*
has a more than traditional function and works in stranger ways than
in classical prose fiction.

One small but oddly pinpointed *pseudo-iteration* appearing in volume six should warn us to be cautious in taking Powell's *used to*'s as
merely traditional rhetoric. Jenkins reminisces about the wit of

Charles Stringham, a former close friend who remains offstage during the entire volume: "Templer's clothes gave the familiar impression—as Stringham used to say—that he was 'about to dance backwards and forwards in front of a chorus of naked ladies'" (KO, 101). The very first volume, in fact, records this same remark of Stringham's as occurring on one evening some seventeen years before: "But my dear Peter, why do you always go about dressed as if you were going to dance up and down a row of naked ladies singing 'Dapper Dan was a very handy man,' or something equally lyrical?" (QU, 30). No sign of the *pseudo-iterative* or even the plain *iterative* appears in this first full version, placed, as it is, within a highly specific sequence: Templer's after-hours return to his public school rooms on account of his involvement with a London prostitute (QU, 29, 32–33). In spite of small variations between the original comment and the one that Nick remembers, the two utterances seem essentially the same. How, then, can Stringham's words be reported as habitual if he said them only once? We might perhaps assume that he felt so pleased after he spoke them at first that he brought them out whenever Templer wore his fancy clothes—an improbable explanation, given Stringham's verbal inventiveness. In a far more likely reading, the "used to" would indicate that one discrete event has assumed timelessness within the narrator's memory—an eternal Stringhamism transcending its single date, its location, and its circumstance. Stringham's description of Templer as a song-and-dance man cavorting in front of *Folies Bergere* chorus girls achieves a kind of immortality. In a novel that places high value on the witty speech of friends, the *pseudo-iterative* here provides the highest form of compliment: now Stringham belongs to the ages.

No other *pseudo-iterations* within *A Dance* use this peculiar temporal sleight of hand, which transforms a unique occurrence into seeming habituality. Repeatedly, instead, we get such passages as the one where Moreland rejects, memorably, Barnby's scorn for all intelligent women:

"I don't want what Rembrandt or Cézanne or Barnby or any other painter may happen to want," he used to say. "I simply cling to my own preferences. I don't know what's good, but I know what I like—not a lot of intellectual snobbery about fat peasant women, or technical talk about masses and planes. After all, painters have to contend professionally with pictorial aspects of the eternal feminine which are quite beside the point where a musician like myself is concerned. With women, I can afford to cut out the chiaroscuro. Choosing the type of girl one likes is about the last thing left that one is allowed to approach subjectively. I shall continue to exercise the option." (CCR, 46)

This "used to" interrupts a single night's event: Jenkins's introduction to Moreland's future wife, Matilda Wilson, who combines high intelligence with unconventional looks (she is known as a *"jolie laide"*) (CCR, 46). The *pseudo-iterative* passage functions here rather like a flashback, but we cannot tell whether it shifts backward, forward, or a combination of both. Furthermore, the extreme particularity of the "used to" passage makes it hover paradoxically between one and many occurrences, so that it stands, in a sense, both inside time and beyond it. In a novel where analogous repetitions provide consolation for life's mutability, pseudo-repetition provides a similar, if equivocal, consolation. Indeed, *pseudo-iteration* in *A Dance* sometimes revives the dead by allowing their speech to reecho long after they have vanished. Just such a passage toward the end of volume nine reawakens Stringham's voice from beyond his grave in Singapore, where he died a few years earlier:

> "Hymns describe people and places so well," he used to say. "Nothing else quite like them. What could be better, for example, on the subject of one's friends and relations than:
>
>> Some are sick and some are sad,
>> And some have never loved one well,
>> And some have lost the love they had.
>
> The explicitness of the categories is marvellous. Then that wonderful statement: 'fading is the world's best pleasure.' One sees very clearly which particular pleasure its writer considered the best." (MP, 221–22)

In this ghostlike echo we have once again an impossible combination of habituality and absolute uniqueness.

In contrast, however, to *pseudo-iterations* of such length and complexity that they suggest uniqueness, *A Dance* often uses them to introduce one-liners. A few examples will illustrate the many. ". . . As Barnby used to say: 'It's no good being a beauty alone on a desert island'" (BM, 106). "'Women can be immensely obtuse about all kinds of things,' Barnby was fond of saying, 'but where emotions are concerned their opinion is always worthy of consideration'" (AW, 136). "Barnby used to say: 'All women are stimulated by the news that any wife has left any husband'" (AW, 140). "'I myself look forward ceaselessly to the irresponsibility of middle-age,' he [Moreland] was fond of stating" (CCR, 58). The shortness of these supposedly habitual remarks allows us to take their frequency in a literal way. A person could reuse such sayings verbatim. Yet they have an effect similar to extended quotations that are clearly *pseudo-iterative*. These one- or perhaps two-liners float free from specific surroundings to enter into the heaven of *A Dance*'s *iteration:* memorable sayings by unforgettable people. But other brief *pseudo-iterative* quotations lack the slightest trace of cleverness. In volume six, for example, we hear Uncle Giles's fatuous comment about Adolf Hitler: "'I like the little man they've got in Germany now,' he would remark, quite casually" (KO, 142). Stupidity can also earn its niche in the extratemporal realm of unforgettable sayings. Throughout *A Dance*, in any case, *pseudo-iteration* provides a narrative refuge from time's mutability.

Without allowing the computer to take over our procedures, we can describe in simple statistics the overall pattern of *iteratives* and also of *pseudo-iteratives* occurring throughout *A Dance*. Two hundred and twenty-four pages contain some form of one or the other. One hundred fifty-three pages or so use simple *iteration*, and some seventy-one employ the *pseudo-iterative* form, though both occur at times on a single page and some examples hover between the two varieties. If Powell employs the one more often than the other, he uses *pseudo-iteratives* more than most writers do. Purely *iterative* passages, on the other hand, occur most frequently in sections set furthest back in time: twenty-six pages in volume one and twenty-three in volume two, compared with just four within the final volume. (Volume eleven provides the one late exception, with a total of seventeen pages containing simple *iteratives*.) The earliest section in time of all of *A Dance*, chapter one of volume six, has the highest concentration: fourteen pages with simple *iteratives* out of only seventy-four. We would not expect a very young person to find life more repetitive than an elderly one would. Thus, this pattern results apparently from the leveling effects of memory applied to distant times—from Jenkins the teller rather than Jenkins the actor.

If *pseudo-iteratives* form a less-than-clear-cut pattern, they nevertheless appear far more often within the first six volumes than in volumes seven to twelve: forty-nine pages in the first half of *A Dance* and nineteen in the second. Not a single *pseudo-iterative* appears in volume twelve. In this death-filled finale, we are not allowed even the ambiguous consolation of habitual voices from the grave or from the past. Far more important, however, than all such tabulations of frequency in *A Dance* are the highly particular ways in which Powell uses it.

Analogy and Eternal Recurrences

One can hardly avoid connecting this tendency in *A Dance* to tell just once what has happened more than once with an even more pervasive tendency: to find repetition in separate events—a pattern of analogy rather than absolute sameness. The text alludes three times to Nietzsche's theory of repetitive reality. "Or is it," asks Pennistone of his chance reencounter with Nick, "just one of those eternal recurrences of Nietzsche, which one gets so used to?" (SA, 98). "We parted company," the narrator says later, "agreeing that Nietzschean Eternal Recurrences must bring us together soon again" (SA, 106). And some thirty years later Jenkins comments to Canon Fenneau that "Nietzsche thought individual experiences were recurrent . . ." (HSH, 129). The philosopher's speculations from *The Will to Power* have relevance to repetition in Powell's novel:

If the world may be thought of as a certain definite quantity of force and as a certain definite number of centers of force—and every other representation remains indefinite and therefore useless—it follows that, in the great dice game of existence, it must pass through a calculable number of combinations. In infinite time, every possible combination would at some time or another be realized; more: it would be realized an infinite number of times. And since between every combination and its next recurrence all other possible combinations would have to take place, and each of these combinations conditions the entire sequence of combinations in the same series, a circular movement of absolutely identical series is thus demonstrated: the world as a circular movement that has already repeated itself infinitely often and plays its game *in infinitum*.[7]

Nietzsche's eternal recurrence differs fundamentally from that other theory of repetitive reality to which Nick specifically compares it within volume twelve—reincarnation (HSH, 128–29). For one thing, if reincarnation posits a repetition beyond a person's life, the change to another body involves the same soul-substance: what seems different is in fact identical. In Nietzsche's eternal return, by contrast, an endless combination of forces in the universe might reproduce a person seemingly identical to a long-vanished one, but the new person could not have the same soul-substance, for in Nietzsche's view, no such substance exists within the entire cosmos. As a result, a Nietzschean return has an oddly spectral quality: it looks the same as its forerunner but does not share its essential nature, for neither has any essential nature to share.[8] Paradoxically, though, if believers in reincarnation sometimes consider it a calamity (who wants to be reborn as a frog?), Nietzsche finds comfort in his ghostlike recurrence within an endless flux:

To me, on the contrary, everything seems far too valuable to be so fleeting: I seek an eternity for everything: ought one to pour the most precious salves and wines into the sea?—My consolation is that everything that has been is eternal: the sea will cast it up again.[9]

Apart from what may happen after death—the "secret harmonies" of volume twelve—repetition in *A Dance* tends toward the spectral Nietzschean form, and Powell usually treats it as a basic consolation.

Another important contrast between reincarnation and Nietzschean recurrence is relevant to *A Dance*. In doctrines of transmigration, the soul's previous behavior determines the fact of repetition as well as its form.[10] A Nietzschean return, however, results from sheer blind chance—a repetitious dice game given plausibility by the vast age of the universe. Repetitions in *A Dance* often seem accidental. Frequently they involve chance reencounters, such as the one between Pennistone and Jenkins that the text itself calls Nietzschean. A few striking examples will illustrate the rest: just when Jenkins has lost track of his great friend Moreland, he shows up at Lady Molly's as her charity case (KO, 238–40); Widmerpool crops up in the army as Jenkins's superior officer (VB, 239–43); Stringham turns up as Jenkins's army waiter (SA, 68–69); and after more than a decade, Jean Templer Duport reappears outside St. Paul's on Victory Service Day as the wife of a Latin-American colonel (MP, 232–33). Although the span of the novel can hardly compare with that of Nietzsche's unending and repetitive universe, twelve whole volumes and more than half a century give somewhat more plausibility to these frequent reencounters than a short and time-compressed narrative could manage to convey. Chance in Powell has a rather extended opportunity to reproduce its human combinations. Powell's use of these coincidental meetings resembles that of another huge *roman-fleuve*—*A la recherche*, of course. Proust, too, distributes his fortuitous reencounters over a rather long time span and thus mitigates their unlikelihood. But perhaps even more than in Proust, they serve in Powell as the crux of the story itself.

Other repetitions in *A Dance* seem to spring from a character's basic nature and behavior—rather more like the theory of reincarnation than anything in Nietzsche, but confined, of course, to a single earthly life. An inner compulsion causes Widmerpool to involve himself masochistically with Barbara Goring (BM, 65–73), Gypsy Jones (BM, 83, 232), Mildred Haycock (LM, 320–32), Pamela Flitton (TK, 261–63), and the bisexual Scorpio Murtlock (HSH, 265–69). This series repeats itself, not because of chance, but rather because of the character's bizarre inner self—a Widmerpoolishness to which he is forever condemned. In a similar way, Pamela Flitton's urge to give men hell leads her to torment a series of lovers or would-be lovers: Odo Stevens (MP,

135–36), Widmerpool himself (TK, 261–63), X. Trapnel (BDFR, 219–26), Louis Glober (TK, 256–59), and Professor Russell Gwinnett (TK, 171–74). The repetitive lives of both Widmerpool and Pamela result from what we might call psychological karma. Yet an important comment by the narrator undercuts the either/or of character versus chance: ". . . In a sense," he tells us, nothing in life is planned—or everything is—because in the dance every step is ultimately the corollary of the step before; the consequence of being the kind of person one chances to be" (AW, 63). Seemingly opposed explanations of coincidence and karma merge into one another in a disconcerting way. One unplanned step that leads to all the others resembles Nietzsche's chance combinations, yet the dancer, after all, wills each individual step. The "kind of person" that the dancer is seems very much like karma, yet the narrator explains character as an outgrowth of chance.

Apart from explaining the pattern of repetition by a blend of character and chance, the narrative, at times, seems to suggest the possible third alternative of a basically subjective pattern within the observer's mind. In volume one, for example, Jenkins confuses one puppy love with another in a virtual hallucination of recurrence:

> Suzette was small and fair, not a beauty, but dispensing instantaneously, and generously, emotional forces that at once aroused in me recollections of Jean Templer; causing an abrupt renewal—so powerful that it seemed almost that Jean had insinuated herself into the garden—of that restless sense of something desired that had become an increasing burden both day and night. (QU, 113).

Just a few pages later, as Jenkins goes to bed, the two young girls unite within his drowsing mind: "The images of Jean Templer and Suzette hovered in the shadows of the room, until they merged into one person as sleep descended" (QU, 120). If chance has substituted one young woman for another in Jenkins's casual encounters, his thoughts alone cause him to perceive a fair-haired Englishwoman and a fair-haired Frenchwoman as absolutely identical. The two, in fact, differ quite significantly. Obviously enough, they speak different languages and come from different cultures, but Jenkins's wish-fulfilling vision stresses just their resemblances abstracted from many points of dissimilarity. As the old saying goes, all cats are the same in the dark, and young Jenkins's knowledge of females remains sunk in darkness. A later scene, however, mocks his inexperienced tendency to confuse one woman with another. Rushing to say good-bye to a female whose face is concealed by Suzette's straw hat, he finds himself holding hands with the middle-aged wife of Monsieur Dubuisson instead of with Suzette. Yet "it was almost as if Madame Dubuisson had, indeed, been the focus of my interest while I had been at La Grenadière. I began to feel quite warmly towards her . . ." (QU, 164–65). Whether repetition takes the form of a worldwide dice game, an inner compulsion, or a merely subjective impression, it tends throughout *A Dance* toward comic effect: the incorrigible human race at it once again, colliding into sameness or creating sameness or perhaps just perceiving it within time's endless flow.

We might finally consider one very special variant of recurring events within Powell's text: a repetition by this fictional autobiography of a string of events from the author's own life yet also a divergence from them. In Powell's own *Memoirs* he describes Nicholas Jenkins as "a man who had shared some (though not necessarily all) of my own experiences" (MD, 114). We must also stress an even more basic distinction—the difference between a life and one described in words and inserted into a fictional story. Yet *A Dance* repeats the external details of Powell's own life quite insistently, at least up to a certain point. Both Jenkins and Powell have army officer fathers and a family that lives in a haunted country house (KO, chap. 1). Both attend public schools and then the university (QU, chaps. 1 and 4), and both take a history degree (AW, 95). Both start off in publishing (BM, 78–79). Both get their first novels into print by 1931 (AW, 23). Both marry in 1934 and remain permanently married in a world where divorce has become very prevalent (CCR, 56). During World War II both undergo the identical sequence of military service: a posting with a Welsh regiment (VB, chap. 1), training in Northern Ireland (VB, chaps. 2 and 4), and a liaison position in London with army intelligence (MP, chaps. 1–5). Just after the war both start to write scholarly books—Jenkins, on Robert Burton (BDFR, 2–3); and Powell, on John Aubrey. We could list other items in this long string of parallels between the narrator-character and Powell himself—a meticulous chain of fictional repetitions from the author's own life.[11]

The two series lack symmetry at one highly significant point, however. The novel avoids repeating the one most important event in all of Powell's life—the writing of *A Dance* itself. Although Jenkins narrates the twelve-volume work, nothing indicates that he has written it or anything else like it. As Powell himself has put it, "*A Dance to the Music of Time* is told, so to speak, over the dinner-table, rather than as recorded history."[12] If the "so to speak" winks at the literal complications of unfolding a vast narrative during dinner-table talk, Powell's remark nevertheless suggests a spoken form of narration. In contrast to those traditional narrators who address a "dear reader" and in contrast even to Proust's Marcel, Nick never speaks of his narrative as written. He is the teller of the story—not its author.

Perhaps most revealingly, the time of *A Dance*'s story line extends into the years when the author was writing the work and Heinemann was publishing it. Volume ten's chronology reaches 1947, and volume eleven starts in 1958. Because Powell actually published *A Dance*'s first four volumes from 1951 to 1957, an equation of real and fictional time would put their publication in the story-line gap between volumes ten and eleven. The concluding two volumes cover 1958 to 1971, and in the equivalent span of Powell's own life, he wrote and published volumes five through ten. He published the last two volumes in 1973 and 1975, so that their writing and publication stretches beyond the time of their own story line. If we persist in considering Jenkins the author of the work, bewildering contradictions arise between the rival time schemes of life and of fiction. In any case, no one within the novel itself, not even its narrator, mentions or even hints at his writing or publication of a huge sequence novel—a negative kind of evidence that is nonetheless decisive.

If Jenkins were, indeed, the author of the novel, surrealistic clashes could break out in the story—odd interactions of different narrative levels. Pamela, for example, might complain to Jenkins within volume eleven about his unfair presentation of her in *The Military Philosophers* and *Books Do Furnish a Room*. Jean Templer [Duport] Flores might protest in volume twelve against the narrator's exposure in volumes six and seven of her endless promiscuities. And in that same final volume, Widmerpool might denounce all of *A Dance* as a worthless expression of conventional decency and morality. None of these actions, of course, takes place. In spite of many details from the author's own experience, Jenkins is not Powell. Just as in his other games with time and reoccurrence, Powell uses repetitions from his actual life with a clear awareness that a series of resemblances do not imply absolute identity.

4

Departures from Chronological Order

Complex Time Shifts

ALTHOUGH *A Dance*'s sequence of volumes moves quite steadily forward from 1921 to 1971, the order of telling within each volume often departs from the story line's chronology—usually in fairly short passages but twice, at least, for entire chapters (CCR, chap. 1; KO, chap. 1). Most novels of memory do use time shifts, yet Powell employs them with his own special subtlety. One remarkable medley of such temporal shifts appears at the start of volume five. This opening narrative of changing years swings back and forth in time while remaining fixed in space: a Soho pub where Jenkins first met his best friend, Moreland—dead at the narrating instance, but within the many periods of the story line, remarkably alive. The section begins with a highly evocative passage:

> Crossing the road by the bombed-out public house on the corner and pondering the mystery which dominates vistas framed by a ruined door, I felt for some reason glad the place had not yet been rebuilt. A direct hit had excised even the ground floor, so that the basement was revealed as a sunken garden, or site of archaeological excavation long abandoned, where great sprays of willow herb and ragwort flowered through cracked paving stones; only a few broken milk bottles and a laceless boot recalling contemporary life. In the midst of this sombre grotto five or six fractured steps had withstood the explosion and formed a projecting island of masonry on the summit of which rose the door. Walls on both sides were shrunk away, but along its lintel, in niggling copybook handwriting, could still be distinguished the word *Ladies*. Beyond, on the far side of the twin pillars and crossbar, nothing whatever remained of that promised retreat, the threshold falling steeply to an abyss of rubble; a triumphal arch erected laboriously by dwarfs, or the gateway to some unknown, forbidden domain, the lair of sorcerers. (CCR, 1)

As in Powell's archaeological metaphor for the bombed-out pub, the reader must sift through many time levels within chapter one. We can locate the opening description as late 1959 or after: a poignant reference on the very next page to the "memory" of Moreland hints at his death, which occurs toward the close of 1959, near the end of volume eleven (TK, 275–77). As the description of the ruined pub continues, a blonde singer approaches on crutches and breaks into the same "Kashmiri Love Song" with which she had serenaded Moreland and Jenkins on a nearby street in 1933. For a moment the two times almost seem to fuse. The singer herself has "hardly" been "altered by the processes of time," and Moreland had played similar tunes on the pub's "mechanical piano" (CCR, 1–2). Then the narrative shifts decisively to 1933 and Moreland's whimsical comments about the song's exotic lyrics and his aunt's trilling of them to her pianoforte accompaniment. On the 1933 public street, he imitates her long-vanished performance of the song, so that now three eras come very close to merging: 1959 or later, 1933, and the unspecified time of Moreland's childhood or adolescence (CCR, 3–4).

The ruined pub and the song become the equivalents of Proust's *petite madeleine*. Just as in *A la recherche*, these emblems of distant eras release flooding memories of times within times. The narrative remains at 1933 for four-and-a-half pages, marked by Moreland's important announcement that he is getting married (CCR, 3–7). After a brief section of indeterminate moments including one "used to" (CCR, 7–8), a parenthetical description leaps beyond the time of the ruins to an unlocatable "now" and a resurrected, though uncongenial, pub: "the Mortimer (now rebuilt in a displeasingly fashionable style and crowded with second-hand-car salesmen)" (CCR, 9). The "now" takes us up to the instance of narrating—later, of course, than Moreland's death in 1959 and perhaps as late as the 1970s.[1]

Next the narrative flows back to the furthest reach of time within the entire chapter—1928 or 1929—and confines itself to it for thirty pages: the night when Jenkins first encountered both the pub and Moreland himself, each in their prewar glory, long since gone (CCR, 9 38). The section contains a still more spectacular resurrection: the painter Edgar Deacon, who died from a drunken fall downstairs toward the end of volume two (BM, 228–31). In the 1928–1929 flashback, however, he remains very lively—a lost fictional friend whom we gladly reencounter. Before the segment departs from 1929, it shifts location to the nearby eating place that gives the volume its name: Casanova's Chinese Restaurant. As the narrator himself points out, this ludicrous amalgam links "the present with the past" (CCR, 29), a central technique of chapter one itself. Not only does the name suggest a twenties Chinese restaurant presided over by an eighteenth-century Venetian, but the place, in fact, has merged two distinct restaurants from several years before: a Chinese one just up the street, and the New Casanova, which served Italian food (CCR, 28). In a volume full of merging and of shifting times, Casanova's Chinese Restaurant itself epitomizes a temporal double exposure.

The last extended time shift within chapter one covers sixteen pages. It moves ahead to 1933 again, a few weeks after Moreland has announced his marriage plans, but the scene leaves the pub and Casanova's Chinese Restaurant. This final segment, from 1933, recounts Jenkins's introduction to Matilda Wilson, Moreland's future wife. Then the chapter concludes with a one-sentence leap into 1934 and Jenkins's own marriage (CCR, 40–56). This takes us back to the year when the previous volume ended. If we consider volumes four and five together, most of chapter one in *Casanova's Chinese Restaurant* works as a long flashback (with back-and-forth zigzags) that finally rejoins the present of the previous story line in the very closing sentence.

If we put chapter one's events into a chronological order, we can better visualize their temporal relationships:

(1) Jenkins visits the pub for the very first time, first meets Moreland, and together with others they go to Casanova's (1928–1929).
(2) Jenkins and Moreland hear the blonde street singer, and Moreland speaks of his coming marriage (1933).
(3) Moreland takes Jenkins to meet Matilda Wilson (some weeks later in 1933).
(4) Jenkins gets married (1934).
(5) Jenkins looks at the bombed-out pub and again hears the blonde singer (in or after 1959).
(6) The pub has been rebuilt and has become a vulgar place (an indeterminate time, perhaps as late as the 1970s).

What does Powell achieve by shuffling this sequence into 5, 2, 6, 1, 3, and 4? By beginning with a scene that includes the bombed-out pub and the still-alive singer, Powell suggests in a symbolic way the survival in the narrative of persons and places dissolved by time and death. To have started, say, with the reconstructed and ungenial pub would have stressed, instead, the debasement of the past by the present. To have begun, on the other hand, with the pristine pub of 1928–1929 would have undermined our sense of nostalgic recreation of long-vanished moments. Then, too, the singer-pub combination (late 1959 or afterwards) branches off neatly into two distinct memories: the singer—1933 and Moreland's marriage announcement; the pub—1928–1929 and Jenkins's meeting with Moreland. The final section resolves the enigma raised by the flashback to 1933—the identity of Moreland's future wife—and returns us at last to the story line's present. Clearly enough, the crooked way of telling works far better here than a straight chronological method.[2]

It seems no accident that many sly allusions to time itself appear within this segment of *A Dance*—a segment that stresses narrative games with time. During the flashback set in 1928–1929, Moreland holds forth on "Problems of Time and Space"—a "fashionable" Einsteinian topic of the period (CCR, 34, 39).[3] Mr. Deacon has an appointment with an acquaintance at the pub to buy a reproduction of Bernini's statue, *Truth Unveiled by Time* (CCR, 13). The narrator refers to Bronzino's painting in the National Gallery—the *Allegory of Venus and Cupid*—with "Time in the background, whiskered like the Emperor Franz-Josef," looming "behind a blue curtain as if evasively vacating the bathroom" (CCR, 16). In the second 1933 flashback, Norman Chandler reads Wyndham Lewis's diatribe against a time-dominated literature—*Time and Western Man* (1927)—a self-mocking and self-relexive allusion in a time-obsessed chapter of a time-obsessed novel (CCR, 48). "What nostalgia," Moreland exclaims in this segment that recaptures the past through highly evocative time shifts (CCR, 3). His words will reecho just before his death in the second-to-last volume when he complains of being killed by "nostalgia" (TK, 230). In effect, chapter one of *Casanova's Chinese Restaurant* keeps calling attention to its own games with time.

Flashbacks

As we have seen, the opening chapter of *Casanova's Chinese Restaurant* combines flashbacks with flash-forwards. It gives us the following specific pattern: flash-forward, flashback, flash-forward, flashback, flash-forward, and a final return to the present—a perfect zigzag pattern. *A Dance* often uses leaps ahead in time with as striking effect as its many backward movements. Nevertheless, as in almost all narratives, its longest flashbacks extend over many more pages than even its longest flash-forwards.[4] Let us consider some examples of flashbacks and analyze how they work in *A Dance*.

As we have already noted, the single flashback in *A Dance* with the largest number of pages appears in chapter one of volume six and serves a unique function. It provides a 1914 parallel with the volume's concluding events in 1939. Here, though, we must concentrate on the temporal shift itself rather than on the complex thematic analogies with later narrative segments. Although *A Dance*'s previous volume ends in 1937, the start of *The Kindly Ones* swings backwards two decades and more in time. This flashback to Jenkins's childhood runs for seventy-four pages. If chapter one itself contains zigzag movements, these time shifts remain in 1914, except here and there for a sentence or two and also in the chapter's closing roll call of characters killed during the First World War (KO, 74). Next the volume jumps to approximately 1928 for only a few pages and then settles firmly down in a period running from 1937 to 1939. Chapter one of volume six forms a special temporal island in *A Dance* as a whole—one that starts and finishes long before the times of its adjacent segments. It also functions as an island in the story line itself—an island cut off from direct connection with later events.

Generally, however, Powell's flashbacks maintain a clear and distinct connection with the surrounding narrative. As we might expect, he often uses them in traditional ways. He may employ them as background for newly introduced characters: for example, Louis Glober's sexual act with Mopsy Ponter some three decades earlier on a cluttered dining room table (TK, 71–72). A flashback in the novel may also supply the narrator's own free thematic associations. For instance, the interruption of a wartime sequence tells how Jenkins, at the war's very start, bought an army coat from a costume store (SA, 1–4). Another traditional use of the flashback is somewhat rare in *A Dance:* to reveal the delayed significance of a past event. Perhaps the clearest case of this occurs in volume seven. It recalls from a vanished decade Jean Templer Duport's complaints about a dull dinner outing away from her lover, Jenkins—an occasion, as he finally learns, when she met her next lover, for whom she dropped Jenkins. In the context of the present, the flashback exposes her habit of telling lies (VB, 128–32).[5] Another kind of flashback seems to stress an occurrence's pastness—a stress transcending the inevitable temporal distance of any first-person narrative. For example, Powell starts the closing chapter of *A Dance*'s final volume with Jenkins's burning of a pile of recent papers and his reading in the flames a headline account of the Deacon Centenary exhibit. A few pages later the flashback description of the exhibit itself takes on the air of slightly faded news. And the second-to-last page of this final volume returns us to that bonfire—a reminder of the fleeting quality of even recent days (HSH, 243–51, 271).

The most frequent and perhaps the most curious type of flashback running throughout *A Dance* revives in brief an event described in full within an earlier passage. This device works as a flashback but also as a special kind of repeating narrative, telling more than once what has happened only once, rather like a passage marked *da capo* in music. In the most striking examples, these flashbacks repeat a sentence or two verbatim from the previous occurrence. For instance, in volume two, when Barbara Goring dumps sugar on Widmerpool's head, Jenkins remembers Stringham's anecdote of Widmerpool's receiving a banana in the face—an account told some five years before. Yet in spite of temporal distance, this music-like recall matches Stringham's exact words: "Do you know, an absolutely *slavish* look came into Widmerpool's face" (BM, 72; cf. QU, 11). The second passage even mimics the italicized stress of *"slavish"* (though a comma not present in the original slips in after "know")—a surprisingly exact repetition after half a decade. As we have seen in chapter two, Jenkins narrates the story but does not write it down, so that he cannot do what the author and the reader can easily do—turn back the pages and look. This narrative convention of miraculous memory goes all the way back to Homer, yet Powell employs it in his own special way.

Just as a musical recall can occur more than once, one of *A Dance's* matching pairs provides a double recall—verbatim flashbacks stretching over the years. Within the fourth volume, in 1934, Templer praises Betty, his own pretty date, although he cannot even remember her married name: "Rather a peach, isn't she?" (LM, 187). By 1938 in the sixth volume, Templer has married Betty and is driving her literally crazy with flagrant infidelities, and Nick recollects Templer's words of four years before: "Rather a peach, isn't she?" (KO, 115). And in 1942, within volume nine, Templer's brutal revelation that his wife has become psychotic recalls to Nick's mind the same identical phrase: "Rather a peach, isn't she?" (MP, 21). Each time that it turns up, the quotation becomes more and more sexist and disturbing. It is short enough for Nick to repeat it exactly, and in any case, the narrator makes some rather slight changes in surrounding words within his second version: "I can never remember her married name. Taylor, is it? Porter? Something like that" (LM, 187); "A Mrs. Taylor or Porter . . ., I can't remember which" (KO, 114–15). Yet even though this repetitive flashback makes some small changes for the sake of verisimilitude, the result seems quite similar to total recall. Three passages separated by time, space, and a distance of many pages somehow coalesce. They interact with one another in spite of separations. They create a strange oneness in three highly different scenes. With a paradoxical effect rather like *A Dance's* *pseudo-iterations*, these verbatim flashbacks move beyond time into a realm of narrative quasi-eternity.[6]

Flash-Forwards

As we have already seen, Powell sometimes locates flash-forwards in especially strategic places, such as a volume's opening pages, where they may establish a mood for its entire length. Consider, for example, volume two's elegiac beginning, on the auction of Deacon's paintings (BM, 1–4). As already noted in this study's first chapter, the scene remains unplaceable in time until the last volume gives a temporal clue "just after the second war" (HSH, 246). In relation to volume one's 1924 ending, the Deacon sale jumps more than twenty years forward, and the rest of volume two finally settles down to 1928–1929. Unlike the indefinite time sequence at the start of volume one—the street-repair episode, which has nothing that comes before it and no markers of the future and consequently functions as the present (QU, 1–2)— the Deacon auction serves as a genuine flash-forward. It describes the nadir of the dead man's reputation before we have even met the living Mr. Deacon. The displaced future casts ironic light on subsequent events in the present, including the efforts of poor Mr. Deacon to assert his self-importance. The flash-forward here has a somewhat similar function to the one at the start of volume five that we have discussed earlier: a bombed-out pub that then shifts back to its long-vanished avatar in which dead men walk and talk (CCR, 1–29). Many other flash-forwards in *A Dance* disarrange the usual relationships of the living and the dead.

An occasional brief flash-forward provides the reader with a kind of narrative contract, a promise that a character will later reappear, an unusual constraint in a work that tends toward creative open-endedness. For instance, in volume one, the narrator informs us that "this was the last I should see of Stringham for a long time" (QU, 229). Included in Nick's regret over this parting of their ways lies an implication that Stringham shall return, as, indeed, he later does. With far more specificity, another place in volume one tells us that Sonny Farebrother will turn up again in about two decades: "He piled his luggage, bit by bit, on to a taxi; and passed out of my life for some twenty years" (QU, 105). By volume eight, during World War II, Farebrother reemerges pretty much on schedule (SA, 22–23). In a more complex way, a parenthetical and *iterative* flash-forward at the end of volume two predicts Jenkins's relationship with Jean several years before it happens: "the game of Russian billiards, played (as I used to play with Jean, when the time came) on those small green tables" (BM, 274). The "used to" forecasts their habit of togetherness when they have become lovers. But this *iterative* flash-forward is also advance notice for a later singular scene when, on a night in volume three, Nick and Jean play billiards at Foppa's (AW, 148). The flash-forward here gives an image of the future before its time has come.[7]

A number of significant flash-forwards in *A Dance* (quite a few in volume nine) work, rather like traditional flashbacks, to slip the narrator's own amusing comments and memories into the narrative out of chronological order. For instance, an encounter in 1942 with a War Office virtuoso of entangled red tape, the mind-numbing Blackhead, is preceded by a scene from long after the war: a senior civil servant tells Jenkins that official rules prevented them from firing Blackhead, so that they stuck him in Jenkins's section, where Blackhead could do little harm, and then they made jokes about him (MP, 41). To sense the full comedy of Blackhead's obfuscations, we need advance notice that they do not really matter. A similar flash-forward occurs just after Jenkins and Kernével anticipate their release from wartime paper-shuffling: several years later, Kernével—technically a member of Intelligence—receives a medal with a secret citation, along with ludicrous praise. "You people," declares the Chief of the Imperial General Staff, "were the real heroes of that war" (MP, 239–41). The temporal double exposure allows a comic effect of incongruous juxtaposition.[8]

A brief flash-forward toward the close of volume eleven creates a special kind of temporal paradox. After Jenkins's final meeting with his dying friend Moreland, the narrator makes an assertion about his own future life: "That morning was the last time I saw Moreland. It was also the last time I had, with anyone, the sort of talk we used to have together" (TK, 276). Obviously enough, the narrator's "last time" for having done something takes us very close to the narrating instance. Yet a gap still remains between the moment of narrating and what it describes, for Powell has kept to the past tense and written "I had" rather than *I have had*. *Have had* would have meant simply that, between the time of the story line and the instance of the telling, Jenkins has lacked conversations like those with Moreland. By contrast, "the last time I had" seems to throw the very being of the narrator into a vanished realm. He cannot have a knowledge of what he will always lack unless he speaks from a vantage point beyond his own life or, at least, from its final moments. Not a single hint, however, anywhere else in *A Dance* suggests a posthumous or last-grasp telling. The narrator seems to have reached, nevertheless, beyond his own future—an anomaly that requires willing suspension of disbelief on the part of a time-conscious reader.

One especially strange passage within volume four works like a flash-forward, yet it claims instead merely to record Jenkins's deepest thoughts in the present of the story line—a moment of love at first sight:

Would it be too explicit, too exaggerated, to say that when I set eyes on Isobel Tolland, I knew at once that I should marry her? Something like that is the truth; certainly nearer the truth than merely to record those vague, inchoate sentiments of interest of which I was so immediately conscious. It was as if I had known her for many years already; enjoyed happiness with her and suffered sadness. I was conscious of that, as of another life, nostalgically remembered. Then, at that moment, to be compelled to go through all the paraphernalia of introduction, of "getting to know" one another by means of the normal formalities of social life, seemed hardly worth while. We knew one another already; the future was determinate. (LM, 136)

The narrator's meditation distinguishes between two levels of consciousness within his younger self. On the first or immediate one—normal awareness—he feels attracted to Isobel but nothing more specific. On another, less accessible, level the future seems available to a heightened form of consciousness. As if looking back in time, he has an uncanny sense of their marriage in the future, their later decades together, their subsequent joys and sorrows, and even their familiarity with each other's basic traits. Yet the narrator remains aware that this sense of foreknowledge owes something to his own position far ahead in time. He asks if he has "exaggerated" his younger self's reaction and made it much too definite—a distortion of the present by hindsight—but he still insists that precognition comes closer to "the truth" than anything else. This moment of the story line in 1934 resembles a flash-forward, yet one particular sentence suggests an even more special category of prediction: "I was conscious of that, as of another life, nostalgically remembered." This seems to go beyond a mild conjugal mysticism to hint at a form of reincarnation—a previous existence relived in the present. It reminds one, in any event, of specifically occult foreshadowings scattered throughout the novel: a network of fortune-telling as the story line's equivalent of the narrator's flash-forwards.

Occult Foreshadowings

During the third volume's scene of foretelling by cards, Myra Erdleigh makes several quite precise forecasts concerning Jenkins's future. He will, she says, become significantly involved with a woman whom he has seen only "once or two twice before, though not recently." He will compete with another man, possibly her husband, whom Jenkins dislikes already. His rival will be a businessman who frequently travels abroad. As for physical characteristics, the woman has "medium hair," and the man is "fair," perhaps red-headed (AW, 15). As we later discover, this prediction by Mrs. Erdleigh hits very close to the psychic bull's eye. The woman will turn out to be Jean

Templer Duport, whom Jenkins has met casually on two previous occasions: on a visit to the Templers' ten years in the past (QU, 74) and during luncheon at Sir Magnus Donners' some two years before Mrs. Erdleigh tells Nick's fortune (BM, 190). The male rival will, in a sense, be her husband, Bob Duport (AW, 214), whom Jenkins met and detested seven years earlier, but, in a truer sense, Jimmy Brent, whom Jenkins also encountered and disliked on that very same occasion (QU, 191–93; KO, 178–81). Myra Erdleigh gets other details right: Duport works for a business firm—one dealing in aluminium—for which he travels abroad (BM, 193–94; AW, 214), and Brent is also a businessman with overseas assignments (VB, 131–32). She errs only slightly on just one point—the woman's "medium" hair color—for the narrator calls Jean "fair" (QU, 74). On the other hand, Mrs. Erdleigh's description of the man as a redhead fits Duport's "sandy" coloring reasonably well (QU, 191). In this fortune-telling instance, her knowledge of the future almost rivals that of the narrator, with his vantage point ahead in time.

Her second prediction about Jenkins's future appears to him at first slightly out of focus. " 'There is a small matter in *your* business that is going to cause inconvenience,' she went on. 'It has to do with an elderly man—and two young ones connected with him' " (AW, 16). Jenkins associates this with the troublesome assignment for his art book publishing house of persuading a second-rate novelist, St. John Clarke, to provide an introduction to a third-rate painter, Horace Isbister (AW, 18–23). Clarke seems to be influenced by his young private secretary, Members (AW, 27–28). As a result Nick thinks that Mrs. Erdleigh has gotten things slightly wrong. His troubles appear to involve only one young man and two elderly ones (AW, 16). Yet, again, her forecast turns out right. Roughly a year later, Isbister dies (AW, 30), so that only one old man now remains to frustrate Nick's project. And an unforeseeable change fulfills the rest of the prediction. Without the slightest warning, Clarke dismisses Members and hires a new secretary, Quiggin, an aggressive young Marxist who makes fresh complications for the Isbister introduction by radicalizing Clark (AW, 52–53, 116). "Inconvenience" has, in fact, arisen for Jenkins from "an elderly man" and "two young" men "connected with him." During the fortune-telling session itself, Nick is "not greatly struck by the insight she had shown" (AW, 16). But later events should convince any reader that her "insight" and foresight deserve higher marks than Jenkins seems willing to grant her.

Most of her other forecasts also hit the target. In the same first session, she insists that Jenkins will reencounter her "in about a year from now" (AW, 16–17). Some thirteen or fourteen months and two chapters later, chance does reunite them very close to schedule (AW, 81). In volume nine Mrs. Erdleigh reads Pamela Flitton's palm and predicts that within "about a year" she will marry "a man a little older than" herself, one "in a good position," who will be "a jealous husband" (MP, 134). Mrs. Erdleigh makes her prediction on June 13, 1944—the night of the first V.1 attack against London (MP, 134 and 138)—and it comes true just after the war in late August or so of 1945 (MP, 244).

Her psychic calendar-clock seems once more highly accurate. The man whom Pamela marries, Kenneth Widmerpool, fits Myra Erdleigh's description rather well: he is older than Pamela, will later reach Parliament (BDFR, 13), and will demonstrate his own masochistic form of jealousy (BDFR, 198–204). Another Erdleigh prediction made that night seems almost part of her forecast about Pamela's future husband: that Stevens "will escape" this explosive femme fatale (MP, 131). In any case, Mrs. Erdleigh predicts correctly. The next time that Pamela and Stevens appear together, she completely ignores him (BDFR, 128), and eventually he comes to loathe her (TK, 164–65).[9] In the final volume, another prophecy appears on a rather less crucial matter. The hippie mystagogue, Murtlock, predicts that farmer Gauntlett will find his missing dog, Daisy, by the small grove or "spinney" near "the ruined mill" (HSH, 22). We later learn that Gauntlett found Daisy just where Murtlock had foretold (HSH, 153)—still another psychic flash-forward.

Two other true prophecies, however, seem basically unimpressive as examples of occult foreknowledge. In late August of 1939 within volume six, Duport asks Trelawney whether war will come. The half-sinister, half-ridiculous mystic replies first in metaphors but then gets more specific:

> "The sword of Mithras, who each year immolates the sacred bull, will ere long now flash from its scabbard. . . ."
> "The slayer of Osiris once again demands his grievous tribute of blood. The Angel of Death will ride the storm. . . ."
> "The god, Mars, approaches the earth to lay waste. . . ."
> "The Four Horsemen are at the gate. The Kaiser went to war for shame of his withered arm. Hitler will go to war because at official receptions the tails of his evening coat sweep the floor like a clown's." (KO, 192)

Trelawney utters his words the night before the news of the Russo-German pact (22 August 1939) (KO, 199), so that Britain enters the war thirteen days after his forecast—on September 3rd. (KO, 204). Yet Trelawney's hierophantic language obscures an obvious fact: nonclairvoyant politicians, unmystical newspapermen, and ordinary citizens without psychic powers had been predicting the same thing for quite some time. One need not invoke Mithras, Set, or Mars to foresee the impending results of Adolf Hitler's policies. In a similar manner on a personal level, Mrs. Erdleigh in volume eleven warns Pamela of disaster (TK, 260–61), and she soon commits suicide in a very bizarre way (TK, 269–70). Yet one only needed to watch her present outrageous behavior to foresee her calamity in one form or another. In the words of Shakespeare's Horatio, "There needs no ghost, my lord, come from the grave / To tell us this," or any soothsayer either.

At times in *A Dance*, the treatment of clairvoyance and occult mysticism becomes quite comic without wholly dissipating a certain air of credence. In the third volume an extended passage describes an amusing series of messages from something called a planchette—a board with castors and a pencil that records communications from the supposed spirit world on a blank sheet of paper. As Jenkins himself, Mona Templer, and Jimmy Stripling lightly touch the board, the pencil writes with fluency and neatness. It infuriates Quiggin, a Marxist skeptic, by claiming to speak for Karl Marx himself. It rattles off quotations from him, including "Nothing to the Left" and "Force is the midwife." The angry Quiggin cries fraud. He complains that whoever is faking the message has insulted him intentionally. Yet the planchette shifts suddenly to seemingly personal warnings about his position as St. John Clarke's secretary. The spirit world writes that "he is sick" in "the House of Books." The skeptic at once becomes a convert. He rushes to phone Clarke as the planchette records an indecent monosyllable—a kind of parting shot perhaps suggesting Quiggin's hidden thoughts. Although he does not find out if Clarke is really worse, Quiggin learns enough to send him rushing back. Members, the former secretary, has returned at Clarke's request—not a good sign (AW, 90–101).[10]

One sly detail in the planchette scene amusingly hints at the perpetrator of these spirit-world messages and, by implication, of all the other psychic foreshadowings in *A Dance*:

> Quiggin took a step nearer.
> "Which of you is faking this?" he said roughly. "I believe it is you, Nick."
> He was grinning hard, but I could see that he was extremely irritated. I pointed out that I could not claim to write neat Victorian calligraphy sideways, and also upside-down, at considerable speed: especially when unable to see the paper written upon. (AW, 95)

Quiggin's accusation cannot be true in any literal sense, in view of the narrator's privileged access to his own younger mind. He has, after all, described how the pencil moved without his conscious control, so that he clearly cannot have committed any intentional fraud. A self-referential joke about narration itself nevertheless seems implied. If Jenkins did not write these ghostly communications, he obviously has narrated them along with everything else. Yet, as we have noted in chapter three of this study, he tells but does not write. His disclaimer of having written the spirit-world messages seems true in a double sense. He did not write them or the scene that surrounds them. The author of *A Dance*, Powell himself, wrote the sentences on the planchette, along with the rest of the story. Quiggin's suspicion reminds one, however, of a rather hasty critic—one who confuses Jenkins with Powell, the author.[11]

Although Jenkins is clearly not Powell, the occult foreshadowings throughout *A Dance* have a curious limitation arising from Powell's novelistic practices. Toward the close of volume eleven, Mrs. Erdleigh makes the following boast to Jenkins and his wife, who have stayed happily married for twenty-five years:

> "When I first put out the cards for your husband, I told him you two would meet, and all would be well."
> If my acknowledgment fell short of absolute agreement that Mrs. Erdleigh had seen so far ahead, it also fell much farther short of truthful denial that she had said anything of the sort. Sorceresses, more than most, are safer allowed their professional *amour propre*. (TK, 243)

As we have already seen, the priestess of the Ufford had not foretold Nick's long and happy marriage decades in advance but rather his approaching affair with Jean Templer Duport in which all turned out ill. In other words, Myra Erdleigh lacked the ability to predict nine whole volumes ahead.

Every psychic forecast in Powell's vast novel has a strictly limited access to the future of the text. Mrs. Erdleigh's prediction about Jean and Jenkins comes true within the volume in which it is made—*The Acceptance World*. Within this same volume, Mrs. Erdleigh prognosticates about Clarke, Quiggin, and Templer, and events bear her out by the very next chapter. Her final prophecy at the Ufford—the reencounter of herself and Jenkins in more or less a year—is confirmed two chapters later. Her forecasts in volume nine—on Pamela's marriage to Widmerpool, and Stevens's escape from Pamela—come true by the volume's end. An analogous time limit also applies to Murtlock's lost dog act. In volume twelve's first chapter, he describes in advance Daisy's hiding place, and chapter five reveals that she turned up where he said. Clairvoyance in *A Dance* has a rather short range.

Any magical foreknowledge in a fictional work rests, of course, on the author's advance awareness of his story line's future. A writer, for instance, who stuck to a highly detailed outline could easily have made Mrs. Erdleigh see twelve whole volumes ahead. A paraphrased interview, however, by James Tucker with Powell describes his insistence on creative spontaneity: "he had no overall, detailed plan because this would not have allowed each book to develop its own life."[12] Myra Erdleigh and the other psychic characters cannot make forecasts far ahead in the text because of Powell's own unwillingness to commit himself in advance to detailed schemes about as-yet-unwritten volumes. Yet within these amusing and self-imposed restrictions, A Dance treats fortune-tellers with essential respect. Their limited clairvoyance is less a matter of the clouded crystal ball than a crystal ball that lacks a telescopic lens.[13]

We have seen that time plays a central role in Powell's narrative method. A Dance begins open-endedly, and for two thousand pages and more, its omnipresent narrator does not know the end of his very own story in the future's distant span. Yet the slowly accumulating past of this volume-by-volume narrative remains unchangeable and frozen in time once each volume has unfolded, or to put matters more precisely, the past changes only through later additions and subsequent new perspectives. Most strikingly of all, a pattern of repetitions gradually develops over time's broad expanse: surprising reemergences of long-vanished persons and events with sharp resemblances to earlier ones. If these reoccurrences often seem comic—characters moved in patterns beyond their control—they also provide a stay from time's continual losses. Finally, A Dance's extraordinary flashbacks and flash-forwards across many years transcend at privileged moments time's essential limits through an effect of virtual narrative simultaneity.

A Dance is, of course, a novel and not a philosophic treatise on the mysteries of temporality. Through its treatment of a large cast of characters over an extended duration, Powell's work richly evokes the common human experiences of love and friendship and the loss of them both over life's broad span. Yet the novel gives us a basic consolation for this endless mutability that even the most profound philosophers cannot provide. By its long and elaborate games with time itself, A Dance triumphs over it in fiction's special way by telling a story about time's disappearances to which we can go back again and again in a reader's eternal return.

Part III
Time's Choreography

5

Youth

A Dance's volumes are separate and sequential and yet are not self-contained. We may read them in order, but we must also later think them through again—this time with an awareness of all twelve volumes. Indeed, a dedicated reader of *A Dance* may actually go through it many times and see new interconnections with each fresh reading. Above all, such a reader needs to remember a string of events in temporal sequence and to recall them in simultaneous space. In discussing "narrative open-endedness and closure," we have already noticed how one small joke concerning Pamela Flitton spread out for more than fifteen hundred pages in three distinct brief segments (see chapter two of this study). In dealing with "analogy" and "eternal recurrences," we have found a pattern of surprising reencounters extending over many volumes. (see chapter three of this study). In the case of "*iterative* flashbacks" and "*iterative* flash-forwards," we have seen how two sections, hundreds of pages apart, can reflect each other's words verbatim. (see chapter four of this study). To read time's complexities in each distinct volume, we need a double consciousness of both the near and the far—the future and past along with the present. Or to put things in another way, we must look for a far-more-scattered story than we find in conventional novels with traditional plots.

A reader of this vast and subtle work must also forego another usual reward of traditional storytelling: immediate identification with a single central character. The only figure appearing in all twelve volumes—the narrator-character Jenkins—remains essentially a passive spectator of acquaintances such as Stringham, Templer, Moreland, Trapnel, Widmerpool, and many others. At certain rare moments Jenkins does act decisively—for example, in his passionate affair with Jean Templer Duport (AW, 66, 105, 137–38) and in his engagement and marriage to Isobel Tolland (LM, 203, 218–39; CCR, 56)—yet his own narrating flits quickly over his own private intensities, as though his basic role is watching all the others in time's complex dance rather than watching himself. If we try to read the work as Nicholas

Jenkins's own fictional autobiography, we not only find that his personal life gets shunted to the margins but even at times entirely off the page.

Genette has called attention to the important narrative device of skipping parts of a story, of devoting zero pages to events taking place over a certain story-line span of time.[1] Most surprisingly, such gaps tend to occur at especially key moments in Jenkins's life. His affair with Jean breaks off in the void between volumes three and four. Early in the fourth volume, the narrator briefly notes that "things had been 'over' with Jean for some time by then. . . ." (LM, 14). Unlike Proust in *A la recherche*, who gives hundreds of pages to Marcel's falling out of love, Powell dismisses the end of the affair in three laconic sentences about Nick's controlled regret (LM, 14–15).

A still more surprising blank occurs at the center of Jenkins's most important and most enduring relationship: with Isobel Tolland, who becomes his wife. Between his love-at-first-sight of her (LM, 135–39, 143, 145, 149, 152–53) and his offhand mention of their later engagement (LM, 203), not a single word appears about their days of courtship. At the end of volume four, even the long sequence about their own engagement party avoids all description of Isobel herself (LM, 218–39) and, indeed, alludes to her only twice and then very briefly: "friends of Isobel" (LM, 218) and "Isobel Tolland—over there" (LM, 220). In a similar way, volume five omits the wedding of Isobel and Nick and refers to their newly married state in a single casual sentence: "Not long after, perhaps a year, almost unexpectedly, I found myself married too; married to Isobel Tolland" (CCR, 56). In curious contrast, Powell later devotes fifty-three pages to the wedding of the Jenkinses' nephew—a figure who has never appeared in the text and who, in fact, remains offstage even in this sequence (HSH, 187–239). Clearly, Nick has no reticence about marriages in general—only about his own. Although the Jenkinses' marriage endures for thirty-six years from volumes five through twelve, Isobel appears so sparingly within these many pages that she seems, in effect, just a minor character. Paradoxically enough, her closeness to Nick, the narrator-character, works to shunt her off to the margins of the novel.

An early essay by Freud about literary creation—"Creative Writers and Day-Dreaming"—suggestively applies to the self-abnegation of Jenkins as a central figure. Freud connects the daydreaming urge to see oneself as hero at the center of events with storytelling's basic pleasure as well as the pleasure of reading others' works of fiction. Freud also notes that skilled writers and the most perceptive readers prefer some disguise of the daydreaming impulse, and he adds that certain stories seem to depart altogether from a wish-fulfilling pattern:

Certain novels, which might be described as "eccentric," seem to stand in quite special contrast to the type of the day-dream. In these, the person who is introduced as the hero plays only a very small active part; he sees the actions and sufferings of other people pass before him like a spectator. Many of Zola's later works belong to this category. But I must point out that the psychological analysis of individuals who are not creative writers, and who diverge in some respects from the so-called norm, has shown us analogous variations of the day-dream, in which the ego contents itself with the role of spectator.[2]

Apart from that final cautious hint about a possible spectatorial or even voyeuristic syndrome (and voyeurism plays a central role with *A Dance* itself, especially in volume eleven), Freud's essay illuminates the reading challenge of a fictional protagonist as mere detached observer. A spectator figure such as Jenkins blocks our desire for easy wish fulfillment through simple identification with a hero. Unlike ego-centric novels, *A Dance* deflects us away from what Freud calls amusingly "His Majesty the Ego" toward the many other characters who pass before its vision through time's relentless changes. Yet the reader's renunciation of an immediate kind of wish-fulfilling pleasure will later result in a subtler pleasure that slowly develops in its own unique manner from *A Dance*'s frequent encounters, departures, and reencounters over twelve whole volumes and more than sixty years.

A Question of Upbringing

Because of their opening place in a vast time structure, the events of volume one appear, at first reading, meandering and inconclusive. Chapter one introduces the public school acquaintances of young Nicholas Jenkins—Stringham, Templer, and Widmerpool. Throughout the volume, these stand out in a rather large cast including family relations, friends, and other assorted persons whom Jenkins briefly meets. Amid amusing incidents at school, we soon understand that of the three Nick prefers Stringham because of his engaging whimsy and wit. Nick likes Templer next best for his daredevil attitudes, and Nick has the least respect for the gauche and clumsy Widmerpool. From the beginning to the end of the volume, only minor changes occur in Nick's first impressions. He visits Stringham's family and finds some unexpected tensions there (QU, 54–63). He also visits Templer's family, meets their eccentric friends, and learns of Templer's sexual sophistication (QU, 73–105). In order to practice French, Nick stays with a family in France, and Widmerpool shows up there, so that Nick can observe his third school acquaintance in quasi-domestic surroundings (QU, 106–66). During Nick's first university year, Stringham drops out early; and Templer and Widmerpool skip college altogether (QU, 167–219). By the closing pages Nick regretfully perceives that he and Stringham have drifted apart, yet Nick still likes Stringham very much (QU, 229). By this same concluding section, Nick feels distaste for Templer's commercial acquaintances but continues to consider him a rather close friend (QU, 201). In the second half of the volume, Nick first notices Widmerpool's imperiousness yet cannot take it seriously (QU, 157). The movement of these three relationships within volume one remains quite small.

In subsequent volumes, however, the three former schoolmates emerge from time to time in altered relationships that drastically transform our perception of volume one itself, although *A Dance* as a whole does not focus on these three exclusively. As a rule, the interlinking of their widely distant scenes differs from the workings of traditional plots. Little consecutive narration appears concerning Stringham, Templer, or even the more frequently onstage Widmerpool. Instead, they drop from the novel, sometimes for hundreds of pages, and reemerge later in surprising metamorphoses that have already happened in voids within the text—a persistent form of storyline ellipsis. We can, of course, find similar effect in such picaresque novels as Defoe's *Moll Flanders*. In *A la recherche* Proust also uses these scattered reappearances—most unforgettably in the offstage transformations between the party of a youthful Duchess de Guermantes and her gathering years later of withered old acquaintances.[3] Unlike Defoe and rather more like Proust, Powell uses intermittent transmutations as a fundamental principal of structure. Later scenes in *A Dance* so alter our reading of those in volume one that only rereading can do justice to these changes.

When volume one ends, we still see Stringham in a simple and more-or-less positive way as a man who tosses off first-rate jokes in any situation. Well into the following volume he shows up as a very drunk man about town (BM, 92–148). He reappears toward the next volume's close, now so helpless and dazed from drink that he has to be put to bed (AW, 184–209). Two volumes later he needs a keeper to control his still-disastrous drinking (CCR, 161–85). And three volumes further on, Stringham reappears as a reformed alcoholic who has squeezed his way into the army onto the lowest rung—as a mess-hall-waiter private (SA, 75–78). These widely dispersed moments in his decline and fall transform our view of him within the first volume. His schoolboy prank of getting his housemaster arrested stands revealed now as a symptom of almost manic-depression (QU, 45–50). His gloom at the university now clearly foreshadows his years of escape into drink (QU, 173). Even his cutting of a dinner date with Jenkins discloses itself now as a sign of future trouble—a forecast of intoxicated irresponsibility stretching over nearly a decade (QU, 226). When we reread these scenes with a knowledge of the future, they no longer look mild or aimless.

Something quite similar happens with Templer. When we first read volume one, he strikes us as rather uncomplicated: a likable extrovert. His precocious sexual exploits with a young London prostitute and then with the widow of his father's business partner appear quite harmless—displays of early self-confidence (QU, 32–35, 81, 99–101). Two volumes later Templer reappears, now married to a beautiful model—a strident-voiced woman with a certain basic coarseness (AW, 40, 54, 57). By the end of the volume, she has run away from him (AW, 170–72). Towards the next volume's close Templer reemerges in the company of a beautiful young married woman whose last name he forgets (LM, 184–87). Two volumes later he himself has married this woman, but his constant infidelities have reduced her to hysteria (KO, 132–133). Three volumes further on, he reappears to announce that his wife "went off her rocker" and now is "in the bin" (MP, 21). And near the end of the volume, we learn that his failure to seduce young Pamela Flitton had caused the despairing Templer to volunteer for a high-risk overseas mission on which he has been killed (MP, 187–89). These broadly spaced vignettes of his sexual misadventures reshape how we see him within volume one. The encounter with the prostitute foreshadows his later habit of using his sexual partners as somewhat impersonal props for his own self-esteem. His complacent satisfaction at sleeping with a woman far older than himself no longer appears just boyish: it foretells his lifelong drive for new sexual conquests. Once we know the pattern of his troubled later life, the Templer of volume one changes. The healthy young extrovert becomes, instead, a self-centered male, prideful and self-destructive.

When we reread volume one, a knowledge of later events sharply alters our view of Widmerpool as well. Throughout our first reading, he seems a harmless figure of fun. We smile at his clumsy overcoat (QU, 5), his dogged and futile athletic attempts (QU, 3–4, 6), and his pompous mediation of a very silly quarrel over a game of tennis (QU, 139–42, 153–57). One volume later, however, this apparently ridiculous man has won a high place in a large corporation (BM, 205). In volumes six through twelve he keeps reappearing on progressively higher rungs of power as an army captain (KO, 218–21), Deputy-Assistant-Adjutant-General (VB, 239–43), Cabinet Offices official (MP, 9–11), member of the House of Commons (BDFR, 13), Life Peer (TK, 35), and Chancellor of a new university (HSH, 43–46). He behaves abominably in all of them. He betrays his former schoolmate, Stringham, by sending him to die in a dangerous zone of war (SA, 189–90, 215; MP, 204). Widmerpool betrays Templer as well, another former schoolmate, by arranging his death on an overseas mission. (MP, 211). And Widmerpool betrays England itself by repeated acts of espionage (TK, 210–11, 217, 262–63). With an awareness of his later power-mad behavior, we can no longer mistake him within volume one for just a harmless oaf. His grotesque overcoat becomes, retrospectively, an outward sign of his inner deformity. His lonely efforts at sports reveal a self-centered will, and his seemingly absurd tennis court diplomacy foreshadows his taste for power over other human beings. The apparently benign young man becomes something alarmingly repellent.

One highly specific example will demonstrate in miniature how distant interconnections transform earlier segments even in their smallest components. In volume one's first chapter the comic episode of Braddock alias Thorne contains a seemingly innocent detail that assumes a darker look when we know of a later scene toward the end of volume eleven. In volume one Stringham tricks the police into arresting Le Bas, a school housemaster, because of his resemblance to a wanted criminal. Knowing nothing of the trick, the astonished Widmerpool observes the arrest and excitedly tells his schoolmates. He serves, in effect, as assistant narrator, for Nick does not see this specific event. But one strange aspect of Widmerpool's behavior escapes our first reading. He watches Le Bas, the approaching policeman, and the unexpected climax from a safe hiding place in an open field. "I kept behind the hedge," Widmerpool explains. "I didn't want to get mixed up with anything awkward" (QU, 48). His furtiveness contrasts with the very different behavior of two other witnesses: "A soldier and a girl appeared from a ditch and watched them [the policeman and Le Bas] go off together" (QU, 48). Obviously enough, the soldier and the girl had been making love together in their ditch. Even so, they hasten out to watch the strange arrest. Yet the solitary Widmerpool remains well hidden. On a first reading, his deviousness appears unimportant—an understandable caution for a student of Le Bas's.

More than ten volumes later, however, we learn that Widmerpool has a startling kind of voyeurist compulsion. A strong hint of it appears in the middle of volume eleven. His wife, Pamela, urges him to inspect Tiepolo's ceiling—a portrayal "of a man exhibiting his naked wife to a friend." She also taunts him for hiding secret dirty photographs in a locked desk drawer, and Widmerpool turns "brick red" (TK, 110–11). The final revelation about his shameful habits comes near the volume's end. Pamela says that she noticed him peering from a curtain as she tried to have sex with a mutual acquaintance—a liaison set up by Widmerpool himself: "Watching your wife being screwed. Naturally it wasn't the first time. It was just the first time with a blubber-lipped Frenchman, who couldn't do it, then popped off. Of course he had arranged it all with Léon-Joseph beforehand . . ." (TK, 262). Public details of this embarrassing death clearly confirm her story (TK, 45–46). And she immediately connects it with another revelation: that Widmerpool has spied for the Communists and betrayed his fellow spy (TK, 262–63).

Although a vast textual gulf divides the two scenes—Braddock alias Thorne and Widmerpool's later disgrace—the second reorients the first. The schoolboy who hides behind a handy hedge and watches a policeman humiliate Le Bas behaves already like a master voyeur, a spy, and a traitor. In the light of later events, his reaction to what he sees becomes in itself unsavory. He is so stirred up that his eyes expand and he pants like "an elderly lap-dog" or "an engine warming up" (QU, 46–47, 48). What excites him most about the arrest of Le Bas is a sense of hidden shame. Amid his own heavy breathing, he keeps on asking one titilated question: "What *could* he have done?" "What can Le Bas have done?" ". . . Tell me what you think it is" (QU, 48). A subsequent reading directs our attention to Widmerpool's own grotesqueness. The knowledge to come colors even the rather small detail of the soldier and girl who climb out of their ditch. Widermpool observes them from his place of concealment as they themselves emerge to watch Le Bas. With more experience, this prurient young man might even have spied on the lovemaking pair before they left their ditch. The panting Widmerpool blends, in short, with his much later self: a spier of copulations, a betrayer of vital secrets.

Even the title of this very first volume, *A Question of Upbringing*, reserves its full significance until much later.[4] The first volume itself simply does not show the decisive effects of childhood training and nurture on Stringham, Templer, and Widmerpool. These do not emerge until hundreds of pages later. Subsequent volumes will reveal, retroactively, that the child or schoolboy is father of the man or, more precisely, that the drunkard, lecher, or Widmerpoolish monster of many years after fathers an altered version of that very same schoolboy. When we learn to read the narrative backwards and even simultaneously, "a question of upbringing" telescopes itself into a question of downfall.

A Buyer's Market

Not until *A Dance*'s very last pages do we learn the full significance of volume two's beginning—the auction-sale of Mr. Deacon's paintings that forms a flash-forward of nearly two decades at the start of *A Buyer's Market*. Although Deacon appears frequently enough within this second volume, he is hardly its protagonist in any conventional sense. Instead of having an immediate importance for the plot, the scene about Deacon has subtle interconnections that expand throughout the volume and continue to expand until the end of *A Dance*. By the time of the auction, the artist's reputation has sunk so low that a dealer buys four Deacon paintings all lumped together for only "a few pounds"—more for the gilded frames than the canvases themselves (BM, 1–4). Nick's mind flashes back to his childhood years when Deacon still painted with moderate success (BM, 4–8). Then the narrative flashes forward to a time still in the past when he no longer painted but supported himself instead by selling antiques (BM, 9–14). By the year of the posthumous auction, Deacon's reputation appears to have sunk to absolute zero. Nevertheless, Nick tells us that it would have distressed him if the men at the sale had laughed at these quaint works of art from a now-faded era (BM, 3). Volume two gradually shows us why Nick feels so protective about them. They have such complex interrelations with his own youthful days that to laugh at Deacon's paintings seems almost like laughing at Nick's vanished youth itself.

Mr. Deacon and his painting interlace all four chapters that make up the volume. In the first chapter Nick's boyish infatuation with capricious Barbara Goring—the central focus of the section—finds an explicit symbol in the small Deacon canvas called *Boyhood of Cyrus:* "its significance being attained simply and solely as symbol of the probable physical proximity of Barbara Goring. . . . . . Even years after . . . I could not hear the name 'Cyrus' mentioned . . . without being reminded of the pains of early love . . ." (BM, 15). Toward the chapter's close, after Barbara has disgusted Nick by dumping a stream of sugar over Widmerpool's head (BM, 70–73), Deacon himself shows up on the public street outside (BM, 82–84), and *Cyrus* now stands for a love that has ended. In the second chapter the painter accompanies Nick and others to a rather wild party at Milly Andriadis's, where Nick observes the flirtations of worldly men and women but feels left out. Mr. Deacon has only a tenuous connection with events in chapter three, yet a reference to him opens it: Nick visits Deacon's shop, learns of his absence, and meets Barnby there—Deacon's young tenant who wishes to seduce Baby Wentworth, a beautiful young woman first glimpsed by Nick at Mrs. Andriadis's (BM, 162–74). This complex grouping related to Mr. Deacon provides a connecting thread to chapter three's climax: Nick's visit to the Stourwater party, where he finds Baby Wentworth and her friend Jean Duport (BM, 194), but again feels barred from a realm of erotic liaisons. Once we have discerned this network of connections, we can understand the sequence of the Deacon auction-sale as a plea not to scorn Nick's early sexual fumblings: poor things perhaps but the narrator's own. Yet the close of volume twelve undermines any simple reading such as this.

The twelfth volume presents an astonishing reversal in Deacon's artistic reputation. A revival occurs in 1971—a century after his birth and almost half a century after his death. His once-despised paintings now receive glowing praises: "unique," "fearless sexual candour," "broodings in paint that grope towards the psychedelic," "a most remarkable artist" (HSH, 244–45, 249). Nick recognizes two of the most praised works as coming from the batch "so summarily dismissed at the down-at-heel auction rooms" a quarter century earlier (HSH, 246–47). And if the first Deacon painting that Nick had ever seen—the *Boyhood of Cyrus*—had so little merit with its owners then that they "skyed" it out of sight in a hall "beyond the staircase" (BM, 15, 85), the gallery's head in 1971 considers this emblem of Nick's early love "one of Deacon's best" (HSH, 249). It seems significant, too, that, on volume twelve's very first page a reference appears to the *Boyhood of Cyrus* and its once-humble place in the hallway—a sly preparation for its closing reappraisal into an Edwardian masterwork.

This belated upending of all our old assumptions about Deacon's art as seen in volume two (now even Nick himself is "more impressed than" he "should have been prepared to admit"—HSH, 248) makes us rethink the entire second volume. If the *Boyhood of Cyrus* symbolized love for Barbara Goring, perhaps that too had a quality that escaped us at the time. Perhaps those parties at Milly Andriadis's and also at Stourwater now may assume a retrospective glow. With the hindsight of almost half a century, even grubby Gypsy Jones may take on retroactively a certain nostalgic charm. If the auction-sale at the start of volume two shows how one era can devalue the past, the Deacon Exhibition demonstrates the opposite: that an era can exalt a long-vanished time. To achieve balance, we need to read the present and the past together. Nick attempts to do so at the Deacon Exhibition. He combines his new respect for the paintings with his former doubts concerning Deacon's technical skill: "at the same time trying to restore self-confidence as to an earlier scepticism by noting something undoubtedly less than satisfactory in the foreshortening of the slave boy's loins" (HSH, 248). In a metaphorical way, volumes two and twelve equate aesthetics with the process of judging and rejudging human lives. If the equation looks fanciful, we need to recall that *A Dance* takes its overall title from a painting. And as a literary work of art of a very special kind, the novel itself demands the aesthetic second thoughts of careful rereading. In other words, the concept of artistic reappraisal refers back to the way that the twelve-volume novel transforms its own past.

A perspective limited to only volume two will seriously mislead us concerning Barbara Goring, Jean Templer Duport, and Gypsy Jones—the women who interest young Nick. Of the three, at first Barbara appears the most glamorous and popular, as an amusing youthful mixture of flirtatiousness and primness who entices four young men to compete for her attentions: Tompsitt, Widmerpool, Pardoe, and Nick himself (BM, 15–69). Although she and Pardoe become engaged by the volume's end (BM, 266–69), at least two of her suitors have already defected—Nick and Widmerpool (BM, 73, 79). The rest of *A Dance* mentions Barbara only fleetingly. In the fourth volume a onetime friend pities "poor Barbara" because of her troubled marriage with the clinically depressed Pardoe. Yet she holds the marriage together until her husband recovers (LM, 92–93; MP, 244), and then she vanishes from the text altogether—no longer an emblem of capriciousness and, in fact, the most innocent of volume two's women and also the least important.

The most important woman in Nick's early life—Jean Templer Duport—receives the smallest space in this particular volume. When he first met her in volume one many years before, Nick had felt attracted to this then-unmarried girl, but nothing had developed between them (QU, 74, 100). During their brief reencounter in volume two, he again finds her attractive, yet he assumes that her marriage puts her out of reach (BM, 190–95, 213–14). Time proves him wrong. By volume three he begins a passionate liaison with this now-estranged wife of an unfaithful husband and even thinks of marrying her himself (AW, 64–67, 104–5, 35–36). By the next volume the affair has ended, apparently for reasons beyond the control of either Jean or Nick (LM, 14–15). But three volumes and six years later, he learns a shocking secret. Not just after their involvement but during it as well, Jean had an affair with another rival male (KO, 176–80). By the end of volume seven, when we know the full details about her chronic infidelities (VB, 126–33), the deceptively sedate young Jean of volume two makes Barbara Goring seem, by comparison, a harmless little flirt, an epitome of innocence itself.

If we confine our focus to volume two alone, our view of Gypsy Jones also remains misleading. In *A Buyer's Market* itself she looks like a major figure—a left-wing femme fatale who seems destined to play an important role within the later volumes. She first appears on the page as a pamphlet-selling gamine with a dirt-smudged face, who curses Widmerpool for trodding on her toes (BM, 83–88). She later captivates Widmerpool and then tricks him into paying for her medical abortion of another man's child (BM, 128–30, 232). At Mrs. Andriadis's Gypsy flirts with the not-very-interested Nick (BM, 127). At Deacon's birthday party she slips off the lap of Howard Craggs to accuse Nick of snobbishness and also to persuade him to embrace her (BM, 247–59). During her final emergence in the volume, she wears a flesh-colored costume as a biblical Eve and provides young Nick with a sexual experience—perhaps his very first (BM, 255–60). Within *A Buyer's Market* itself, she appears to have a more significant place in Nick's early life than either Jean or Barbara. With later perspectives, however, Gypsy fades in importance to an astonishing extent. Throughout the rest of *A Dance*, she returns in only a few scattered pages, and she never develops as a character. During almost half a century of Soviet oppressions, she remains a stalwart Communist, a party-line parrot, who ultimately dies on a trip to Czechoslovakia (KO, 227–29; BDFR, 36, 142–43, 269, HSH, 104–5). Her sexual behavior also displays a similar monotony. Within *A Buyer's Market* she has sex with Nick in spite of her involvement with Craggs. By volume ten she has finally married Craggs after years as his mistress, but she seems to have had an affair with Erridge (BDFR, 35–36). And toward the close of volume ten, the now–Lady Craggs has still another affair—this time with a former Trotskyite—yet she keeps an understanding with her husband through it all (BDFR, 132). In Nick's own words, Gypsy is always "essentially the same" in either love or politics (KO, 227). In spite of her apparent centrality within volume two, her basic lack of development disqualifies her for any major role in this twelve-volume work about time's slow surprises. In *A Dance* as a whole, Gypsy has almost as little importance as young Barbara Goring.

Until we know events from later volumes, one scene of volume two remains an enigmatic fragment: Nick's reencounter with Jean. Art hovers over this meeting—sixteenth-century tapestries of the Seven Deadly Sins—just as the *Boyhood of Cyrus* played a similar role in Nick's vanished love for Barbara. At the Stourwater luncheon he sits opposite the tapestry illustrating lust, and Jean, on his right, jokes about it. At first reading, little connection seems to exist between the slim, reserved Jean Duport, who slightly resembles a "secretary" out "of musical comedy" (BM, 191), and the buxom *Luxuria* or lechery, "portrayed in terms of a winged and horned female figure, crowned with roses, holding between finger and thumb one of her plump, naked breasts, while she gazed into a looking-glass, supported on one side by Cupid and on the other by a goat of unreliable aspect" (BM, 189). At this point we may think that the tapestry reflects only sexual doings at Stourwater: that is, Sir Magnus Donner's rumored sadistic orgies with a long succession of mistresses (BM, 201–2). A few pages later Jean's obvious unhappiness in her own married life suggests another reading of the tapestry as a hint of Duport's unfaithfulness to her (BM, 192). But only the juxtaposition of many subsequent volumes with this scene about the tapestry allows us to see it as a portrait of Jean herself—"winged and horned" lust.

A series of shocks throughout the remainder of *A Dance* establish the details of this surprising resemblance. After Nick (in volume three) has begun to sleep with this seemingly ill-used wife, she reveals that she once had a secret affair with repulsive Jimmy Stripling (AW, 142–43). Nick learns in volumes six and seven that during their own apparently idyllic romance Jean had betrayed him with repulsive Jimmy Brent and, in fact, even wished to run away with Brent (KO, 178–81; VB, 126–32). By volume ten Nick cynically assumes that Jean also cuckolds her South-American-colonel second husband: "with the gauchos or whatever was . . . most tempting to ladies in that country" (BDFR, 97). As we reread volume two with our subsequent knowledge, we at last understand why Jean makes jokes about the ménage à trois in the tapestry—a copulating couple and their helpful little satyr: "All newly-married couples have someone of that sort about. Sometimes several" (BM, 191). Her own private satyrs turn out to be Jimmy Stripling, Jimmy Brent, Nick himself, and also nameless gauchos. Two other small details support Jean's association with the tapestry's goddess of lasciviousness. In volume two Jean's attitudes remind Nick "immediately of her brother" (BM, 193), and in volume six at Stourwater, the entire dinner party acts out a fancy-dress series of tableaux on the Seven Deadly Sins for Sir Magnus Donners' camera as Peter Templer portrays lust (KO, 122–33). Lust evidently runs in this family. These widely spread-out interconnections give retrospective meaning to the juxtaposition within volume two of Jean Templer Duport and *Luxuria*.

A Buyer's Market clearly draws its title from the opening auction-sale of Mr. Deacon's paintings. In the economic conditions of any buyer's market, the supply of commodities so outruns demand that goods decline in price and become readily available. If Mr. Deacon's works will later find an extraordinary seller's market in which they rank as masterpieces, a few pounds can now purchase four canvases as a bunch (BM, 3). Yet the application of supply and demand to *A Buyer's Market* as a whole remains at first obscure. In a volume centering around erotic and amorous quests, Nick believes himself pretty much excluded; to him, it looks like a seller's market. With the perspective, however, of the subsequent volume and his passionate affair with Jean, we can see that such experiences have already begun without his even knowing it. Life has become, in fact, a buyer's market for Nick; but to read the title correctly, we need to know occurrences that stretch beyond the limits of volume two itself.

The Acceptance World

If volume three centers around two parallel love affairs—those of Nick with Jean and of Quiggin with Mona—it creates a misleading impression of both. At first reading, Nick's liaison with Jean seems momentous and fulfilling, and Quiggin's elopement with Mona appears highly decisive. Only later volumes disclose the transitory nature of these romantic soap bubbles. Within *The Acceptance World* itself, the characters have little inkling of love's decline and fall. Early in the relationship of Jean and Nick, the mere pressure of her arm against his hand gives him "an assurance that all would be well" (AW, 79). A brief, distant echo eight volumes later provides an ironic perspective on love's misplaced confidence. Myra Erdleigh claims to have predicted at the time of volume three that once Nick met Isobel—the woman whom he marries—"all would be well" (TK, 243). The sorceress reproduces his unexpressed thought about Jean from twenty-eight years before yet applies it retroactively to a far different woman. In fact, Mrs. Erdleigh foretold Jean and Nick's affair but not its long-term outcome (AW, 15). Taken together in a subsequent reading, these widely spaced uses of "all would be well" serve as subtle reminders of love's mutability. In a much more obvious way, a sequence beyond volume three undercuts the apparent uniqueness of Mona's elopement with Quiggin. She later runs away from him in turn with still another man (LM, 204).

In this volume about the deluded hope of lovers to live happily ever after, the act of fortune-telling itself connects the two couples. *The Acceptance World* starts with Myra Erdleigh's prediction of Nick's affair with Jean (AW, 1–18), and Mona flirts with Quiggin during the fortune-telling session within chapter three (AW, 74–101). In addition, many other details link Nick and Jean's affair with that of Quiggin and Mona. At the Ritz in the second chapter, Nick reencounters the still-married Jean for the first time in roughly three years (AW, 57–58), and

Quiggin reencounters the now-married Mona after having glimpsed her once some three years before (AW, 54–55). In the third chapter, at Peter Templer's house, Nick begins to sleep with Jean (AW, 73), and Mona takes steps towards seducing Quiggin (AW, 76–78, 101). In chapter four Nick and Jean have an assignation (AW, 137–38), and the runaway wife, Mona, shows up with Quiggin in public (AW, 129–32, 138–40). And in chapter five Nick and Jean have another tryst (AW, 210–14), and Quiggin and Mona take a cottage together (AW, 173). In spite of the interlacings of these extramarital couples, they appear, at first reading, diametrically opposed. Nick and Jean seem involved in a truly grand passion, and Quiggin and Mona seem rather less than grand in their comically incongruous alliance.

Later volumes reveal, however, that Nick's supposedly serious affair with Jean and Quiggin's ludicrous one with Mona have disconcerting resemblances. If Jean justifies adultery with Nick by Duport's own unfaithfulness, she betrays Nick with Brent withut any such pretext (KO, 178–81; VB, 126–32). And her choice of a high-ranking military man for her second husband (he begins as a Latin American colonel and becomes his country's dictator—MP, 232–33; TK, 234–35) reveals a chameleonlike quality in one who liked books and the arts (AW, 135). She even assumes a "foreign accent" to match that of her husband (MP, 233). Mona also goes through similar changes of orbit. If Templer's notorious womanizing may conceivably extenuate her elopement with Quiggin, her betrayal of Quiggin with Erridge lacks any such excuse (LM, 204). And in a startling transformation for a former artist's model (AW, 55), Mona ends with a high-ranking military man for her second husband. If Jean marries a future generalissimo, Mona marries an Air Vice-Marshal. With a chameleonlike flair similar to Jean's, Mona even sprinkles her conversation with air force small talk (BDFR, 46).

When we reread volume three with these later perspectives, the apparently sharp contrasts between Mona and Jean turn out to be merely illusory. If Jean has an aura of mystery, reserve, and intelligence and if Mona has one of violence, vulgarity, and silliness (AW, 57–60), these differences hide the same fickle lust. Although Jean never openly complains about her husband and although Mona complains at the slightest excuse (AW, 103), both women have a readiness to jump into bed with others and then to run away with them. By learning to read time backwards, we perceive the serious Jean and the frivolous Mona as more than just sisters-in-law: they are, in fact, sisters under the skin.

Two particular scenes in *The Acceptance World* yield their full implications only with a knowledge of *A Dance*'s distant future. An image that accompanies Nick and Jean's first kiss at the time seems merely vivid and amusing yet later assumes the perspective of erotic disillusionment:

> The exact spot must have been a few hundred yards beyond the point where the electrically illuminated young lady in a bathing dress dives eternally through the petrol-tainted air; night and day, winter and summer, never reaching the water of the pool to which she endlessly glides. Like some image of arrested development, she returns for ever, voluntarily, to the springboard from which she started her leap. A few seconds after I had seen this bathing belle journeying, as usual, imperturbably through the frozen air, I took Jean in my arms. (AW, 64–65)

Only after subsequent volumes disclose Jean's chronic promiscuity can we perceive the connection between her way of life and the diver's recurrent uncompleted motions. Again and again Jean plunges into new sexual liaisons. Yet, in a metaphorical sense, "she returns for ever, voluntarily, to the springboard from which she started her leap." She breaks off her relationship with Nick and goes back to Duport, but only as a cover for her new affair with Brent in which Duport serves as a handy conjugal "Springboard" (KO, 178–80; VB, 126, 128–33). When her second husband, the Latin American dictator, is "killed by urban guerillas," she does not languish abroad but instead comes back to England and again begins to see "a good deal of" Duport (HSH, 252)—a return to her starting point within volume three. With an awareness of these later events, even the apparently offhand phrase "image of arrested development" takes on special relevance. Not only do all of Jean's loves suffer from what we might call "arrested development," but she herself has an emotional lack—a basic incapacity for permanent attachment.

The image of the diver's "eternally" futile movements ironically contrasts with the unmoving image of "eternal" lovers at the close of volume three (AW, 213)—a passage occurring in A Dance's last description of Nick and Jean's liaisons. Jean sends him an erotic French postcard to tell him when to come for their next assignation. Nick's thoughts about the card appear at the time to have only general significance, but later events provide a specific application. In the postcard's picture a dressed young woman sits smiling on the knee of a dressed young man. Nick thinks the pose false—an exclusion of love's real tensions—yet he grudgingly admits a partial likeness between the card's "crude image" and the various loves mentioned in the volume:

> Some of love was like the picture. I had enacted such scenes with Jean: Templer with Mona: now Mona was enacting them with Quiggin: Barnby

and Umfraville with Anne Stepney: Stringham with her sister Peggy:
Peggy now in the arms of her cousin: Uncle Giles, very probably, with
Mrs. Erdleigh: Mrs. Erdleigh with Jimmy Stripling: Jimmy Stripling, if it
came to that, with Jean: and Duport, too. (AW, 212–13)

In his complex listing of couples, the narrator has slyly inserted,
without comment, a movement of unfaithfulness. Each partner has, in
turn, run off with a new one. Even the odd punctuation suggests a
round of love: a series of arrowlike colons, each of which points to yet
another pairing. On first reading, though, this generalized succession
of lovers diverts our attention from Nick's specific problems with
Jean. Then, too, it seems a history rather than a prognosis. It lists past
and present romances and says nothing of the future. But an
awareness of later volumes permits us to continue this long erotic
series and apply it to Nick's affair with Jean. With *A Dance* as a whole,
she takes the following succession of partners: Jimmy Stripling: Duport: Nick and then Jimmy Brent simultaneously: Colonel Flores and
nameless others simultaneously: Duport. Compared to this expert at
cyclical adultery, the Jean of the postcard segment appears almost
chaste. The passage, however, contains a further cunning hint concerning her promiscuity—one that remains obscure until subsequent
unveilings: " 'Doesn't she look like Mona?' Jean had written on the
back" of the postcard (AW, 211). This linking of Mona with Nick and
Jean's affair has, at the time, only limited suggestiveness: both women
appear to have made a simple erotic move from husband to lover. Yet,
as we have noted already, Mona goes through her own cycle of unfaithfulness—Templer: Quiggin: Erridge: and an Air Vice-Marshal. If
the card looks like Mona, Jean behaves as Mona does. In short, *The
Acceptance World*'s passage about the "eternal" lovers misleads us at
first but on a second reading, assumes sardonic clarity.

Volume three's title, *The Acceptance World,* comes from the corpo-
rate name of the bill-brokers' house that Widmerpool has joined—a
house that advances money for overseas transactions (AW, 45). *Acceptance* refers technically in finance to a willingness to pay a time draft or
bill of exchange. The narrator explicitly associates the term with life's
metaphorical engagement to deliver present happiness or some other
present value at unknown future cost: "the world in which the essential element—happiness, for example—is drawn, as it were, from an
engagment to meet a bill" (AW, 170). In the narrator's playful analogy,
sometimes happiness is "delivered," sometimes it is not, and sometimes it costs too much (AW, 170). During Nick's affair with Jean he
gains short-term happiness, yet he pays for it with subsequent mortification: the discovery that she left him for fat Jimmy Brent and lied
to Nick's face about Brent from the start (KO, 178–81; VB, 126, 128–

32). Mona's elopement, on the other hand, fails to deliver apparently even temporary bliss. By the next volume she quarrels with Quiggin just as she quarreled with Templer (LM, 123–24).

The theme implied by "The Acceptance World" analogy—an elusive pursuit of happiness—explains why the volume starts with a fortune-telling scene. Mrs. Erdleigh makes two kinds of forecasts—those involving business and those connected with love—the literal and metaphorical senses of "The Acceptance World." She correctly foretells Nick's business troubles and his love affair with Jean (AW, 13–16). The time-draft metaphor for life helps explain, in addition, Widmerpool's absurd and uninvited speech at the Old Boy's Dinner towards the close of volume three. As he boasts to the guests about his bill-brokerage work, he expounds the need for governmental planning in controlling "domestic prices," but out of his mouth comes a laughable farrago of economic jargon:

> "Now if we have a curve drawn on a piece of paper representing an average ratio of persistence, you will agree that authentic development must be demonstrated by a register alternately ascending and descending the level of our original curve of homogeneous development." (AW, 193)

If the psychic forecaster, Myra Erdleigh, spoke clearer English than this, she also showed more caution in describing the details of a still-unfolding future. Widmerpool represents the supreme example of "a man of will" in the novel—one who thinks to impose his own special wishes on time's inescapable uncertainties.[5] His double talk expresses in comic form his hubris about controlling the future. His financial gobbledygook embarrasses everyone, and it ends with Le Bas's small stroke, and the confused dispersal of the Old Boy's reunion (AW, 191–97). In fact, Widmerpool has failed to foresee the immediate results of his own prognosticating speech. And in the long term, he will suffer more than any other character from time's unexpected reverses.

If in the end we have to reread all of A Dance's volumes to develop an awareness that cuts across the whole, the work also tends to divide in front of our eyes into three-volume units, each dealing with a time of life: the youth, maturity, wartime years, and middle and old age of Nick and his generation. Volumes one, two, and three take him from about sixteen to about twenty-seven—a span in which he and his acquaintances see only a brief segment of time's unfolding pattern. Toward the end of volume three, one very important section suggests the approaching close of youth. Strategically placed at the center of the very last chapter, the Old Boy's reunion brings together once again the first volume's three main characters: Templer, Stringham, and Widmerpool. Enough time has passed so that significant changes have at last become apparent. "A chap who looked . . . like something the cat had brought in" (AW, 175)—Quiggin—has won a sexual rivalry over Templer, the public school Don Juan. In contrast to this cuckolded early philanderer, a once-bashful Nick keeps on cuckolding Bob Duport, Templer's own brother-in-law (AW, 214). Stringham, who "derided" Widmerpool in volume one is, in turn, "derided" and put to bed by him as a helpless, pathetic drunk (AW, 206–10). But compared to later changes, these seemingly sharp alterations will appear just minor ripples of early manhood. In a period of far more decisive change, the older Templer's fear of impotence will lead to his actual destruction (MP, 187–89), and Widmerpool will help to effect the deaths of both Templer and Stringham (SA, 189–96, 215; MP, 204, 211)—much more drastic reversals than those of the first three volumes. At the close of *The Acceptance World*, a still quite young Nick has perceived the mere first stirrings of time's transforming dance.

6

Maturity

At Lady Molly's

VOLUME four, *At Lady Molly's*, unfolds a complex pattern of seemingly random encounters that lead to a chain of others and, ultimately, at the end of all the chains, to decisive personal outcomes. This movement of distant social interaction resembles a complicated sequence of colliding balls in a game of pocket billiards: one strikes another, which strikes others, until, at last, a ball falls into the pocket. Because a billiard shot takes only seconds to unfold, we can easily comprehend its series of collisions. But the collision of human billiard balls within volume four spreads out across 238 pages and takes up much of a year. Without a view of the entire chain at once, each separate encounter seems aimless, and even when we finally perceive the whole volume's pattern, relationships trail off into subsequent volumes.

Volume four's very first sentence describes a diffuse network of social interconnections:

> We had known General Conyers immemorially not because my father had ever served under him but through some long-forgotten connexion with my mother's parents, to one or other of whom he may even have been distantly related. (LM, 1)

Until far into the volume, the significance of this link is even more unclear than its original genealogy, for the general has, basically, a minor role in the narrative. In an opening flashback-encounter of Nick with General Conyers, the general's sister-in-law, Mildred Blaides, steals the center stage from him. This cigarette-smoking World War I nurse strikes Jenkins, at roughly eight years old, as romantic and even seductive (LM, 7–10). Both then and afterwards, however, Mildred's relationship to Nick remains indirect and distant. In 1914 she arrives at General Conyers's with a message from the future aunt of Nick's future wife (LM, 8–9), and twenty years later Mildred shows up at Aunt Molly's place as the over-aged fiancée of Widmermpool, Nick's former schoolmate (LM, 43). In a pattern of similar indirection, both of the general's later appearances within volume four (at his own house and at Lady Molly's) revolve around the troubled engagement of Widmerpool and Mildred—an event tangential to Nick's own life. At the general's house conversation hinges on what sort of husband Widmerpool will make for Mildred (LM, 70–71, 72–75, 77–78). And at Molly's house Conyers drops a bombshell revelation about Widmerpool and Mildred. She has canceled their engagement because of his sexual fumblings and impotence (LM, 227–34). In spite of the opening connection with Nick and the Jenkins family, General Conyers seems more central to the other human chain—the Mildred-Widmerpool one.

Nick becomes involved in his own chain of collisions within volume four, yet he remains, for the moment, completely unaware of the billiard-like caroms that bounce him toward his marriage. This complex movement starts with his happening to know Chips Lovell—a fellow scriptwriter for films that never get made (LM, 12–14). Nick accompanies Lovell on a visit to Lovell's Aunt Molly—an aunt only through her long-past marriage to his long-dead uncle (LM, 15–17). Through a similar tangle of circuitous ties, Molly also turns out to be an aunt of Isobel's—Nick's future wife. Molly's sister has become stepmother to Isobel, so that Isobel has an even less direct link to Molly than Chips Lovell has (LM, 31). Furthermore, Nick feels receptive to meeting "lovely girls" at Lady Molly's house because Jean Templer Duport has "some time" ago ended her affair with him because of her affair with Brent (LM, 14–15; KO, 178–81; VB, 26–32)—another network of happenstance connections. And even though Lovell specifically suggests that Isobel might turn up at Lady Molly's gathering and that Nick "might like" her (LM, 19), the billiardlike sequence brings him instead within the orbit of Isobel's uncle and sister but not of Isobel herself (LM, 29, 36, 42, 48). Without Nick's awareness, this complex circle of in-laws begins to prepare him for becoming an in-law himself within Isobel Tolland's multibranched family.

A visit to the now old General Conyers continues Nick's insertion into Isobel's group—an Isobel whom he has yet to meet. Although Nick does not feel like paying this unexciting call (LM, 68–69), it introduces him to still another Tolland: Isobel's eldest sister, Frederica (LM, 75). Frederica then drives him to another sister of Isobel's, Norah, just because she rooms with Eleanor Walpole-Wilson—a onetime best friend of Nick's early love, Barbara Goring (LM, 89; BM, 17). The interconnections become so complex that we almost need a scorecard to identify the players in this tangled social game, but they do not know that they are playing a game, for the pattern unfolds without their conscious intent. Even the reader cannot perceive the aim of this social tournament until he has finished more than half the volume.

The pattern of Nick's quest for Isobel Tolland reveals itself only retrospectively. Neither we nor Nick at the time have any comprehension that he is looking for her. He attends various gatherings out of what appears to be just aimless gregariousness or, at times, mere politeness. As he meets more and more of the Tollands, he remains unaware that one special family member—his wife-to-be—has come tantalizingly close to making his acquaintance. His ultimate encounter with Isobel occurs through a series of random caroms—nothing so direct as finding her at Molly's.

Standing on a movie line with an unnamed female date, Nick encounters a former college schoolmate, the Marxist writer Quiggin— a highly unlikely link to Isobel Tolland or to anyone else from society's upper reaches. Because Quiggin naively believes that Nick's film-writing job gives him special influence with motion picture heads, Quiggin invites Nick for a weekend stay, so that Nick can help Quiggin's discontented mistress—Templer's ex-wife—to become a film star (LM, 98–100, 110–11). Nick unwillingly accepts the invitation because a studio strike robs him of a ready-made excuse: too much take-home work (LM 100–1). Any small variation of circumstances would have broken the chain that leads at last to Isobel: a differing taste in movies on the part of Nick and Quiggin, an awareness by Quiggin of the facts of movie life, or even a strike settlement. When Nick visits the rent-free cottage that Quiggin has on loan from a wealthy radical patron, this until now unnamed socialist benefactor drops in unexpectedly and turns out to be Erridge—Isobel Tolland's eccentric eldest brother (LM, 108–10, 112–15). But this unfraternal aristocrat recoils at Nick's mention of the Tolland sisters— "the world of his relations no doubt caused him chronic dissatisfaction" (LM, 118)—so that he appears an unlikely conduit for Nick's encounter with Isobel. In addition the secretive Quiggin attempts to keep Erridge from including Nick in a dinner invitation (LM, 120– 21). During his visit to Erridge's as a third social wheel, Nick finally encounters Isobel. She arrives unexpectedly with another of her sisters, Susan, to a halfhearted welcome from Erridge (LM, 135). A complex chain of social machinery has labored for months and years to achieve instant enchantment between Isobel and Nick—proverbial love at first sight (LM, 136).

An equally intricate sequence of tangential caroms leads Mona to Erridge. This trick billiard shot of colliding human beings began a few years earlier with the visit of a minor character, St. John Clarke, to Lady Molly's house. He met Erridge there long before Quiggin had entered Mona's bed or become involved with Clarke (LM, 124). Quiggin's best friend, Members, first brought Clarke and Quiggin together (AW, 124), but the treacherous Quiggin supplanted his friend as Clarke's private secretary (AW, 152–53). In addition, this very same friend, Members, first introduced Quiggin to Mona (AW, 545)—the woman whom Quiggin later steals from her husband, Peter Templer (AW, 170–73). Clarke himself had first introduced Quiggin to Erridge, and Quiggin has exploited this Marxist lord as a patron (LM, 124–27). Now Mona runs off with Erridge (LM, 204–6), but she stays with him only briefly. (CCR, 65–66). In the final bounce of this billard-like sequence, St. John Clarke dies and leaves his money to Erridge (CCR, 225–29), completing in this way a circular return to the very first encounter of the series.

Only after the reader has finished volume four and even gone beyond it can he note the single key to virtually all its movements: the relationship of in-laws. We have already seen how marriages—Molly's own and that of her sister—have linked Aunt Molly to both Lowell and Isobel and have thus helped create the network that Nick at last joins. In volume four Nick and Lovell begin as mere work-place acquaintances (LM, 12); but, by the sixth volume, two separate family mergers have made them brothers-in-law, as Nick marries Isobel (CCR, 56), and Lovell marries her sister, Priscilla (KO, 86). Other potential in-laws hover in the background without quite entering the chain, though they dominate much of the narrative. Toward the end of volume four, as Mona runs off with Erridge and his sister and Nick become engaged (LM, 203–4), it begins to look as if Mona will end up as Nick's own sister-in-law though she hardly ranks high in his favor. The marriage of Mona and Erridge never, in fact, comes off. As a sister-in-law, she remains merely hypothetical. Indeed, the Tollands disagree among themselves about whether she would have made a good wife for Erridge or merely embarrassed them them all (CCR, 66). Widmerpool, too, very nearly becomes the brother-in-law of General Conyers—a weathered campaigner old enough to be his grandfather (LM, 39). And marriage to the general's sister-in-law might even have inserted Widmerpool into Nick's own family network, for the first page tells us that the general "may . . . have been distantly related" to the parents of Nick's mother (LM, 1). With the perspective of the final volumes, we can see that any family link, however vague and distant, with this impossible human being would have deeply distressed Nick. By the end of A Dance, Widmerpool comes to represent everything that Nick despises. Yet only Kenneth Widmerpool's humiliating impotence keeps him from entering this web of affinities.

A simile that describes Widmerpool early in volume four seems mere comic playfulness until subsequent volumes reveal the complete extent of his sexual incapacity—not just the one-time failure with Mildred. The passage occurs when Widmerpool shows up at Lady Molly's as Mildred's surprising fiancé:

> Scarlet in the face, grinning agitatedly through the thick lenses of his spectacles, he advanced into the room, his hand on Mrs. Haycock's arm. He was wearing a new dark suit. Like a huge fish swimming into a hitherto unexplored, unexpectedly exciting acquarium, he sailed resolutely forward: yet not a real fish, a fish made of rubber or some artificial substance. There was something a little frightening about him. That could not be denied. (LM, 43)

Because Widmerpool's ugly face has a certain fishlike look, earlier volumes have already used a marine-life simile for it, but without the suggestion of a synthetic creature. Volume one describes him as the proverbial fish dumped out of water, an awkward and heavy-breathing man: "to all intents and purposes, a fish recently hauled from the water, making powerful though failing efforts at respiration" (QU, 49). In the second volume he retains "that curiously piscine cast of countenance, projecting the impression that he swam, rather than walked, through the rooms he haunted" (BM, 29). Also in volume two Rosie Manasch sees him as a somewhat different specimen of watergoing life: "the Frog Footman" from *Alice's Adventures in Wonderland* who receives a huge letter from an equally strange Fish-Footman (BM, 60).[1] In volume three, though, the narrator continues to see Widmerpool as piscine rather than amphibian: "He nodded, puffing out his lips and assuming the appearance of a huge fish" (AW, 179). In any case, none of these aquatic metaphors quite prepares us for the rubber fish of *At Lady Molly's*—an image that at first seems whimsical and arbitrary.

We do not begin to grasp the simile's implications until volume four's final major episode: the exposure of Widmerpool's sexual fiasco (LM, 230–32). His impotence reduces him to a mere rubber fish in Molly Jeavons's aquarium—a man who aims at becoming a husband without even minimal sexual capacities. Later volumes confirm this tentative diagnosis. When he finally does marry (BDFR, 13), he chooses a woman with her own spectacular sexual problems—the frigid nymphomaniac, Pamela, who "wants it all the time, yet doesn't want it" (BDFR, 225). His life as a husband is ultimately revealed as a psychosexual mess. He combines the roles of pimp, cuckold, and sneaky voyeur—a man who gets gratification from "watching" his "wife being screwed" (TK, 262).

Sexual kinks and ineptitudes on such a grand scale might well have produced comic pathos in a manner similar to Bloom in James Joyce's *Ulysses*. But the rubber-fish passage specifically adds that "there was something a little frightening about him. That could not be denied" (LM, 43). Widmerpool has already shown excessive competitiveness, but that hardly can justify the epithet "frightening" even when modified by "a little." Only subsequent volumes reveal his full menace. In volume eight he sends Stringham off to die and virtually murders Templer within volume nine (SA, 189–90, 215; MP, 204, 211). Helped by these later perspectives, we at last understand the frightfulness of this "fish made of rubber or some artificial substance." In spite of its comic appearance and its synthetic nature, this fish is a killer.

Volume four's title—*At Lady Molly's*—refers to the place around which the story's complexities revolve. To further complicate matters, however, not just one but two of Lady Molly's homes—stately and humble abodes widely spaced in time—play important roles in this game of interconnections. A third home in the volume—Lord Erridge's Thrubworth—has a similar function and a small, amusing connection with Lady Molly's own perpetual open house. In effect, the volume presents a tale of two or even three sites for a game of human billiards.

Molly's present home is a modest red brick, where she lives in South Kensington with Jeavons—her unassuming, unrich, and unelegant second husband. It serves as a meeting hall for all sorts and conditions of guests: "No one was ever, so to speak, turned away from the Jeavons table. The place was a hinterland where none of the ordinary rules seemed to apply and persons of every sort were to be encountered" (LM, 155–56). Here Nick finds an attendant of the British royal court (LM, 31), a retired general (Conyers) (LM, 225), a professional literary man (LM, 218), as well as an ex-governess and many nondescripts (LM, 161–62, 26). Yet years before, as the wife of Lord Sleaford, Molly had lived at Dogdene—a sumptuous mansion described in Pepys's Diary, depicted by Constable, and visited only by the social elite (LM, 10, 11–12). One of the couples in volume four— Widmerpool and Mildred—gravitates in orbit around both houses: Lady Molly's unpretentious present place and her former great mansion. In the 1916 flashback at the volume's very start, Nick (as a boy) meets army nurse Mildred, who not only occupies a Dogdene wing serving as an officers' hospital, but approaches her own sister, General Conyers's wife, at Lady Molly's request (LM, 7–9). Almost two decades later Widmerpool first meets Mildred in Molly's red-brick house, yet he meets his sexual Waterloo with Mildred at Dogdene (LM, 58, 229–32), and news of his impotence surfaces at Molly's present red brick place, where he himself arrives to brazen out his shame (LM, 231–32, 237–39). In short, the Widmerpool-Mildred engagement spans both of Molly's homes.

Nick's own developing relationship with Isobel has whimsical connections with Molly's present house. Although he first meets Isobel at Erridge's rather than at Molly's, a diverting circumstance associates the sadly run-down Thrubworth with Molly's jumble of a place: both use the same drunken butler, Smith, whom Erridge loans out to Molly (LM, 20–21, 127–28). This link underscores a more basic point of connection: the usually inhospitable Erridge serves in volume four as a stand-in for the perfect hostess, Molly, almost in spite of herself. He, and not South Kensington's great social entertainer, introduces Nick to Isobel (LM, 15, 136–37).

Even the Quiggin-Mona-Erridge triangle has small, droll connections with Lady Molly's house. After all, Quiggin's onetime employer, St. John Clarke, began the whole thing by becoming acquainted with Erridge at Lady Molly's (LM, 124). And although neither Quiggin nor Mona actually visits Molly, she has bought a pet monkey with a certain resemblance to Quiggin and keeps it in her bedroom (LM, 160–61): "There was something of Quiggin in his seriousness and self-absorbtion: also in the watchful manner in which he glanced from time to time at the nuts, sometimes choosing one specially tempting to crack" (LM, 164). The narrative even suggests a basic political affinity between Quiggin and the monkey. Quiggin is a pro-Russian Marxist, and the monkey is named " 'Maisky,' after the then Soviet Ambassador" (LM, 164). A kind of Rube-Goldberg narrative contraption—a tangential character and a tangential joke—links Mona's affair to Lady Molly's place.

In this twelve-volume exploration of time, At Lady Molly's gets its title from location rather than the temporal process itself. Only one other volume title comes from an actual place—Casanova's Chinese Restaurant (volume four)—although further titles in A Dance invoke metaphorical places: The Acceptance World, A Buyer's Market, and The Valley of Bones. Given the nature of language, it is difficult, perhaps, to talk about time without on occasion resorting to metaphors of space: span, juncture, interval, or stretch, to choose just a few at random. Still, A Dance employs such titles—metaphorical or otherwise—in a half-joking way. In this comic-narrative vision, time will use everything and anything at all to accomplish its slow surprises—even the spaces of Lady Molly's houses.

Casanova's Chinese Restaurant

Just as in the earlier sequences of *A Dance*, volume five presents a pattern of changing partners that becomes clear only over time. In *Casanova's Chinese Restaurant*, however, it hinges upon incongruous pairings: a male with suicidal tendencies and a female perpetual survivor, a sophisticate and an ingénue, a woman in fancy dress and a man in old tweeds, an incessant talker and a man forever at a loss for words, a heterosexual female and a homosexual male. At one point, the volume's central character, Moreland, explicitly remarks on the frequency of oddly matched couples: "those fascinating mutual attractions between improbable people that take place from time to time" (CCR, 52). But Moreland hardly remains just an observer of this pattern, for he himself becomes caught up in the dance of strangely matched partners.

In volume five's opening chapter, the aesthetically fastidious Moreland adores Matilda Wilson, a "not . . . very 'finished' actress," who, furthermore, lacks the "conventional good looks" that he usually insists upon in women (CCR, 45, 46). In addition, this very jealous male has chosen a wife widely known in the past as Sir Magnus Donners's mistress (CCR, 41–42, 49). She also remains "on easy terms with a world which Moreland, in principle, disliked, indeed entered only for professional purposes"—that of fashionable society (CCR, 53). Although the two have a deep affection for one another, their marriage entails habitual dissension. ". . . What a business married life is," Moreland laments (CCR, 104), and Matilda echoes his complaint: "It is fun to be married to anyone?" (CCR, 157). And, indeed, this marriage of true but less than unified minds begins to break apart when Moreland falls in love with young Priscilla Tolland—herself not at all "the sort of girl Moreland usually liked" (CCR, 156, 160–61).

In the last two chapters of the volume, the unconsummated pairing of Moreland with Priscilla seems at least as incongruous as his marriage to Matilda. As an unintellectual and sheltered young thing, Priscilla has shown little taste either for musicians or other women's husbands (CCR, 137, 156), and Moreland, who lives for music and is someone else's spouse, has never much liked debutantes (CCR, 155–56). When at last we reach the perspective of the volume as a whole, we can note a certain symmetry of strangely matched loves. If the opening chapter centers around Moreland's enchantment with Matilda, a section near the close hinges upon his equivalent enchantment with Priscilla. Love in volume five, in the beginning and the end, makes him yearn for inharmonious sweethearts.

In the course of the volume, the shrewish Mrs. Maclintick has often clashing relationships with three quite different males. This female virtuoso of chaotic pairings performs most vividly in a long-endured marriage with the music critic Maclintick. The two contrast in extraordinary ways. He mutters (CCR, 110); she shouts (CCR, 115). He tends towards silent lugubriousness and she toward voluble ferocity (CCR, 116). He crams his overweight body into old, ill-fitting suits (CCR, 116, 151), but his rather small wife wears eccentric, frilly clothing (CCR, 108, 150). He wallows in filth and disorder (CCR, 206), but she strives fanatically for neatness (CCR, 117). In the course of almost a decade, he has sweated over a book on musical theory that she considers hopeless and utterly impractical (CCR, 116–17). He has, in fact, devoted his entire life to music, but when she first learned that this was his career, she simply said, "Oh, God" (CCR, 209). They fight about politics, too. Maclintick scorns the Loyalists in the Spanish Civil War as mere Communist dupes, but she wholeheartedly supports them. (CCR, 119–21). On every possible topic, they sharply disagree, yet domestic warfare seems to have a masochistic charm for them, or at least for Maclintick himself. When his wife runs off without warning, he proclaims her his "ideal in a sort of way" and kills himself in despair (CCR, 211, 216–17).

The brief encounter of Stringham and Mrs. Maclintick compresses into only a few minutes or so the funniest cross-pairing of the volume. In clothes absurdly wrong for Mrs. Foxe's formal party, Audrey Maclintick looks like a guest at a costume ball with a "medieval or Pre-Raphaelite" cap and "a fluffy, pale pink dress covered with rosettes and small bows, from which her arms and neck emerged surrounded by concentric circles of frills" (CCR, 150). Stringham, on the other hand, "in a very old tweed suit and woollen jumper," somehow achieves a "rather distinguished" appearance in spite of "ancient" clothing (CCR, 162). If Audrey Maclintick exudes "cold rage" (CCR, 166), Stringham sweeps her and everything else before him with a kind of "controlled . . . madness," a drunken "exhilaration" (CCR, 163). Even their flirting techniques contrast very sharply. Stringham teases her about her cap and frills by calling her "Little Bo-Peep" and pretends to mistake her for a very young child: "Fancy a little girl like you being allowed to come to a grown-up party like this one. . . . You ought to be in bed by now I'm sure" (CCR, 166–67). Yet she responds with unchildlike gestures of explicit sexual seductiveness: "She flushed with pleasure, contorting her body into an attitude of increased provocation" (CCR, 166–67). And their dialogue together keeps twisting into comic cross purposes. She always swings back to complaints about her husband, but Stringham ascends into whimsical generalizations about the ills that married flesh is heir to (CCR, 174–

79). One excerpt from their dissonant duet will serve to illustrate the whole:

> "You should have seen Maclintick's sister," said Mrs. Maclintick, "if you are going to grumble about your sister-in-law."
> "We will visit her, if necessary, dear lady, later in the evening," said Stringham. "The night is still young."
> "You can't," said Mrs. Maclintick. "She's dead."
> "My condolences," said Stringham. (CCR, 175)

Stringham turns her hostile comment into a project of empirical research for the evening on this unsatisfactory sister-in-law. Audrey's blunt reply that the sister-in-law is dead leads to Stringham's amusingly inappropriate condolences. This flirtatious dialogue is structured around laughable discordances. Yet to appreciate fully the comic depths of the scene, the reader needs a vision that cuts across time, an awareness that these two are only a single mismatched couple among many others in the volume.

When Audrey's brief flirtation with Stringham has ended, the man with whom she does run away—Carolo, the violinist—appears as odd a partner for this small explosive woman as the whimsically drunken Stringham or, indeed, as her husband, the lugubrious Maclintick himself. "Pale," "drawn," and out of touch with his surroundings, the down-at-the-heels Carolo, a former child prodigy, seems, in his few short appearances, almost entirely tongue-tied (CCR, 20, 121). Amid the swirling talk around him, he confines himself to minimal responses and brief, conventional remarks: "I must be going too" (CCR, 24), "How have you been, Moreland?" (CCR, 119), "Got to remove myself" (CCR, 121), and "Coming?" (CCR, 186). When Carolo runs off with the voluble Mrs. Maclintick, the scene occurs offstage; but one can imagine him sunk in catatonic silence while she rages on about her undeserved afflictions from him and other men. Carolo and Mrs. Maclintick provide yet another example of love's ill-sorted unions: the most nervously talkative woman in the volume and its most inarticulate male.

Mrs. Foxe and Norman Chandler form the oddest of odd couples in all of volume five. Norman is a homosexual young dancer-actor-musician, and wealthy Mrs. Foxe is a beautiful, middle-aged woman married to someone else (CCR, 22, 50–52). Moreland provides a well-phrased description of Norman's epicene appearance: "pure Picasso—one of those attenuated, androgynous mountebanks of the Blue Period" (CCR, 52–53). On the spur of the moment, he takes little fay "leaps in the air" (CCR, 48). Though he seems an unlikely partner for this heterosexual woman, Norman cares for her very much. Yet he fears the ridicule of his homosexual friends concerning his surprising ties to Mrs. Foxe (CCR, 52). As time goes on, he and she are "continually seen about together, linked in a relationship somewhere between lover with mistress and mother to son" (CCR, 90). If by the end of volume five, Chandler has become, to all intents and purposes, this woman's assistant husband (CCR, 146), everyone still wonders at their peculiar arrangement:

> It was not that anyone supposed that Chandler was "having an affair" with Mrs. Foxe—although no one can speak with certainty . . . about two people in that connection—but, apart from any question of physical relationship, she obviously loved Chandler, even if this might not be love of quite the usual sort. (CCR, 147)

An already odd alliance becomes even odder with the perspective of later time spans and subsequent volumes. In *The Valley of Bones*, Mrs. Foxe resolves to divorce her longtime husband and "to live in a workman's cottage" near the wartime camp where the army has stationed Norman Chandler (VB, 165). In volume eight we learn that she still lives with Chandler in these rather humble lodgings and has even risen daily "at half-past five . . . to cook his breakfast" for him (SA, 79). Surprisingly enough, their relationship endures when somewhat less incongruous ones have all split apart. By the end of volume six, Matilda leaves Moreland (KO, 242–45). As early as the close of volume five itself, Moreland breaks with Priscilla (CCR, 219–21), Audrey Maclintick deserts her husband, he kills himself in grief (CCR, 203–4, 216–17), and Audrey's bizarre flirtation with the drunken Stringham leads to absolutely nothing (CCR, 185–86). And although she runs off with Carolo in this very same volume (CCR, 203–4), he, in turn, escapes from her by the middle of volume eight (SA, 118–19). In brief, the odd couple to end all odd couples—Norman Chandler and Mrs. Foxe—has far and away the greatest staying power of them all.

In volume five's second half, news and comments appear about a very famous incongruous couple of 1936: Edward VIII of England and Wallis Simpson. Before the Abdication crisis, Widmerpool proudly reveals his acquaintance with Mrs. Simpson (CCR, 126–27). Other characters—Barnby, Roddy Cutts, Frederica and Robert Tolland, Members, Quiggin, and Moreland—discuss the pros and cons of King Edward's possible marriage to this Baltimore divorcée (CCR, 135–37). Later Robert Tolland and then the drunken Stringham chat about the Abdication after it has happened (CCR, 153, 165–66), and Widmerpool laments the exalted opportunities closed off to him by the failure of Mrs. Simpson to become the royal consort of a still-reigning king (CCR, 195).[2] Only with an overall temporal perspective that includes the strange pairings of Moreland and Matilda, Moreland and Priscilla, Maclintick and Mrs. Maclintick, Stringham and Mrs. Maclintick, Carolo and Mrs. Maclintick, and Mrs. Foxe and Norman Chandler can we recognize the wedlock of this once-royal person and a divorced transatlantic commoner as a public and historic grace note to the odd-couple theme.

Even the bravura passage describing the four-way conversation between Stringham, Mrs. Maclintick, Moreland, and Priscilla gains comic enhancement from later perspectives that cut across time. When we first read the scene itself, Stringham seems securely paired up with Mrs. Maclintick, and Moreland with Priscilla. Stringham taps Audrey's knee with a rolled music program and calls her "little rogue" (CCR, 178), and she looks "thoroughly pleased with herself" at having attracted him (CCR, 173). Priscilla looks "enormously happy" as Moreland sits "beside her," obviously "very taken with" this pretty, young debutante (CCR, 173, 174). Yet, in volumes eight and eleven, we discover that the future gives the lie to these impressions. The only permanent couple emerging from this foursome turns out to be a wholly unexpected combination. It is Moreland and Mrs. Maclintick who live happily ever after in friendly incongruity for almost two decades until, at last, death parts them (SA, 117–19; TK, 275, 276–77).

The volume's title, *Casanova's Chinese Restaurant*, itself refers specifically to an amusing union of absolute contrarieties. The composite name belongs to a large Chinese restaurant that has moved to the quarters of a former Italian one—the New Casanova—and has kept the French-style murals of the famous Venetian lover (CCR, 28, 29–30). In the narrator's own words, "the name . . . offered one of those unequivocal blendings of disparate elements of the imagination which suggest a whole new state of mind or way of life" (CCR, 29). All along this hodgepodge of a restaurant, "panels depicting scenes from the career of the Great Lover" stare out over "chopsticks," "eight treasure rice," and "bamboo shoots fried with pork ribbons" (CCR, 28), and the place becomes an emblem of love's incongruities. It even fills up with a mishmash of ethnic clientele: "Chinese businessmen," "Indian students," "Negroes . . . with very blonde white girls," and "a sprinkling of . . . ethnically indefinable races" (CCR, 30). At first Moreland patronized this place because of a pretty, young waitress who at last rebuffed his attentions (CCR, 28–29). But when he teasingly compares the woman-hunting Barnby to the Great Venetian Lover—a literary favorite of Moreland's—Barnby strikes back by approaching the waitress himself (CCR, 34–35).[3] In the climactic event of the restaurant sequence, Moreland glumly watches as Barnby persuades the waitress to pose for him in his studio (CCR, 36–38). Eventually the painter has a "love affair" with her, but "he always insisted she was 'not his type,'" was "too thin for" his "taste," and had legs too "poorish" for his personal requirements (CCR, 38–39, 31, 30)—yet another case of love's incongruous pairings.

Only when we have finished all of volume five can we see that the restaurant passage sets forth a theme—love's incongruous couples—that spreads itself out in distant ramifications throughout the entire volume. Just like Barnby, two of the other diners in that poly-ethnic place have already made or later will make their own discordant pairings: Maclintick with Mrs. Maclintick, and Moreland with Matilda, with Priscilla, and at last, most surprisingly, with Mrs. Maclintick. Jenkins, though, is present in the restaurant scene as hardly more than an observer; he will not join the odd couples' dance. His marriage to Isobel Tolland brings together like with like, and fittingly enough, gets very little space within volume five. Their well-matched life together remains a marginal exception. In the fifth sequence as a whole, love makes strange bedfellows.

The Kindly Ones

By volume six, an insistent pattern of fortuitous reencounters and analogous events has begun to emerge from time's choreography.[4] Within The Kindly Ones itself, a web of remeetings and similar occurrences spans a quarter of a century—a one-volume paradigm for the scattered repetitions of the three thousand or so pages within A Dance as a whole. Volume six, however, has its own unique time scheme determined by history's recurrence: world war for Britain. Chapter one flashes back to 1914 just before Sarajevo, and chapters two, three, and four move forward, respectively, to the Munich agreement of 1938, the Nazi-Soviet pact of 1939, and the days shortly after Great Britain declared war on Hitler. Within each chapter, an extended social gathering provides a comic sequence of petty disasters that counterpoints war's approaching enormities. In an amusingly complex way, each subsequent gathering echoes an earlier one either by an improbable recombination of guests or a reenactment of similar misadventures. If world calamity repeats itself within volume six, so do private embarrassments.

The volume presents an archetypal mishap at a luncheon entertainment in 1914 and analogous mishaps at subsequent gatherings. The opening sentence of the 1914 section introduces Albert, the Jenkinses' cook—a true virtuoso at entertaining guests (KO, 1, 7). Because the isolated Jenkinses seldom invite visitors to their less than spacious bungalow (KO, 8, 34–35), Albert plans to cook a special mousse for a rare Sunday luncheon with a food-loving general and his wife who are scheduled to arrive 28 June 1914 (KO, 9–10, 69). Chapter one unfolds a tangle of servant problems that threatens to make a mess of the cook's great performance. Albert scorns the maid, Billson, who, in turn, adores him; and she scorns the manservant, Bracey, who, in turn, loves her (KO, 15). She keeps vowing to quit because of late-night hauntings by the ghosts of the Jenkinses' house (KO, 3–6). Albert's very position as the family cook is threatened by a persistent "girl from Bristol" who intends to marry him and take him from the family (KO, 6–7, 45–46). And from time to time, the manservant Bracey slips into paralyzed ineptness because of his almost psychotic depressions, benumbing "funny days" (KO, 12–14). An odd local nuisance causes further trouble among these three servants: Dr. Tre-lawney's religious and vegetarian cult that occasionally jogs by the Jenkinses' house in "artistic" "pastel" clothing. Its half-starved disci-ples are sometimes reduced to begging back-door snacks, and when Billson gives a seed-cake to one of Trelawney's urchins, Bracey con-demns the charity as unauthorized by the family, Albert defends it, Billson cries, and dissension smolders on (KO, 28–34). On the day of Sarajevo, these small comic troubles all coalesce in one amusing muddle that detracts from Albert's triumphant lunch.

Each small disaster builds onto the next to form a slightly bigger one, and the accumulated mess finally crashes down on the guests in the drawing room. The predawn reappearance of a household ghost makes Billson somewhat jumpy (KO, 42–43). Later that morning Albert gives notice of a month or so in order to marry the Bristol girl (KO, 43–44)—a double-barreled proclamation that distresses lovelorn Billson but also disturbs the Jenkinses. To make matters worse at this moment of confusion, Bracey starts to have one of his "funny days" (KO, 49). And the already tense Mr. and Mrs. Jenkins receive an infuriating telegram—an announcement that Uncle Giles, the Jenkins family bore, will intrude on their house in just a few hours, even though he and the scheduled guests despise one another (KO, 46–49). With everyone ruffled by this tangle of events (KO, 55), the general and his wife arrive for Albert's fine cuisine, but the heartsick Billson almost ruins the occasion as she waits on the family table. Her extreme agitation makes the general drop a potato, she herself drops a ladle, and she slams down her tray and rushes from the room (KO, 55–56, 57–58). After lunch, in the drawing room, a free-floating edginess explodes in comic disaster. With her sanity shaken by both Albert and the ghosts, Billson walks into the drawing room absolutely naked and declares that she has quit as maid—at once an erotic statement and an on-the-job protest (KO, 57–61). Yet, in spite of the Jenkinses' embarrassment and pain, it looks for a time as though Uncle Giles will miss his special chance to annoy them further. The general and his wife begin to drive off before Giles appears, but another ludicrous problem delays their departure. Dr. Trelawney and his whole crazy cult come running so abruptly up a hill in the road that the general's car almost hits him, and during the confusion and the resulting conversation, Uncle Giles arrives (KO, 63–66). With his usual obtuseness, Giles tells of Franz Ferdinand's assassination during a motorcar visit to Sarajevo as a simple illustration of the troubles caused by cars (KO, 69–70). On this day of domestic absurdity, the messenger of war turns out to be a clown.

As World War II approaches twenty-four years later, a new cast of characters within chapter two attends a dinner party with a ludicrous conclusion. Near the chapter's opening, a simile connects this new impending war with the phantoms that harassed the maid in the house called Stonehurst twenty-four years before:

> Like one of the Stonehurst "ghosts," war towered by the bed when you awoke in the morning; unlike those more transient, more accommodating spectres, its tall form, so far from dissolving immediately, remained, on the contrary, a looming, menacing shape of ever greater height, ever thickening density. (KO, 87)

Stonehurst had been built around 1900 by a soldier "retired" from India (KO, 5), so that Billson's ghosts may well have been soldiers, and the metaphorical specter of World War II may connect especially closely with these previous literal ghosts.

Amid recurring world conflict, still another love triangle sets off once again an outbreak or explosion of after-dinner madness. During an entertainment at Sir Magnus Donners's castle, Templer's wife displays distracted jealousy as her husband flirts with Anne Umfraville, Donners's present mistress (KO, 115–16, 138). Amid symbolically appropriate works of art, such as *Cupid Chastised* and the *Seven Deadly Sins* (KO, 110, 117–18), pathetic Betty Templer has a nervous collapse very much like Billson's. Templer's wife cracks up at the climax of a pantomime on the Seven Deadly Sins played out by the guests: ". . . Lust is the star part," Anne Umfraville declares (KO, 126). As Anne and Templer enact a tableau of "impotent desire" on the tabletop, Betty howls like a dog, weeps uncontrollably, and scampers from the room (KO, 131–33). The narrator explicitly notes how this bizarre event resembles Billson's crazy nakedness: "Betty wanted

Templer's love, just as Billson wanted Albert's; Albert's marriage had precipitated a breakdown in just the same way as Templer's extravagances with Anne Umfraville" (KO, 133). Yet the narrator keeps silent about another recurrence of chapter one's pattern right after Betty's breakdown—Widmerpool's arrival at the castle—so that we ourselves must make the unexpressed connections. Widmerpool serves on page 133 as the analogue of Giles on page 66. Just like Uncle Giles, Widmerpool was expected as an after-dinner caller (KO, 107), and bumbles in after the highly embarrassing climax. Further reenacting the role of Uncle Giles, Widmerpool becomes a messenger of war—a war only months away. His faux pas of entering the castle in his Territorial uniform makes him seem "a sinister, threatening figure, calling the world to arms" (KO, 133). With an obtuseness like Giles's concerning Sarajevo, Widmerpool believes that the Munich appeasement has averted war "for five years at least" (KO, 137). Also like Uncle Giles, Widmerpool shows up merely to "talk business" (KO, 46, 107, 136)—not to proclaim the imminence of World War II. But, without his own awareness, he serves as the herald of the "Furies."

Almost a year later, within chapter three, four of the characters from that day of Sarajevo come together again in another troubled time, in the midst of global conflict and private fiascoes. At a seaside hotel where Giles had spent his last futile years, Nick arrives for his uncle's seriocomic funeral. There Nick reencounters Albert, the cook; Trelawney, the mystagogue; and the figurative "spirit" of clownish Giles himself (KO, 202). Albert runs the hotel now, Trelawney is its most disreputable guest, and Giles lingers on in his personal effects—a shabby and embarrassing collection (KO, 141, 152–53, 155). Ironically enough, by the time of this reunion and reworking of the past, Albert has forgotten most of what occurred in 1914, including Billson's naked protest (KO, 150–51). Nevertheless, at the climax of this section set in 1939, Dr. Trelawney has an attack of hysteria somewhat reminiscent of Billson's comic breakdown and also of Betty's collapse. He locks himself by accident in a hotel bathroom, begins to wheeze with asthma, and needs calming down before he can manage to turn the key correctly (KO, 183–86). Once again, an absurd anxiety attack occurs within a framework of impending world war—a war, incidentally, that foolish Uncle Giles had insistently denied would ever take place (KO, 191–92).

The messenger of World War II in this chapter turns out to be Bob Duport—Nick's despised (but only slight) acquaintance and Jean's former husband, who has actually appeared just once before at the first volume's close (QU, 191–99). As a chance fellow guest at Albert's hotel, Duport brings the news of the Russo-German pact: a conspiracy of powers that means certain war (KO, 199–200). Appropriately enough, in a chapter with a mere chance messenger from long-vanished days and many chance reencounters, Myra Erdleigh reappears as yet another hotel guest—an eerie clairvoyant with detailed foreknowledge of who will meet whom and when (KO, 152–53, 195–96). Indeed, she claims to have had a mystical preawareness that Nick would show up at this very time and place (KO, 196).

In a well-known essay on time and space in the novel, the Russian critic Bakhtin has noted that fortuitous meetings in plots ruled by chance "are better understood" by the characters "through fortune-telling" and other similar means rather than rational "analysis."[5] Expressing a parallel thought, A Dance's final volume quotes a saying of Trelawney's: "coincidence was no more than 'magic in action'" (HSH, 35). Ostensibly, however, the magus in A Dance speaks of life itself rather than of novels.

Just as in most of the other twelve volumes, fortuitous encounters within volume six take place during social occasions such as luncheons, dinners, and the like. In his essay on what he calls "chronotope" or novelistic time and space, Bakhtin sketches the way that novels over the centuries have shifted from mere chance meetings of travelers on a road (as in picaresque novels) to less random meetings in "parlors" and "salons" (as in Balzac and Stendhal).[6] In A Dance, though, even encounters at these indoor meeting places have an on-the-road kind of fortuitousness. We must note, however, that in chapter three of The Kindly Ones the various chance meetings occur at a hotel—the indoor extension of a narrative highway, the end of a traveler's road. Within the long history of the English novel, we can point to a similar pattern, for example, in Fielding's Tom Jones: the inn at Upton as a central switching point for many random meetings.[7] For Giles, of course, in A Dance and also for Trelawney, Albert's place serves as a residence hotel—the end of life's road. Powell's narrator adds another whimsical touch that transforms the hotel into a residence in motion, a place where travelers come together but also one that itself can move. Its "battleship-grey" makes it seem absurdly like an ill-built boat, "resolutely attempting to set out to sea"—a sort of hotel cruise ship (KO, 149).[8] The "magic in action" within volume six finds a highly appropriate setting at Albert's hotel—a sort of cross between a picaresque road and a parlor or salon.

If The Kindly Ones sets up repeating correlations between its various chapters, it also develops further interconnections with far-more-distant passages and volumes. A single extended example well illustrate the rest. Seven full pages at the start of chapter three deal with odds and ends in Giles's old Gladstone bag, including certain things that withhold their full significance until we connect them with widely spaced details. Amid a fairly self-explanatory jumble of objects, such as Giles's unfavorable horoscope, overdrawn bank account, enema tube, and late-Victorian appointment to army second lieutenant (KO, 156–59), other items yield their secrets in full only with a view that cuts across the volumes. The outdated batches of company reports stuffed throughout the bag require the details of distant correlation (KO, 155). As far back as volume two, when Nick encountered Giles at dawn on a scruffy London street, Giles pulled out of his "pocket a handful of documents, looking like company reports, and glanced swiftly through them" (BM, 156)—an unlikely time and place for an instant reappraisal of one's financial worth. The scene suggests that ridiculous Uncle Giles carries his portfolio crammed inside his pocket at every shabby moment. Because the Gladstone bag as described in volume six holds the "gratifying prospects" of "endless financial projects" and also the "inevitable losses" that ensued (KO, 155), we can, of course, deduce that those same "company reports" from the dawn of volume two end up in the posthumous rubbish heap. The widely distanced passages coalesce here to shed amusing light on Giles's stumbling ways.

When juxtaposed with earlier details, one apparently insignificant item in the bag takes on new importance: old letters involving a subpoena of Uncle Giles as a witness to an automobile accident (KO, 159). At the climax of chapter one, an unknowing Giles brought news of Sarajevo in a very offhand manner: "Some royalty in a motorcar have been involved in a nasty affair today." Indeed, in this passage, he worried not at all about impending world war but only about automobiles: "Not too keen on 'em. Always in accidents" (KO, 69). In light of this previous scene, the fact that Giles kept outdated correspondence about an automobile collision suggests an old obsession—a motorcar phobia over the years. But the long-feared automobile itself becomes an emblem of Giles's absolute obtuseness: his automobile-obsessed and blinkered disregard of the signal for World War I.

One final object in the Gladstone bag—a privately printed copy of *The Perfumed Garden of the Sheik Nefzaoui or The Arab Art of Love* (KO, 160–62)—casts sudden light on a far-distant scene. Over the years Nick has wondered at times about the sexual habits of his bachelor uncle. Nine hundred and thirty-six pages before Nick uncovers his uncle's Arab manual, Nick encountered Giles in the small morning hours on a block overrun by prostitutes' flats. Nick himself had a perfectly innocent reason for being in that place—he lived in rooms across the way—but his uncle's explanation might well inspire a flicker of a doubt. He had just arrived in London at daybreak, he asserted, and was strolling to his club (BM, 154–57). The posthumous evidence from Uncle Giles's bag of *The Arab Art of Love* undermines his abili of a chaste dawn stroll through a red-light district. Once again in *A Dance,* a far-removed passage rewrites an earlier one.

Volume six's title, *The Kindly Ones,* provides a literal translation of the Greek euphemism for the war-bringing "Furies"—an ancient "flattery intended to appease their terrible wrath" (KO, 2). But here the expression has a somewhat different nuance. Although set against a horizon of impending world wars, volume six tells an essentially comic story. A title such as *The Furies* would have been far too grim for a book that hinges on Billson's naked protest, Betty's jealous howls, and Dr. Trelawney's entrapment in the lavatory. In spite of its melancholy background, *The Kindly Ones* remains a very funny book. Instead of working merely as a simple euphemism, its title transposes and shifts itself into a comic key.

The closing sentence of *The Kindly Ones* declares that "another stage of life" has "passed" (KO, 254). Volumes four, five, and six center around a time of early manhood or maturity for Nick's whole generation—the 1930s: an era for them of settling down into a realm of work, of establishing families, and of sorting out one's friends and one's basic social circle. World War II will break up this pattern of maturation. To his fellow soldiers in wartime, Nick will seem quite old, someone past his prime. And the war will separate Nick and the rest of his generation from their proper line of work, their families, and the party-going rounds of *A Dance*'s social circle.

7

Wartime

The Valley of Bones

THE wartime experiences in most of volume seven return us to an all-male setting that, in spite of class differences, resembles and repeats the all-male one at *A Dance*'s beginning. Surprising yet basic correlations unfold between Jenkins's six months in a 1940 training camp of raw Welsh recruits and his long-vanished years in an English public school almost two decades earlier. Indeed, a sergeant briefly appears who looks a bit like Templer (VB, 8, 11), Nick's public school friend, and an actual school acquaintance, Widmerpool, turns up in the end as Nick's new superior officer (VB, 239–41). As in volume one's opening chapters, the standard plot interest that propels most novels—boy meets girl—remains almost nil in *The Valley of Bones*. What matters here most is man's relationship to man. At one point, the narrator comments at length on the strong male bond arising in the army:

> The relationship seems to develop a curious state of intimacy in an unintimate society; one, I mean, far removed from anything to be thought of as overstepping established limits of propriety or everyday discipline. Indeed, so far from even approaching the boundaries of sexual aberration or military misconduct, the most normal of men, and conscientious of officers, often provided the most striking instances. Even my father, I remembered, had possessed an almost mystic bond with Bracey, certainly a man of remarkable qualities. It was a thing not easily explicable, perhaps demanded by the emotional conditions of an all-male society. Regular officers, for example, would sometimes go to great pains to prevent their servants suffering some deserved minor punishment for an infringement of routine. (VB, 71)

Volume seven hinges upon Nick's subaltern relationship to Captain Rowland Gwatkin, a likable man who idealizes the army yet makes a mess in the Company's Command. When he invites just Nick to share a small sleeping space in the Company's working office, the two men

110

grow quite intimate (VB, 50–51). In an important scene, the fuss-budget Company Commander wakes up after dark and starts to pile the contents of his confidential box on Nick's adjacent bed in search of a newly issued codeword. Among stacks of official documents, Nick discovers a copy of Rudyard Kipling's *Puck of Pook's Hill*, and a slightly defensive Gwatkin confesses admiration for its tale of "a Roman centurion." Nick says that he too likes this story, which he read "ages ago" (VB, 56–59)—most likely a tactful reference to having read it as a boy, for *Puck of Pook's Hill* is, indeed, a children's classic.[1] Three of its chapters tell of a Roman centurion stationed in England by Hadrian's Wall, who defends his post bravely over the years at the personal request of the Emperor Maximus. The emperor's successor, Theodosius, has Maximus put to death yet offers the faithful centurion command of a whole legion under the new regime. Although the hero turns it down out of loyalty to the dead, the new emperor still honors this paragon of all the military virtues with a glorious Triumph in Rome.[2] The adolescent quality of this Gwatkin-Kipling dream of wartime army glory seems clear enough here, but the immediate juxtaposition of the Kipling passage with the one in which Gwatkin searches for the code word connects the whole segment with a much later scene that makes the would-be hero a figure of some pathos—an object of Nick's pity as well as his amusement. One hundred and fifty pages further on, Gwatkin messes up the whole codeword sequence—a comic conglomeration of unheroic terms, including *Fishcake, Buttonhook, Bathwater, Leather, Toadstool*, and *Walnut*. He even forgets to reveal them to his staff. Instead of a Triumph of Kiplingesque glory, he loses his command and ends up in the rubbish heap of military discards (VB, 208–10, 216–18).

In still another way, Gwatkin's final debacle connects with a further allusion to Kipling's book for children. Only Nick knows that the captain's lapse about the Battalion's codewords has largely come about from his helpless infatuation with a local Irish barmaid, and Gwatkin himself links sexual temptation with words from a poem in *Puck of Pook's Hill:* "keep us pure till the dawn" (VB, 90–91). When the poor dismissed Gwatkin discovers his barmaid in the arms of one Corporal Gwylt, Nick says that Gwylt has special need of Kipling's prayer, and Gwatkin begins to laugh. By keeping his sense of humor in spite of all indignities, the captain shows a certain plucky "style" (VB, 229–30), yet events have virtually unmanned him. One hundred sixty-four pages earlier in the volume, Gwatkin had employed a laughable comparison when urging his men to "take care of" their "rifles": ". . . a soldier is no longer a soldier when his weapon is gone from him. He is like a man who has had that removed which makes him a man, something sadder, more useless, than a miner who has lost his lamp, or a farmer his plough" (VB, 66). It seems no mere phallic coincidence that, in Gwatkin's moment of pathetic shame at messing up the code words, the narrator's eyes focus on the captain's private parts: "Gwatkin stepped quickly out of bed. His pyjama trousers fell from him, revealing sexual parts and hairy brown thighs" (VB, 208). Nick's quick gaze at the poor, naked Gwatkin suggests a pitying affection, the compassion of male for male, though not at all homosexual: a bemused commiseration for "something sadder" and "more useless" than a soldier without his gun—a captain deprived of his visions of glory and his childish dreams of manhood from *Puck of Pook's Hill*.

The story of the captain's pathetic decline and fall gains special poignancy from Jenkins's own complex feelings about him: a simultaneous amusement and compassion. When Gwatkin, for example, attempts to reform the Company's perpetual "bad character," Private Sayce, Nick perceives the lecture as virtual slapstick comedy, yet he also understands that this laughable charade springs from Gwatkin's boyish idealism (VB, 60–65): "Those stylized pictures of army life on which Gwatkin's mind loved to dwell did not exclude a soldier of Sayce's type" (VB, 61). When Irish marauders steal Deafy Morgan's rifle, Nick connects the captain's exaggerated despair over a trifling misadventure with his "homily about rifles" and, by implication, his nervousness about removing from a man "that . . . which makes him a man" (VB, 68, 72–74, 66). During a segment where Gwatkin bungles Company maneuvers and expresses his frustration by depriving Nick of lunch, Nick can see a touching magnanimity in Gwatkin's later apology and compensatory gift of "a sizeable bar of chocolate" (VB, 77–82, 85–87). And the possible death by suicide of depressed Sergeant Pendry—Templer's look-alike—gives Nick further insight into his captain's vulnerability. "I blame myself too," Gwatkin says. "I should have foreseen it." "This," adds the pitying but also amused Jenkins, "was another of Gwatkin's ritual sufferings for the ills of the Battalion" (VB, 100–2). Nick's sly displacement of *Company* by *Battalion* suggests an amused compassion for a Company Commander who takes upon his shoulders the sins of the larger unit, the sins of the military world, as pathetic Gwatkin tries hard to become an army saint.

Although the Nick-Gwatkin friendship stands at the volume's center, the narrator treats their relationship with British understatement: e.g., "I gave him a salute for the last time, feeling he deserved it" (VB, 234). For the full significance of the strong male bond between Nick and his pathetic captain, the reader must supply distant correlations

from other times and scenes. From Nick's early closeness to the witty
Charles Stringham in *A Dance*'s opening volume to Nick's later pleasure in Moreland's witty talk throughout volume five, we can see that
the narrator-actor has his own special gift for lasting male friendships.
Such masculine connections mean a great deal to him; and within
army life, Gwatkin fills the void left by Nick's separation from his old
peacetime friends.

Within *The Valley of Bones* itself, the single exception to a virtually
all-male milieu comes in chapter three, where Nick, on leave, visits his
sister-in-law, Frederica. Yet even here the stress falls on man-to-man
encounters, and the chapter's prelude to this gathering of the sexes—
Nick's week at Aldershot for a quick training course—remains as
wholly male as a men's locker room. This preliminary section includes
a brief reencounter with a bookish man named Pennistone, who will
later become one of Nick's closest friends in the army (VB, 103–9); an
introduction to young Odo Stevens, an aggressive young man with off-
putting ways (VB, 115–17); and a chance remeeting with one Jimmy
Brent, whose sexual revelations about Jean Templer Duport revolve,
in fact, around his own hero worship of Bob Duport, Jean's ex-
husband (VB, 118–20, 124–33). When Nick finally gets to his sister-
in-law's gathering of both men and women, he spends the most time
chatting with Dicky Umfraville, an epitome of rake-hell manliness
(VB, 140–44, 149–56). In this male-dominated chapter, even Nick's
reunion with his own expectant wife takes no more than four and a
half pages out of sixty-two in all (VB, 144–48, 167).

Within volume seven, one character alone serves as a comic exception to Nick's generalization about the entire decorum of army male
relationships: "far from even approaching the boundaries of sexual
aberration" (VB, 71). Shabby Lieutenant Bithel transgresses those
"boundaries" almost from the start. At the climax of the scene that
first introduces him, a drunken Bithel performs a homoerotic dance
around a male effigy flung together in his bedclothes by the Company's practical jokers. "Love 'o mine," chants Bithel as he covers its
sponge-bag face with innumerable kisses (VB, 25–28). In a novel with
the title *A Dance to the Music of Time*, Bithel's whimsical choreographic turn stands out from the others that crop up here and there: the
workmen's opening dancelike movements (QU, 1), Poussin's painting
of Time's choreography (QU, 2), an actual ballroom dance (TM, 57–
75), dance metaphors for social pairings and chance reencounters
(BM, 174; AW, 63), and a musical chairs simile for death's interruption
of all these complex patterns (VB, 196). Except for a later obscene
dance by a naked band of hippies (HSH, 164–69), men in all these

images pair off with women or encounter male friends without "approaching the boundaries of sexual aberration" (VB, 71). Yet Bithel nonchalantly transgresses those "boundaries."

Allusions and phrases about homosexual men occur in various places like verbal iron filings drawn to the magnet of Bithel's mere presence. In *A Dance*'s very first reference to Proust's *A la recherche*, Nick describes Bithel's cap as "cut higher than normal (like Saint-Loup's, I thought)" (VB, 32)—of course, one of Proust's secret homosexuals. When it suddenly occurs to Gwatkin that the *Puck of Pook's Hill* prayer about keeping "pure till the dawn" might allude to sex with women, the narrator adds his own wry comment: "I controlled temptation to make flippant suggestions about other, more recondite vices, for which, with troops of such mixed origin as Rome's legions, the god's hasty moral intervention might be required" (VB, 91). Even in the single chapter where Bithel remains completely offstage—the one about the training week and Nick's weekend leave—a homosexual theme emerges once again in a rather amusing passage as if Lieutenant Bithel has influenced the text even from afar. Here we learn that retired General Conyers, an armchair dabbler now at psycholanalytic theory, has composed an article specifically on "heightened bi-sexuality in relation to early religiosity" (VB, 158–59). In view of the general's hypothesis that too much childhood religion cause sexual inversion, it seems hardly an accident that, at Bithel's reemergence in *A Dance*'s final volume, this aged homosexual chants the same devotional hymns sung by his old Welsh Company three decades before:

> Open now the crystal fountain,
> Whence the healing stream doth flow:
> Let the fire and cloudy pillar
> Lead me all my journey through.
>
> (HSH, 216–17; VB, 237)

> When I tread the verge of Jordan,
> Bid my anxious fears subside,
> Death of Death and hell's destruction,
> Land me safe on Canaan's side.
>
> (HSH, 238; VB, 102)

One suspects that this old homosexual finally has returned to an "early religiosity"—a psychosexual symptom or joke linking six entire volumes and thirteen hundred and seventy-two pages. One other amusing homosexual detail goes far back beyond *A Dance*'s own era—over one hundred and twenty-five years before it. Nick reads a fragment from a letter of Lord Byron's—actually a pastiche concocted by Powell—that twits Lady Caroline Lamb for alleged attentions to her by Hercules Mallock, the owner of Castlemallock: ". . . Spare me an account of his protestations of affection & recollect that your host's namesake preferred *Hylas* to the *Nymphs*" (VB, 170–71). This refers to the classical Hercules's love for a boy whom he snatched from a band of beautiful nymphs. Within this web of learned allusions, the ancient Greek demigod, the nineteenth-century lord, and even Byron himself share Bithel's homosexual tendencies.

These scattered textual references to homoerotic men foreshadow Lieutenant Bithel's big comic scene in chapter four. Having drunk himself silly, he pleads with an army waiter for still one more whiskey, although the bar has closed:

> . . . Bithel lunged his body forward, and, either to save himself from falling, or to give emphasis to his request for a last drink, threw his arms round Emmot's neck. There, for a split second, he hung. There could be no doubt about the outward impression this posture conveyed. It looked exactly as if Bithel were kissing Emmot—in farewell, rather than in passion. Perhaps he was. Whether or not that were so, Emmot dropped the tray, breaking a couple of glasses, at the same time letting out a discordant sound. Gwatkin jumped to his feet. His face was white. He was trembling with rage.
>
> "Mr. Bithel," he said, "consider yourself under arrest." (VB, 203–4)

As in many other places in this vast, complex work, to get the scene's full impact, we need to recollect some far distant ones. Perhaps not surprisingly in a twelve-volume novel filled with artists and Bohemians, homosexuality crops up here and there, and Nick always treats it with tolerant amusement. He remains on friendly terms with his epicene acquaintances: the painter, Edgar Deacon (BM, 122; CCR, 13–14, 17, 21); the dancer-actor-musician, Norman Chandler (CCR, 22, 52, 53, 141); and a Noel Coward-like nightclub performer, Max Pilgrim, who sings double-entendre songs about "pansies" and "fairies" (BM, 115, 118, 120, 148–49; SA, 154).[3] Even if the *Manual of Military Law* condemns such behavior, Bithel's kiss of the startled army waiter teeters somewhere between perversity and a merely comic stumble by a very drunken oaf: "This may have been a stumble, since some of the floorboards were loose at that place" (VB, 203). The tolerant Nick, indeed, begins "to laugh" until Gwatkin trembles "with rage" (VB, 203–4). In the context of *A Dance*'s amused broad-mindedness, the captain's tense reaction seems utterly absurd. Then, too, this scene has comic interconnections with an earlier one in the volume: Gwatkin's equation of a weaponless soldier and a man with "that removed which makes him a man" (VB, 66). In the military degradation ceremony for Bithel's "crime"—a "crime" that Gwatkin defines as kissing "an Other Rank" (would it have been acceptable if drunken Lieutenant Bithel had "kissed" a fellow lieutenant?) (VB, 205)—Gwatkin strips the culprit of his gun "He will not wear a belt, nor carry a weapon," the captain declares, and Bithel reacts with "a despairing look, as if cut to the quick to be forbidden a weapon" (VB, 204). Because of the captain's bumbling ineptness, this scene of mock castration stays unthreateningly absurd. In the chaos of his other mistakes, Gwatkin forgets to file immediate charges and has to drop his case against Bithel (VB, 213–15).

Darker comic connections with other distant volumes further affect our reading of Bithel's "kissing" scene. At the end of the volume that follows—*The Soldier's Art*—an officer far more ruthless than pathetic Rowland Gwatkin, the detestable Kenneth Widmerpool, hounds Bithel from the army for simple drunkenness (SA, 186–88). If homosexuality plays no direct role in Bithel's last undoing, a web of interactions from very distant volumes inserts it retrospectively. In *A Dance's* final volume, the hippie guru Murtlock has Widmerpool do penance for wrongs against two men with homosexual pasts—Bithel himself and Sir Bertram Akworth (HSH, 223–25). If Widmerpool had driven Bithel, weeping, from the army (SA, 187), a much younger Widmerpool in the very first volume had triggered the public school expulsion of young Bertram Akworth for trying to send a love note to another male student (QU, 13). Within this broad context of almost three thousand pages, we can put together a corollary to the army's special rules against "sexual aberration" (VB, 71). In *A Dance's* own implied rules of conduct, sexual intolerance ranks as a serious infraction against balanced broad-mindedness and a healthy sense of humor.

The seventh volume's title comes from Ezekiel 37: 1–10, the text of Chaplain Popkiss's sermon as chapter one closes (especially in view of Bithel's later "kissing" episode, the unmajestic name of *Popkiss* has comic reverberations). With a Church-of-England hopefulness, the chaplain prophesies that the "bones without flesh and sinew, bones without skin or breath" of the ragged Welsh Battalion will "come together" to make "an exceeding great army" (VB, 37–38). In *The Valley of Bones* itself, Popkiss's prediction seems way off the target. Throughout the entire volume, a chain of markers from World War II history suggests the increasing menace that the men must someday face, yet the ragtag Battalion shows very few signs of pulling itself together. Juxtaposed with the Nazi invasion of Denmark and Norway (9 April 1940—VB, 98), Deafy Morgan loses his rifle (VB, 72–74), the pedantic Gwatkin spoils the Company's maneuvers (VB, 77–80), and depressed Sergeant Pendry dies, perhaps by his own hand (VB, 100–

2)—deeds hardly worthy of the great historic challenge. As Germany invades the Netherlands (10 May 1940—VB, 179), as the Nazis drive toward the Channel ports (15 May 1940—VB, 181), as Belgium abruptly surrenders (28 May 1940—VB, 195), as Italy joins in against France and England (10 June 1940—VB, 216), and as the Nazis overrun Paris (14 June 1940—VB, 243), Gwatkin forgets the code, and his Company stumbles badly through their training maneuvers (VB, 207–13). Amid gathering world disasters, these soldiers in the valley of bones seem hardly more than clowns in a military farce. Yet astonishingly enough, two volumes later, when Nick reencounters his former Welsh Battalion and the present commander of his former Welsh Company, they have seen heavy action near Caen and have produced a genuine hero, one Elystan-Edwards, who has won the Victoria Cross, Britain's highest decoration for military valor (MP, 172–77). Absurd Chaplain Popkiss has managed somehow to prophesy correctly. In spite of the chaos of those 1940 days, the "bones without flesh and sinew, bones without skin or breath" finally have become "an exceeding great army" (VB, 38).

The Soldier's Art

Throughout volume seven the war remained distant from Nick's army training, but in a central sequence of volume eight, German bombs rain death on Nick's acquaintances and friends. As early as page five, an air raid foreshadows the pivotal role that bombings will play in subsequent events (SA, 5–18); and later in chapter one, another raid occurs as a narrative reminder (SA, 42–43). At the second chapter's climax, bombing deaths darken and utterly transform an up-till-then comic story (SA, 155–66). In the third and last chapter, still one more German air raid adds a final touch to Bithel's ludicrous downfall (SA, 184–86). Within The Soldier's Art as a whole, the public events of worldwide struggle crash down unexpectedly upon private lives.

The opening description of an air raid in Northern Ireland is distinctly understated—a mild beginning to a later deadly sequence. The narrator devotes just one subordinate clause to "our first local blitz," when "a thousand people" died, and he passes on instead to a less alarming raid several nights afterwards (SA, 5, 16). Bithel even likens it to a thrilling tale for children in Chums or the Boy's Own Paper, and Nick reveals in turn that, during his own childhood, he lived through Zeppelin raids in World War I (SA, 13–15). Even with its spectacular searchlights, bursts from anti-aircraft, and flares dropped from planes, the present raid seems an adventure to them both, almost a childish game (SA, 11–12). Only "a deep, rending explosion" and a few smaller ones remind us and them of the danger— a Nazi deus ex machina waiting in the sky to distribute random death on the characters below (SA, 12, 17).

From A Dance's first volume onward, coincidence assumes an increasingly central role, but in volume eight's long middle chapter, the mere chance placement in space and time under random Nazi bombs becomes the plot's be-all and end-all. Unaware of his own approaching death from a haphazard bomb, Lovell meets Nick at the Café Royal and asks him to become executor of a newly drawn will (SA, 106)—a task that will fall upon Jenkins with almost indecent speed. Complaining of his wife's affair with Lieutenant Odo Stevens (SA, 107–11), Chips tells of a scheme for surprising her that evening into instantaneous reconciliation. He will approach her in a nightclub called the Madrid, at Bijou Ardglass's fortieth birthday party, to which he and his wife have been separately invited, though she does not even know that he is in London. He counts upon a sentimental circumstance to revive her wifely feelings: when they first became engaged several years before, they celebrated together at the very same Madrid (SA, 111–12). During Bijou's nightclub party, some half dozen persons will die all at once from a single German bomb (SA, 111, 156–57). Because Priscilla detests the Madrid's current act—the same Max Pilgrim who, in volumes two and four, quavered out ballads about "fairies" and "pansies" (BM, 114–15, 118, 119; LM, 183, 185–86)— she unexpectedly balks at the birthday invitation, even though Stevens particularly wants to see Pilgrim perform (SA, 145). Except for this disagreement over Max Pilgrim's act, the wife, the lover, and the husband all would have perished at the ill-fated nightclub. By another fortuitous circumstance, however, Priscilla and Stevens arrive at the Café Royal only minutes after Lovell has left for Bijou's birthday party (SA, 116, 124). If the lovers had arrived while Chips still remained, a quarrel would undoubtedly have broken out among them, yet neither Priscilla nor Chips would have died in the bombings.

Throughout the entire chapter, death and life depend on an intricate web of chances that the reader must perceive across many scattered pages. In one striking instance, when Stevens goes off for a moment from Priscilla, Nick informs her that her husband is in London and has just left this table to find her at the Madrid (SA, 132–32). As an apparent result, she abruptly cools towards Stevens (SA, 139–42), though he cannot know her reason. Before he returned to the table, she had, indeed, resolved to "get in touch with Chips tomorrow" (SA, 132). Yet she soon has an eerie intuition that something appalling has occurred outside. Above the dining room clatter, she detects the noise of "a blitz," although others at the table insist that she has merely imagined it (SA, 137–39). Subsequent details confirm that Lovell's sudden death at the nearby Madrid took place at about the moment when Priscilla went "white" over air raid noises, felt "suddenly rather odd," and rushed away from her lover into the street (SA, 137–42). Later we learn that Max Pilgrim had intended to join the Café Royal diners after his "early" performance at the Madrid—a performance occurring at approximately the time when Nick and the others wait for their food (SA, 145). But the bomb killed Lovell and the assembled party guests right "in the middle of" Max Pilgrim's "act," and the horrified singer fled to the room that he rents from Moreland and Mrs. Maclintick (SA, 155–56). When Nick visits Moreland's flat, Pilgrim describes the deaths at Bijou's party, and Moreland exclaims at Priscilla's strange clairvoyance: "So there *was* a blitz earlier in the evening" (SA, 156). Her strong premonition leads immediately, however, to her own chance death in the raid. Too upset to remain with her lover at the restaurant, she hurries home in time for another random bomb that kills both her and her aunt (SA, 160–61). If Priscilla had accepted Stevens's last-minute offer at the restaurant to take her to a "quieter" place (SA, 139), she would have escaped from death that night. Throughout this powerful sequence—as dramatic as any in all twelve volumes—the metaphor of "a dance" from the overall title assumes disturbing implications. A choice of a lover over a husband, a short excursion down one London street rather than another, a change of dining plans, a brief delay in time—all of these tiny choreographic circumstances determine who shall live and who shall die.

Until chapter two of *The Soldier's Art*, the worldwide carnage has remained rather distant, but death and destruction ironically arrive during Nick's one-week furlough—a leave that he had yearned for as a "magical" escape from army existence (SA, 83). Yet his barrack-room life within volume eight has remained absurdly unwarlike. Soldiers behave like clowns throughout the volume, and civilians get killed like soldiers. This topsy-turvy world blurs the prewar distinctions suggested by the narrator on volume eight's first page as distinctions between the "Civil and Military . . . Work and Play . . . Detachment and Involvement . . . Tragedy and Comedy . . . War and Peace," and finally "Life and Death" (SA, 1).

To get the full meaning of this opening passage—a flashback to Nick's purchase in the early days of war of a military coat at a costume store for actors—we need a broad awareness of all of volume eight. In the shop's tall display case, emblems appear of a tragicomic split that subsequent events tend to refute: "two headless trunks," one of which "wore Harlequin's diagonally spangled tights; the other, scarlet full-dress uniform of some infantry regiment" (SA, 1). In a brief aside, however, the narrator hints that "the headless figures were perhaps not antithetical at all . . ." and that both may encounter the very same fate (SA, 4)—a somewhat veiled comment on the mingling and confusion, during total war, of civilian and military targets. But the passage hints at a further ironic ambiguity when the shop clerk amusingly assumes that Nick needs the coat for a part in a play:

"What's this one for?" he asked. . . .
"Just the war."
"Ah," he said attentively. "*The War.* . . ."
It was clear he had remained unflustered by recent public events. . . ,
too keen a theatre-goer to spare time for any but the columns of dramatic criticism. . . .
"I'll bear the show in mind," he said.
"Do, please. . . ."
"Tried to make a neat job of it," he said, "though I expect the theatre's only round the corner from here."
"The theatre of war?"
He looked puzzled for a second, then, recognising a mummer's obscure quip, nodded several times in appreciation.
"And I'll wish you a good run," he said, clasping together his old lean hands, as if in applause. (SA, 2–3)

With an overview of volume eight, we perceive specific applications of this laughable confusion between actors in a play and soldiers in a war. In spite of Widmerpool's connivings as Deputy-Assistant-Adjutant-General, he retains throughout *The Soldier's Art* the look and manner of a music-hall captain, which the narrator had noted as early as volume six: ". . . He had almost the air of being about to perform a music-hall turn, sing a patriotic song or burlesque, with 'patter,' an amy officer" (KO, 134). And he speaks stock military phrases like a very bad actor whose delivery rings false: " 'Putting you in the picture,' that relentlessly iterated army phrase, was a special favourite of Widmerpool's" (SA, 25–26). His attempt at a "hearty military" manner always seems ridiculous (SA, 22), for his attitudes remain essentially "civilian" (SA, 60). In spite of Widmerpool's mastery of army red tape, he never quite loses the air of "Heather Hopkins got up as an" officer "in some act as the Merry Thought" (KO, 134)—a transvestite man of arms.

Even conscientious Nick seems essentially miscast as a lowly junior officer. Among his fellow soldiers, Nick becomes known as the second lieutenant who likes to read books: "At least admitting to it put one in a recognisably odd category of persons from whom less need be expected than the normal run" (SA, 13). Nick's bookworm reputation has even reached the general of the entire Division. "Book reader, aren't you?" General Liddament asks. When Jenkins admits his un-soldierly love of books, the general inquires about his literary tastes. Although Nick's indifference to Anthony Trollope infuriates the gen-eral, Nick's preference for Balzac's novels prompts General Lidda-ment to ask about his proficiency in French. Then Liddament con-cludes that the army has miscast this lowly second lieutenant: ". . . People like you may be more useful elsewhere," and ". . . it seems a pity not to do the jobs we're suited for" (SA, 45–49). But Liddament's effort to reassign Nick—specifically, as liaison officer to the Free French Mission—fails when Nick flunks an army French exam (SA, 96–98, 100–3). Eventually, though, the general's recom-mendation wins Jenkins a place in the London War Office—an ap-pointment that requires no foreign language skills (SA, 228; MP, 4–5). The ramshackle methods of military casting have found him at last an appropriate role. Yet it has, nevertheless, very slight connection to the soldier's traditional part of kill or be killed. Nick's duties seem, instead, pretty much those of a low-ranking government bureaucrat or clerk.

The most striking case of miscasting in the army involves Private Stringham. The army has assigned a mess-waiter role to this public school graduate with time at the university and a "la-di-da" accent that especially annoys gruff Captain Biggs—a mess-hall diner with the habit of spitting unwanted bits of fat back onto his plate (SA, 67–70). Although Nick suggests to Widmerpool that their schoolmate could be found "a better job " (SA, 72), Stringham himself whimsically de-clares that ". . . I think I have it in me to make a first-class Mess waiter. The talent is there. It's just a question of developing latent ability" (SA, 77). For his own hidden reasons, Widmerpool shifts Stringham to a Mobile Laundry unit—not a glorious promotion, perhaps, but one that at least saves him from the jeers of Captain Biggs (SA, 167–71). Yet Widmerpool converts a miscast waiter into instant laundry man for an utterly malicious purpose: the Mobile Laundry has received secret orders to leave for a dangerous war zone, and Widmerpool wishes to get rid of Stringham (SA, 188–90). Stringham meets his death, however, as a Japanese prisoner-of-war with a bravery transcending his military bit part (TK, 209).

A brief remark by Stringham himself connects the title, *The Sol-dier's Art,* with the actor-soldier theme of the opening flashback about the costume shop. The expression, he notes, appears in Browning's "Childe Roland to the Dark Tower Came": "Think first, fight afterwards—the soldier's art" (SA, 221). Stringham adds that Browning "always gives the impression of writing about people who are wearing very expensive fancy dress" (SA, 221). Apart from this amusing if arbitrary linkage with the Harlequin and regimental costumes of the opening pages (SA, 1), "think first, fight afterwards" has ironic applications to the pattern of the volume as a whole. When Stringham learns that Widmerpool has schemed to get him sent to a dangerous war zone, he himself associates his schoolmate's machinations with "the soldier's art" of Browning's poem: "The old boy's a marvellous example of one of the aspects of this passage . . ." (SA, 221). "Fight afterwards" ironically applies to the noncombatant role of Widmerpool and the others in this training-camp army, and "think first" serves as a droll euphemism for the cynical maneuvers of such sordid Divisional Machiavellis as Widmerpool himself. The squalid endeavor of these small scale army "thinkers" to enhance their bureaucratic power dominates the volume.

Throughout the entire volume, Widmerpool engages in a long-running struggle for power with Captain Sunny Farebrother, an enemy from prewar days, over such trivial matters as "transfers from one unit to another, candidates for courses and the routine of disciplinary cases" (SA, 22–23). And early in chapter one, Widmerpool competes with Colonel Hogbourne-Johnson—a "sour" yet common army type (SA, 29)—over which of them can maneuver their own personal favorite into the command of a brand-new unit (SA, 31). As bitterness grows between these two archconnivers, Widmerpool seeks to prove that the colonel's chief clerk has embezzled army funds (SA, 53–64). In a comic climax toward the end of volume eight, Widmerpool and the colonel both get what they deserve—defeat and humiliation. Upon learning to his chagrin that Widmerpool soon will rise above him in power, Farebrother achieves instant revenge. He reveals that his own candidate, rather than Widmerpool's, has won the new command and that General Liddament has been fully informed of Widmerpool's unethical meddling (SA, 198–207). Colonel Hogbourne-Johnson suffers double mortification over his own failed schemes. His candidate, too, has lost the new command; and the colonel's chief clerk has fled to neutral territory to escape arrest for graft (SA, 211–13). As a coda to this sequence, General Liddament rebukes Captain Widmerpool with a scolding that reduces him to "utter despair" (SA, 214). Throughout volume eight, the so-called "soldier's art" seems little more than bureaucratic scheming—an unheroic craft with purely selfish aims.

The Browning monologue about Childe Harold from which Powell draws volume eight's title suggests, as a whole, a soldierly strength that can triumph in the end over utterly sordid circumstances. In spite of the disgrace and death of all his fellow knights and a hopeless quest across a grotesquely ugly landscape, Childe Roland achieves his goal of facing death bravely. The very same Stringham who applied Browning's phrase to Widmerpool's shameful intrigues also hints at a nobler "soldier's art." When he learns of the death of Nick's brother-in-law, Robert Tolland, in the early days of blitzkrieg, Stringham responds unforgettably: "Awfully chic to be killed." "You can't beat it," he adds. "Smart as hell. Fell in action. I'm always struck by that phrase" (SA, 78). Amid despicable chicaneries, some scattered, brief reminders recall this other role for men of the army. One quick flash-forward reveals that the general's personal messenger to contemptible Captain Widmerpool, the Aide-de-Camp Greening (SA, 207–8), will be "badly wounded at Anzio" (SA, 87). And Stringham himself dies as a prison-camp hero (TK, 209). Perhaps the one supreme "art" of the soldier, after all, is not petty scheming but instead the moral gift of dying well and bravely—the sacrifice of life itself.

The Military Philosophers

Until at least the midpoint of *The Military Philosophers*—the last of the wartime volumes—the narrative seems shapeless and meandering, like a nonfictional memoir by a former army bureaucrat of desk-bound colonels, majors, captains, and reams of trivial paperwork. Only with a subsequent perspective can the reader begin to perceive how a single vivid character, Pamela Flitton, joins many of these seemingly disconnected threads into a meaningful sequence. As army driver and later as secretary attached to an espionage group (MP, 57–58, 203), Pamela not only knows a number of these "military philosophers, "but she knows quite a few of them in a carnal sense. If Nick starts as assistant liaison to the Poles (MP, 4), she carries on her own special kind of liaison with members of the Polish contingent. When she first turns up in chapter one, she has "already" become "quite a famous figure in Polish military circles" (MP, 66): a nameless Polish major has been brought before an army "Court of Honour" because of an entanglement with her (MP, 73), and a Polish rogue and spy named Szymanski has evidently also been her lover (MP, 127).

Pamela's affairs keep deflecting the narrative in unexpected ways—most notably her offstage involvement with Szymanski. This has intricate links with the cloak-and-dagger intrigues of numerous officials: namely, a hinted-at struggle in Cairo between supporters of the Yugoslav Chetniks and those of the Partisans involving Szymanski as a hired assassin with no true allegiance to either side (MP, 126–27, 188–

89). Pamela herself publicly flaunts her sexual relationship with one Prince Theodoric—a royal Yugoslavian supporter of the Chetniks (MP, 101–2). Two of the opposing British agents in Cairo—Peter Templer on the side of the Chetniks and Odo Stevens on the Partisans' side—also contend for Pamela. Indeed, Templer volunteers for this dangerous assignment specifically because Pamela has sexually rebuffed him (MP, 77–78, 82, 188–89). She, in turn, sleeps with Stevens, though she later rebukes him for inadequacy in bed (MP, 135). Still another of Pamela's conquests—Kenneth Widmerpool himself—shows up in Cairo at the center of the intrigue. To aid the Partisans but also, apparently, to dispose of Templer as Pamela's rival lover, Widmerpool blocks Templer's rescue when the Cairo scheme falls through. Partly because of Pamela, Widmerpool, in effect, condemns Templer to death (MP, 116, 189, 211–13). Pamela, in short, provides the key to many seemingly scattered fragments throughout volume nine. Yet because these highly dramatic events remain almost entirely offstage in the blanks between the bureaucratic narrative, this story of foreign intrigue emerges very slowly as a kind of shadowy supplement to the day-to-day trivia of Nick's own duties.

Only our later awareness of Pamela's erotic network and of her many conquests makes retrospective sense of chapter one's intimidating bureaucratic tangle. The first nine pages introduce us to seemingly random problems of the Poles, but they ultimately connect with Pamela, Widmerpool, Templer, and Szymanski. Pages 9 through 24 present the later key conspirators in the Cairo affair, Widmerpool and Templer. Prince Theodoric shows up on pages 47 to 52—another potential conspirator and apparent lover of Pamela. Nevertheless, the link to these apparently unrelated encounters of military bureaucrats, Pamela herself, remains unknown to Nick and to us for almost one fourth of the volume (MP, 58). As a result, the offstage intricacies of Pamela and Cairo do not come into view until we can look back from a later perspective.

In addition to Pamela's not-so-secret network, chance reencounters from Nick's own past form a cross-temporal pattern that enlivens the trivia of day-to-day bureaucracy. Nick's meeting of three old acquaintances at a Cabinet Offices session—Widmerpool, Templer, and Farebrother—reinserts the past into a wartime routine (MP, 12–23). At another such meeting, an acquaintance of Nick's named Tompsitt turns up from volume two and supports Kenneth Widmerpool's despicable attack on the Poles for complaining about Katyn—the Soviet massacre of some ten thousand Polish officers (MP, 104–7). What becomes, in effect, an "Old Boy" reunion meshes here with a bureaucratic treatment of an offstage world occurrence. In the first V-1 bombing of London, Myra Erdleigh reemerges from volume six (MP, 121–38), another surprise visitor out of the past. And when Nick escorts a group of allied attachés across the liberated Continent, he happens to encounter Bob Duport, Jean Templer's ex-husband, who also last appeared within the sixth volume (MP, 150, 185–90). As part of a further network of surprising interconnections, Duport reveals that he himself "stuffed" Pamela Flitton "once," "against a shed in the back parts of Cairo airport" (MP, 190), thus involving himself with the very same woman as his own ex-brother-in-law, Peter Templer. Amid a seemingly aimless chronicle of war's bureaucracy, these complex interlinkings themselves form a story. In the final chapter, an embassy party reinserts momentarily a very important character out of volume six—Moreland's ex-wife, Matilda, one of Nick's favorite persons from prewar days (MP, 207–9). And the closing Victory Service leads to the single most startling reappearance in all of volume nine: Jenkins's former love, Jean, reemerges from volume three with a faint foreign accent as the present wife of a Latin American colonel (MP, 219–21, 231–36)—his country's future dictator and generalissimo (TK, 235). In spite of its seeming randomness, volume nine hangs together, not only through Pamela's complex erotic web, but also through a pattern of elaborate reencounters in time's extended "dance."

One of volume nine's most dramatic events—Pamela's public condemnation of Widmerpool as "a murderer" (MP, 213)—withholds its full significance until the later volumes. The scene occurs shortly after Widmerpool and Pamela have become engaged to be married (MP, 196):

> . . . Plenty of people were close enough. It was no place to allow a scene to develop. Pamela turned to me.
> "Do you know what happened?"
> "About what?"
> "About Peter Templer. This man persuaded them to leave Peter to die. The nicest man I ever knew. He just had him killed."
> Tears appeared in her eyes. She was in a state of near hysteria. . . .
> "How could you utter such rubbish?" he [Widmerpool] said. . . .
> "He put up a paper. That was the word he used—put up a paper. He wanted them to stop supporting the people Peter was with. We didn't send them any more arms. We didn't even bother to get Peter out. Why should we? We didn't want his side to win any more."
>
> . . . .
>
> "I am only a member of the Secretariat, darling. I am the servant, very humble servant, of whatever committees it is my duty to attend."
> "You said yourself it was a rare meeting when you didn't get what you wanted into the finalized version."

"So it is," he said. "So it is. And, as it happens, what I thought went into the paper you're talking about. I admit it. That doesn't mean I was in the smallest degree responsible for Templer's death. We don't know for certain if he is dead."
"Yes we do."
"All right. I concede that."
"You're a murderer," she said.
There was a pause. They glared at each other. (MP, 211–13)

This knockdown-dragout quarrel ought to mark the end of Pamela's engagement to Widmerpool, yet, not long afterwards, the volume's final page announces that their wedding has nevertheless occurred (MP, 244). Only in subsequent volumes do we finally understand that Pamela has married this despicable man precisely because of his betrayal of Templer. Throughout volume ten she torments her husband and finally runs away with another man in especially mortifying circumstances (BDFR, 179–83,188–97). Soon she returns to Widmerpool and again makes him suffer by her presence rather than her absence (BDFR, 238) and throughout volume eleven continues to subject him to marital torture. In a culminating scene echoing her murder accusation within volume nine, she publicly proclaims both his sexual perversity and his treason against England (TK, 261–63). As Dicky Umfraville points out in *The Military Philosophers*, "giving men hell is what Miss Flitton likes" (MP, 74). At last, in volume eleven, we fully understand the motives for her marriage to Widmerpool. Instead of dissuading her from it, the revelation of his guilt concerning Templer's death has strengthened her resolve to become Mrs. Widmerpool—a conjugal avenger, a wifely tormentor, a tenacious household nemesis.

Within the context of the story as a whole, volume nine's title, *The Military Philosophers*, has humorous implications. According to the *Oxford English Dictionary*, the term *philosopher* formerly included "men learned" within nonmetaphysical spheres—say, science, medicine, and warfare. In fact, Powell drew his title directly from an eighteenth-century French usage and equivalent, Casanova's *Le Philosophe militaire*, a manuscript seized by the Inquisitors of Venice but recalled by Powell in his own memoirs (FMT, 89). Most of volume nine's bureaucrats remain far removed from the elevated meaning of philosophy: the love of wisdom, of the one, the true, and the good. For example, Mr. Blackhead, an astonishing virtuoso of War Office red tape, sits in an upper room amid stacks of memoranda and blocks a wide range of military plans by stupifying queries (MP, 38–46). This particular "military philosopher" epitomizes small-mindedness, "the mystic holy essence incarnate of arguing, encumbering, delaying, hair-splitting, all for the best of reasons" (MP, 40). Widmerpool's special army talent consists in writing official papers that persuade his superiors to put in effect his own contemptible aims (MP, 212–13). His rival, Sunny Farebrother, has a similar wartime skill: the ability to charm persons to their faces and betray them behind their backs (MP, 13, 114–15). Even when the volume ascends above the ruck of these bureaucrats, it presents an essentially comic view of supposed master soldiers. Thus, the volume introduces a famous army commander modeled on Montgomery, but it does so with such playfulness as to undermine thoroughly the great man's status of supreme "military philosopher." Annoyed by the unruliness of the Belgian Resistance forces, the marshal blithely threatens to "shoot 'em up" (MP, 179). With less than army omniscience, he misidentifies the emblem on Nick's divisional cap (MP, 180). And, in front of a multilingual group of attachés, the field marshal counsels the avoidance of any foreign language at all (MP, 180). His very "features" "suggest," to the narrator's amusement, "some mythical beast, say one of those encountered in *Alice in Wonderland*, full of awkward questions and downright statements" (MP, 184). Perhaps most disconcertingly of all, the field marshal starts his briefing of assembled attachés with the same army cliché that Widmerpool had favored within the previous volume: " 'Putting you in the picture,' that relentlessly iterated army phrase, was a special favourite of Widmerpool's" (SA, 25–26). "You'll want me to put you in the picture," says the great British commander (MP, 181), and the echo undercuts his military majesty. Within the wartime volumes as a whole, even the very greatest soldiers, such as Montgomery himself, remain essentially comic and unexalted.[4] The ability to laugh at war's grandiose muddle may be the ultimate mark of a "military philosopher"—a "philosopher," in fact, very much like Nicholas Jenkins, who never fails to see the joke.[5]

The wartime volumes form a special great divide in the course of *A Dance* as a whole. The war itself kills off Nick's very oldest friends from public school days—Stringham and Templer. It also reveals the despicableness of another former schoolmate, Widmerpool, and years of army life tend to distance Nick himself from many survivors of prewar days. Thus, right after the elaborate Victory celebration at St. Paul's Cathedral, Nick reencounters Jean, his great prewar love, but she seems like a personage from history, a figure unconnected to Nick in the present, an antebellum ghost of dances past (MP, 232–36). With the fading or death of numerous major figures from the various prewar

volumes, the postwar ones will require an infusion of many fresh
characters, a thorough restocking of the fictional cast. Yet subtle
continuities will remain in effect. Even late-arriving characters will
continue old patterns of chance meetings, long separations, and surprising reencounters. The war may have caused many changes of
partners, but it has not ended the "dance."

8
Middle and Old Age

Books Do Furnish a Room

Eᴀᴄʜ of *A Dance*'s concluding volumes—ten, eleven, and twelve—has a tightly structured plot and climax almost like those of completely traditional fiction: a pattern less dependent on distant interweavings than in any previous part of *A Dance*, even though one with certain loose ends derived from preceding volumes. Yet within these colorful postwar sequences, a basic paradox emerges. The more vivid and dramatic the narrative becomes, the further that Nick, the observer, stands from the center of the action. In *Books Do Furnish a Room*, he has left the army as a middle-aged man, sedate and highly uxorious, a decorous avoider of such erotic escapades as his earlier affair with Jean in volume three. Although the explosive Pamela's sexual attractions dominate most of volume ten, Nick remains exempted from them. Unlike the other men, he never stares lustfully at Pamela's sullen beauty, and she, in turn, makes no attempt to seduce him. She never, for example, grabs Nick "by the balls," as she does in the very next volume to Professor Russell Gwinnett, a man whom she has only recently met (TK, 158). She does not even slip an arm around Nick's waist as she does to another married man, Roddy Cutts, Nick's own brother-in-law (BDFR, 77–78). If Pamela's sexual desires and resentments propel the narrative action, Nick can perceive her spectacular amours only as an outside observer and at times less than that—as a semidetached narrator who relays another's telling or even the telling of a telling. But the further that he drifts from the volume's emotional center, the better he becomes at discerning a story in time's complex "dance."

In volume ten's opening chapter, Nick receives only indirect news about the characters who will later dominate the sequence. Back at his former university to reserve a book on Burton's *Anatomy of Melancholy*, he revisits Professor Sillery, a meddling old pedant introduced in volume one (QU, 167–71). Sillery's literary collaborator, Ada Leintwardine, mentions one Trapnel (BDFR, 24), an upcoming novelist whose later affair with Pamela will energize the plot. As Nick departs by train for London, an editor named Bagshaw shows up on the platform and answers Nick's question about Trapnel's life. Nick has already read and admired Trapnel's first novel but up till now knows nothing about him (BDFR, 33–34). Bagshaw further mentions his forthcoming plans to recruit Trapnel for a brand-new magazine called *Fission* (BDFR, 36). And Trapnel's eventual femme fatale, Pamela Widmerpool—the wife of a *Fission* organizer—has already surfaced in scandalous rumors passed on by old Sillery just a few pages earlier (BDFR, 14–16, 21–23), third-hand stories as grist for the narrator's mill. We later understand that these brief reports about two colorful human beings not only belong together but also form a prelude to everything that follows.

In chapter two, at the funeral of the narrator's brother-in-law, Erridge, Nick glimpses a Pamela Widmerpool who has not yet met Trapnel—a Pamela at her ill-tempered worst. She enters the church with a look of "condescension" and sullen "melancholy" as Nick coolly watches (BDFR, 46). From his own pew, at an undescribed distance, he hears her complain about faintness in a loud and angry voice and sees her rush out in the middle of the service (BDFR, 52–53). As a rather amused bystander, he later contemplates the disturbance that she causes among various men assembled within the Toll-and mansion: a tongue-tied Alfred Tolland, an over-aged German houseboy, Roddy Cutts, and Widmerpool (BDFR, 70–71, 72–73, 77–78). Although Nick himself escorts Pamela from the house, he still seems little more than an uninvolved witness who maintains both his psychic and physical distance even as she vomits into a gigantic vase or vessel belonging to the family. "On such occasions," he explicitly remarks, "there is no way in which an onlooker can help" (BDFR, 82). Curiously enough, within chapter two, Pamela's action most important for the plot—her browsing through a copy of Trapnel's novel—is glimpsed by Nick for a mere unthinking eye blink (BDFR, 74). Only long afterwards does Nick discover from Trapnel himself that Pamela eventually read and liked the novel (BDFR, 163)—a step towards loving its author. Again Nick remains detached and removed from the story's emotional heart.

In chapter three, Nick's spectator vantage point derives from his role as *Fission*'s book review editor (BDFR, 76)—an editor who will hand out assignments to Trapnel himself (BDFR, 111–12). But not until almost halfway through the volume does Nick finally encounter Trapnel face-to-face. Although this vivid scene introduces details about him that will later figure prominently in the Trapnel-Pamela story—his skull's head sword-stick and nonstop volubility—the dialogue clings mainly to literary shop talk and withholds any hints of Trapnel's weakness for sullen femme fatales (BDFR, 105–13).[1] Even when Nick has a close-up view of the very first meeting between Trapnel and Pamela, the witness receives a highly misleading impression of this fateful brief encounter—an impression reflecting only surface appearances. "It was not a success. In fact it was a disaster. From being in quite a good humour, she switched immediately to an exceedingly bad one. As he came up, her face at once assumed an expression of instant dislike" (BDFR, 136). The narrator fails to note that the eccentric, bearded novelist made an equally bad impression on Nick himself at their own first meeting, as an apparent "exhibitionist," with a death's head stick, "an emerald green tie patterned with naked women, . . . grey suede brothel-creepers" (army boots made from old flat tires), "and gruffness of manner" (BDFR, 105–6). Because Jenkins revised his "unfavourable" "impression" virtually "at once" (BDFR, 107), he need not assume that Pamela will go on detesting the colorful Trapnel for more than a brief moment. Yet as though to underscore the meeting's utter nullity, Nick quotes Trapnel's dismayed reaction to Pamela's sharp tongue: "Girls like that are not in my line. I don't care how smashing they look. I need a decent standard of manners" (BDFR, 137). Instead of emphasizing an incipient romance, Nick shifts our attention to Trapnel's audacious borrowing of a pound from Kenneth Widmerpool, almost an absolute stranger (BDFR, 138–40). Only later does this scene take on full significance, when Trapnel cuckolds his creditor—a surprise for which the narrator does not prepare us. In fact, throughout the volume's opening half, he usually adheres to the mere opaque appearance of what he observed at the moment and omits his final knowledge, his ultimate awareness at the story-telling instance.

In chapter four, Nick first retails a lot of second-hand gossip about Trapnel's eccentricities and only then zeroes in on the developing affair with Pamela (BDFR, 143–55). At a meeting with Nick, the self-dramatizing novelist announces his unrequited passion by inscribing Pamela's name on a small slip of paper, like a mystic incantation too holy to pronounce (BDFR, 161). "His face," the narrator comments, "showed that he saw this climax as the moment of truth, one of those high-spots in the old silent films that he liked to recall. . . : the train is derailed: the canoe swept over the rapids: the knife plunged into the naked flesh" (BDFR, 162). These similes of stock motion picture disasters suggested to Nick by Trapnel's overacting foreshadow in their turn the man's ultimate undoing by Pamela. Here, for once, the narrator-observer finds whimsical hints of prophecy because of what he knows from his later place in time. As a spectator at the moment, he remains, however, excluded from any clear awareness of developing events. He suggests, for example, as a simple teasing joke, that Trapnel might use the pretext of repaying Widmerpool's pound as a way of seeing Pamela (BDFR, 165–66), and only later does Nick learn to his surprise that Trapnel has followed, in all seriousness, this mock bit of counsel. Even when Nick arrives on the scene at a crucial moment in the Pamela affair—her desertion of her husband for Trapnel—Nick's sense of Pamela's presence is ultimately revealed as no more than an illusion. Arriving at Widmerpool's flat with Roddy Cutts and Widmerpool himself, Nick hears water splashing in the tub and assumes that Pamela is taking a bath. Her husband even shouts conjugal words through the closed bathroom door. But Pamela has, in fact, run off with Trapnel an "hour or two" earlier and has left the water running as a tactical diversion. This crucial event that Jenkins seems to witness has, indeed, already vanished into the past. Yet "two used glasses" left together on a table permit Nick and us to envision a romantic tête-à-tête not described in the narrative (BDFR, 172–83).

Later in chapter four as the drama unfolds, Nick witnesses events in a more direct way than previously. After he has learned of a ridiculous complication in the Trapnel-Pamela affair—the novelist's parody in *Fission* of the husband's pompous essays (BDFR, 185–87)—Pamela summons Nick to a secret shabby love nest (BDFR, 188–93). Here he observes directly some very important occurrences. Widmerpool shows up shortly after Nick for a laughable confrontation. The cuckold expresses his contempt for Trapnel and asserts that Pamela will come back home "in her own good time" (BDFR, 202). As a melodramatic reply, Trapnel draws his sword, chases Widmerpool from the house, and shouts insults that apply particularly well to the son of a late dealer in farm manure (BM, 58–59)—"Coprolite! Faecal débris! Fossil of dung!"—while Pamela watches silently (BDFR, 202–4). Although Nick is present throughout the whole scene, he does not affect it at all. Both parties, indeed, express satisfaction at his role of detached observer. "I am quite glad to have a witness," says Widmerpool (BDFR, 198). "I'm glad you were here, Nicholas," Pamela declares. "I'm glad it all happened in front of someone" (BDFR, 204). Obviously enough, their comments serve to ratify a narrative necessity. The story line itself requires Nick as a nearby handy witness, a means for achieving the effect of presence at this highly important point.

During a return in chapter five to his former public school, Nick recalls the climax, some six months earlier, of the Trapnel-Pamela affair. But the narrator tells it to us from an even later period, perhaps as long after as a quarter century, and he pictures himself on this visit to the school when his thoughts wandered back to an already old catastrophe (BDFR, 206–7).[2] Besides complex gaps in time between the story line and the telling with resulting effects of emotional distance, Nick saw only the end of these events, for he stood far removed from Pamela's spiteful act that set the catastrophe in motion: dumping the only manuscript of Trapnel's new novel into the Maida Vale Canal, a spectacular form of literary criticism. No one, in fact, witnesses this destruction, but Nick and the others imagine its details from one single page fished out of the filthy water as the manuscript drifts away (BDFR, 211–26). Nick does directly witness Trapnel's dramatic surrender to defeat—his flinging of his sword-stick into the Canal. Yet even this magnificent final gesture has a missing phantom climax, a supreme consummation from Arthurian romance:

> He lifted the sword-stick behind his head, and, putting all his force into the throw, cast it as far as this would carry, high into the air. The stick turned and descended, death's-head first. A mystic arm should certainly have risen from the dark waters of the mere to receive it. That did not happen. Trapnel's Excalibur struck the flood a long way from the bank, disappeared for a moment, surfaced, and began to float downstream. (BDFR, 223)

An even more important event occurs away from Nick's presence: Pamela's abrupt forsaking of Trapnel, an emotional knockout punch. Thus, when Nick and Bagshaw escort the manuscriptless writer back to his Maida Vale pigsty, they find Pamela gone with all her things, including her valuable Modigliani drawing and two prized photographs of her now-vanished self (BDFR, 191, 227). "No doubt," Nick reasons, "she had strolled down to the Canal, disposed of *Profiles in String*, then returned with a taxi to remove her effects" (BDFR, 227). Trapnel himself offers a temporal deduction that rounds out the impression of what we have not observed: "She can't have been gone more than a few hours" (BDFR, 227). Even though these events happen offstage and are further distanced by a narrating lag, the teller creates an illusory sense of presence.

Although earlier volumes play similar tricks at times with the narrator-witness's presence, volume ten and its successors combine a detached observer with a much more dramatic plot than ever before. In spite of this, a reader who began *A Dance* only with volume ten would encounter many unexplained characters and events, numerous narrative threads dangling from the unread previous volumes. Loose ends would obscure an essentially well-made structure. The traditional plot of *Books Do Furnish a Room* remains, in effect, a localized phenemenon as a structure existing within a larger pattern of distant and complex interconnections.

Consider, for example, how a reader new to *A Dance* might puzzle over a scene near the start of volume ten: the narrator-actor's meeting with an old don named Sillery (BDFR, 5–27), who has not appeared since volume three (AW, 128–31). Without some knowledge of his earlier eccentricities, of his skill as supergossip and perpetual busy-body, the reader loses much of the effect: a shock of recognition that this very ancient pedant remains, after almost two decades, an ardent collector of dirty-laundry secrets and malicious private rumors. And a subsequent long section about the funeral of Nick's brother-in-law, Erridge (BDFR, 44–91), would seem a blur of new names and faces for a reader who had never met the large Tolland family, their numer-ous acquaintances, or even Erridge himself—a character who first appeared back in volume four (LM, 112–15). For this reader who began late in *A Dance,* other reappearances from earlier volumes would also become enigmatic: Nick's short scene with Jean (BDFR, 94–99), his paramour from volume three; his fleeting reencounter with Moreland (BDFR, 118–20), Nick's closest friend back in volume five; and the narrator-observer's remeeting with Le Bas (BDFR, 231–36), Nick's former housemaster from public school days, who has vanished from the text for some seventeen hundred pages since vol-ume three (AW, 195–97). In spite of volume ten's highly dramatic plot, a late comer to it, a newly entered reader, would remain excluded from the many complex pleasures of *A Dance*'s vast web.

Even the central plot of *Books Do Furnish a Room*—the Pamela-Trapnel love affair—is not quite complete without the subsequent volume. There at last, Pamela's infatuation with Professor Russell Gwinnett, her now-dead lover's future biographer, suggests, among other things, her lingering feelings for Trapnel himself—feelings, in effect, transferred to the keeper of his flame, his literary alter ego. But Gwinnett, in a sense, becomes the dead man's avenger. Just as Trapnel's love for Pamela caused his later collapse and death, her thwarted love for Gwinnett ends with her own self-destruction (TK, 156–59, 269, 270). In spite of the impression at the close of volume ten that Pamela escapes all retribution, the Pamela-Trapnel story reaches beyond the limits of *Books Do Furnish a Room* to an ultimate twist of poetic justice.

Volume ten's title derives from the comic nickname of *Fission*'s chief editor, "Books-do-furnish-a-room Bagshaw" or sometimes just "Books"—a secondary figure who plays, nevertheless, an important role in the story. Nick's two alternate anecdotes of how this name arose illustrate the complexities and subtle ambiguities of his second hand telling. In the first version, a drunken Bagshaw "overturned" a "massive" upright "bookcase," and "as volume after volume descended" on top of him, he jokingly remarked that "books do furnish a room" (BDFR, 32–33). In the second account, a naked Bagshaw seduced the also naked "wife of a well-known" drama "critic" "in her husband's book-lined study," but a moment before the sexual encounter, Bagshaw murmured an unerotic aside: "Books do furnish a room" (BDFR, 33). Wrapped "in the mists of the past" (BDFR, 32), both forms of the anecdote come filtered through a long chain of telling; and the sexier one, at least, reaches Nick in the end through his old friend Moreland. "Whichever story were true—probably neither," the narrator concludes, "the second had all the flavour of having been worked over, if not invented, by Moreland" (DBFR, 33). In other words, an accurate explanation of Bagshaw's ridiculous nickname most likely lies in a missing third version, a phantom anecdote not in the text.

Even though both variations of the Bagshaw anecdote may, in fact, be false, they have, when taken together, a suggestive connection with the Trapnel-Pamela story. In version one, Bagshaw's mishap takes place within a purely literary framework: an effort to check a poetic quotation (BDFR, 32–33). In version two, however, he annoys his sofa-mate by combining sex with bookishness (BDFR, 33). A similar or analogous wavering between books and eroticism occurs throughout the Trapnel-Pamela affair. When the novelist first meets her at *Fission*'s party, he mistakes Mrs. Widmerpool for a writer (BDFR, 136–37). She later becomes, not only his lover, but also, in effect, his resident critic: a merciless judge of all that he writes (BDFR, 196–97). When she finally destroys his manuscript and then walks out on him, her motives seem literary—a judgment that the work is not good enough. Yet just as in the two opposing legends about Bagshaw's name, books and sex seem interchangeable here. At one key moment, Trapnel describes Pamela's attitude toward his writing as a disconcerting mixture of self-contradictions: "It's almost as if she hates it, doesn't want me to do it, and yet she thinks about my work all the time . . ." (BBFR, 219). In nearly identical words six pages later, he reveals that she combines spectacular nymphomania with a secret and hopeless frigidity. "She wants it all the time, yet doesn't want it" (BDFR, 225). The ambiguous alternate versions of the "Books" Bagshaw legend seem analogous to a far more important ambiguity at the heart of volume ten: does Pamela's dislike of her lover's new novel spring from her own frigidity, or does dislike arise from the work's genuine faults? We cannot disentangle the two opposing motives.

Within the subtleties of *Books Do Furnish a Room*, sexual frustration and literary judgment fuse and blend together into an inextricable whole.

Temporary Kings

In the eleventh and second-to-last volume of *A Dance*, a highly dramatic plot combines with extraordinary complexities of narrating distance surpassing even those of the previous sequence. Here, too, the well-made plot functions within a much larger pattern of surprising reencounters from earlier volumes. In addition to the distancing effects of complex time lapses, tellings within tellings, and cross-temporal patterns that cut across the plot, the eleventh volume uses a complicated mixture of different narrative levels: most importantly, a story depicted in a Venetian painting mingles with the volume's own story. Throughout the twelve-volume sequence, paintings have played significant roles: for example, the Poussin canvas that gives *A Dance* its own title or the Deacon paintings in volumes two and twelve.[3] At a key moment in *Temporary Kings*, however, the narrator calls whimsical attention to an even more thoroughgoing fusion of art and life than earlier in *A Dance:*

> Pamela's own tints hinted that she herself, only a moment before, had floated down out of those cloudy vertical perspectives [of the painting on the ceiling], perhaps compelled to do so by the artist himself, displeased that her crimson and peacock shades struck too extravagant a note, one that disturbed rather than enriched a composition, which, for all its splendour, remained somehow tenebrous too. If so, reminder of her own expulsion from the scene, as she contemplated it again, increasingly enraged her.
> . . . Only a sufficiently long ladder—expedient perhaps employed for banishing Pamela from on high—seemed required to reach the apartment's so trenchantly pictured dimension; to join the trio playing out whatever game had to be gambled between them by dire cast of the Fates. (TK, 82–83)

This jocular confusion of story-line characters with those from a painting approaches the strangeness of what Genette has called "the Robbe-Grillet type of narrative": "characters escaped from a painting, a book, a press clipping, a photograph, a dream, a memory, a fantasy"—"games" that "overstep, in defiance of verisimilitude . . . a shifting but sacred frontier between two worlds, the world in which one tells, the world of which one tells."[4] Powell, to be sure, stops short of transgressing verisimilitude, for Pamela has not actually fallen from the painting. But the painting depicts a story with details very close to Pamela's own troubled sex life—details that we shall later examine in full. For now, let us note the accumulating effects of all these complexities wrapped around the plot: such distancing complications as temporal lapses, frequent retellings, and shifts across different story levels.

In each of the six chapters, at least one dramatic episode (more than one in the opening chapter) is filtered through a complex of indirect tellings. Chapter one quickly sets a strong plot in motion under the eyes of the narrator-character Nick. In Venice for a literary conference, he hears of Pamela's presence there amid scandalous rumors of her sexual liaison, in a London hotel, with Ferrand-Sénéschal, a French intellectual who died hours later, before he could attend the conference. And at Nick's Venetian hotel, Nick encounters Russell Gwinnett, Trapnel's future American biographer, who yearns to interview Pamela for his book. Within this clear framework, a complex embedding of separate narrating acts obscures the details of Pamela's involvement with Ferrand-Sénéschal—fragments muttered or read by Professor Emily Brightman from a Paris scandal sheet and enclosed, of course, in Nick's own telling:

> Fougueuse sensualité . . . étrange caprices . . . amitiés équivoques. . . .
> We never seem to get anything solid.
> Odieux chantages . . . but of whom? Situation gênante. . . . Then why not tell us about it? Le scandale éclate. . . . It never seems to have done so. I am still not at all sure what happened, scarcely wiser than after reading the headline. (TK, 45–46; the ellipses appear in the text itself)

The narrator's own brief paraphrase also stresses the account's indefiniteness: "no details given," "even less specific," "touched on only vaguely" (TK, 46). One might explain all this as simply a means of withholding an important plot-secret about Pamela and the Frenchman until the climactic moment, yet as we shall later see, this ultimate climax itself employs an even more evasive and complex form of telling than muttered newspaper fragments. Just as in volume ten, the more dramatic that events become, the greater the separation that insinuates itself between them and the narrator.

Shortly before the French-scandal-sheet passage, the legend of Trapnel's last mortal binge—an event some five or six years in the past—had received a still more complex kind of telling.[5] In largely indirect discourse with supporting details from many nameless sources, the narrator recounts the drama of Trapnel's death as told to various listeners over the years by the poet Malcolm Crowding, an eyewitness. Thus many tellings are embedded within Jenkins's own retelling. Although this method of narrative presentation resembles a child's game of "telephone"—a message whispered through a long chain of listeners to emerge with amusing distortions—Nick's version makes no claim to express the absolute truth but only a surviving legend, and legends always spring from multiple tellings. The narrator admits that the poet's composite version "had been a little ornamented with the passage of time" (TK, 29), and the narrator's own comments add further ornaments. As a minimum, though, all versions agree on a few "basic facts" (TK, 29). With a windfall of money from someone, Trapnel bought drinks for an army of hangers-on at a pub, launched into a nonstop monologue, collapsed on the pavement outside, and died shortly afterwards (TK, 29–35).

We might well doubt the accuracy of the single most important detail, however: Trapnel's last utterances. The exact transmission of these thirty-six words through countless retellings during roughly half a decade seems at best unlikely. Within this composite account, Trapnel cries out that "I've forgotten my stick. I've lost my stick. My death's head stick," but he realizes then his own confusion. "No. . . . Of course I haven't got a stick any longer, have I? I sacrificed it. Nor a bloody novel. I haven't got that either" (TK, 33–34). In spite of all the indirect tellings, Trapnel's last words establish a point essential to the plot. They explicitly connect his impending death with his years of anguish over Pamela's destruction of his manuscript. Although it took him long to die, she really did kill him.

Most centrally of all, chapter two's description of Tiepolo's imaginary masterpiece, *Candaules and Gyges* (a subject, in fact, never painted by him), becomes itself a second-level tale with complex connections to the main story line. Within the direct gaze of the narrator-spectator, all the major actors in the volume's unfolding plot meet beneath the ceiling of the painting: Pamela herself; her movie-producer lover of the moment, Glober; her future lover, Gwinnett; and her always cuckolded husband, Widmerpool. The painting, in turn, depicts "three main figures" (TK, 83): a reclining naked man with an erection; a naked, hesitating woman near his couch; and a cloaked man about to sneak away (TK, 83–85). The text transforms this visual work of art into a dramatic tale by an intricate weave of narrating methods: the teller-observer's own vivid word-painting, the viewers' excited dialogue about Tiepolo's ceiling, and Professor Emily Brightman's learned exposition. Within this composite second-level narrative, the Lydian king, Candaules, has arranged for Gyges, his chief military officer, to spy on the naked beauty of the queen as Candaules has sex with her, but she suddenly glimpses the hidden voyeur. And in Dr. Brightman's addendum to what the painting shows, the vengeful queen has Gyges kill Candaules and ascend the throne himself as her husband (TK, 85–87). By an idiosyncratic reaction to the painting, Pamela all but reveals its secret resemblance to her own quirky sex life. She denies that Candaules's essential motive had anything to do with displaying the naked beauty of his queen. "What are you talking about? What the King wanted was to be watched screwing" (TK, 88). In volume eleven's climactic scene, Pamela discloses that, during her sex with Ferrand-Sénéschal, she noticed her husband "watching through the curtain" (TK, 261).

The convergence of the Candaules-Gyges myth and Pamela's own love life is complicated, however, by a skein of distinctions and even of reversals—yet another way of insisting upon a subtle distance between two narrative levels. If the husband in the myth is a sexual exhibitionist, Widmerpool, in fact, shuns sex with his wife and spies instead on her sex with other men (TK, 37, 262)—a voyeurist equivalent to Gyges in the painting. Within the Candaules-Gyges myth, the voyeur becomes the queen's second king, but Ferrand-Sénéschal collapses and dies in his frustrating sexual efforts with a frigid nymphomaniac (TK, 262). If Tiepolo's queen has her husband later murdered, Pamela kills merely her husband's reputation (TK, 261–63). Like the Lydian queen, Pamela takes on a new paramour, Professor Russell Gwinnett, but only at the price of her own instant death (TK, 269, 270). And at that fleeting moment, Gwinnett supplants Glober instead of her husband. Amusingly enough, in the final few pages, the text inserts a self-referential comment about the lack of a perfect fit between the myth and the story line—an objection expressed by Nick's friend, Moreland: "No, it doesn't really work . . . —the bearings are more general than particular, in spite of certain striking resemblances . . ." (TK, 270). If we connect these "general" "bearings" with the well-known idea of a Freudian "primal scene," the surface differences appear rather less decisive, however, than basic "striking resemblances." On a level of adult perversity, both *Candaules and Gyges* and *Temporary Kings* reenact an archetypal experience: a child's first awareness of his parents' sexual coupling. Freudian tensions seem very near the surface when Moreland connects the story line and also the myth with two quite familiar sexual anecdotes, both of them sadomasochistic, hoary, and even rather whorish: a man's castration by a pair of strange women and another man's subjection to an audience of secret voyeurs during sex with a female stranger (TK, 273–75). A universal human trauma underlies the story of *Temporary Kings* as well as of *Candaules and Gyges*.

Although the painting exists only in the text, the myth itself derives from other written narratives.[6] Dr. Brightman explicitly cites two modern literary analogues: a conte by Gautier stressing the king's artistic motives and one by Gide stressing instead the politics of master and vassal (TK, 88–89): These two variants are illustrative of the myth's wide range. Gwinnett conflates Tiepolo's imaginary masterpiece with a few actual Tiepolos, most notably *Iphigenia*—"not unlike" his *Candaules and Gyges* "in composition" (TK, 43). The web of mythic connections becomes even more complex with Gwinnett's quirky excitement over the sacrificial death of the beautiful Iphigenia (TK, 22). This connects with a scandal from his undergraduate past. As a young necrophiliac, he had broken in to see, and maybe to caress, the body of a girl suspected of having killed herself, very possibly for him (TK, 49, 50). He also virtually salivates over the memory of a photograph that made it appear as if Glober "was lying" inside of his young wife's grave (TK, 64). And Gwinnett misinterprets bizarrely the Ferrand-Sénéschal scandal—Powell's counterpart of *Candaules and Gyges*—as sex after death rather than before. "The implication is she was in bed with this Frenchman after he was dead" (TK, 45). In effect, both Gwinnett and Pamela interpret their favorite Tiepolos rather like Rorschach tests. By the volume's conclusion, however, he has somehow induced Pamela to sacrifice herself to his own necrophilia, to discard her *Candaules and Gyges* for his version of *Iphigenia*. This network of allusions to paintings and to myths swirls in a complicated pattern around the volume's still center: the Tiepolo ceiling.

Besides these intricacies of narrating method and also of interlaced myths, an extraordinary embedding of many voyeuristic levels, one inside the other, further complicates the scene both in and out of the painting. If Gyges watches the queen and Candaules as well, the viewers of the painting, in turn, watch Gyges and also the two lovers—a voyeur observed by other voyeurs. For his part, Nick looks at both the ceiling and at Pamela herself as she peers up at the painting. In a sense, too, as narrator, Nick looks back in time on his own act of watching. And the reader becomes the ultimate voyeur, gazing, along with Nick, at the viewers of the painting and also at the painting's voyeuristic scene. In spite of the episode's emotional intensity, it remains oddly distanced from a sense of fictional presence by a web of complications rather like those of a Chinese box puzzle.

In chapter three as well, complexities of telling create a sense of distance in a most explosive episode. To begin with, a number of characters meet within Nick's line of vision: characters with a role in Pamela's later story. The old amateur painter, Tokenhouse, has shadowy connections with her husband's espionage (TK, 126, 141, 146,

176). Glober escorts Miss Ada Leintwardine as a hint of his impending break with Pamela (TK, 128–29). A briefly appearing couple, Odo and Rosie Stevens (TK, 159–69), will give the London party at which Pamela denounces her husband. But the chapter's most startling episode—her rendezvous with Gwinnett in San Marco Basilica—is relayed, after a time lapse, by both Gwinnett's reticent telling and the narrator's own laconic questions. Dressed in nunlike black, Pamela led Gwinnett to the church's "darkest" corner, spoke of the lure of religion, and then suddenly pounced (TK, 157–58):

> "She grabbed hold of me," he said.
> "You mean—"
> "Just that."
> "By the balls?"
> "Yeah."
> "Literally?"
> "Quite literally." (TK, 158)

Within this voyeuristic volume, the San Marco scene blocks the reader off from any direct vision. Instead we get a dialogue after the fact—a string of questions and answers. This roundabout way of telling deflects our attention from the sexy scene itself to Gwinnett's embarrassment and Nick's curiosity.

Chapter four creates other effects of distance in its own spectacular climax—Pamela's naked raid on Gwinnett—by enclosing its narrating act with a second telling and also within a third. As a teasing visual prelude, Nick first recounts his own visit to the scene—the Bagshaw household where Gwinnett later rooms—long before the episode itself. In his description of the place, Nick vividly relates how the ultimate eyewitness of Pamela's nude intrusion—Bagshaw's old father—ambles in, sees Nick, and leaves apologetically: old Bagshaw's dress rehearsal for his later confrontation with an undressed femme fatale (TK, 181–82). This preview helps the reader to visualize details of the actual subsequent performance—an event distanced by many complex layers. Old Mr. Bagshaw tells young Mr. Bagshaw, who eventually tells Nick. Additional particulars issue from yet another narrating chain, as Bagshaw's two stepdaughters relate what they saw to Bagshaw, who later informs Nick (TK, 191–95). Nick also hears some preliminary rumors from nameless other sources who must have got it all from Bagshaw, who himself arrived to view things only after Pamela's exit (TK, 191, 195, 199).

Many basic aspects of Pamela's naked foray remain wrapped in mystery. When old Mr. Bagshaw wanders downstairs and sees her without her clothes on, has she just had a sexual encounter with

Gwinnett, perhaps an unsuccessful one? How did she enter in the first place? From where does she retrieve her clothes before she slips away? And does she really murmur about Gwinnett's "dead woman" or something about his "death wish"? Expressions of uncertainty dot the whole composite telling: "may not have," "could have been," "the narrative lacks absolute positiveness," "may also," and "just what happened at this stage is not at all clear" (TK, 191–96).

The uncertainty arises from the lack of key details within the narrating chain, from the blurring effects of several time lapses, and from sheer creative lying. The stepdaughters apparently relate their own story right after Pamela leaves, and old Mr. Bagshaw tells his version the next morning. An immeasurable delay occurs, however, before his son tells anything to Jenkins. The text even hints that Nick's principal source here, Bagshaw, may not have told him anything till after Pamela's death. "By the time Bagshaw told the story himself, a good deal had happened to give opportunity for improving its framework, accentuating high-spots of the narrative" (TK, 195). In other words, he may have invented such striking details as Pamela's departing comment about a "dead woman" or "death wish" to match Pamela's later suicide. Given the uncertainty of this very wayward telling, Pamela's naked pursuit of Professor Russell Gwinnett becomes yet another voyeuristic episode obscured from the reader's sight.

As chapter five builds toward the volume's biggest climax amid rumors of Widmerpool's treason, Nick provides his own direct impression of the Stevenses' musical party. But the climax itself—Pamela's double-barreled exposé of her husband's having spied on her own sexual acts as well as on his country—remains enclosed in labyrinthian tellings. With indirect discourse mainly but also with direct quotation, Nick, at secondhand, mixes slightly varying eyewitness accounts by supersensitive Moreland and tough Odo Stevens. To add to the distance of this complex retelling, Nick provides his own after-the-fact speculations as he weighs both versions. In spite of a split-level narrating source, Nick himself tries for a kind of synoptic unity that will somehow permit the climax to emerge. Outside the Stevenses' house, Pamela warms up for her shocking grand finale by revealing to a crowd of departing guests, including Glober and his present girlfriend, that this movie-magnate lover keeps "a charming little cushion with hair snipped from the pussies of ladies he's had" (TK, 258)—Pamela, of course, among them. Then she turns her fire on Widmerpool and tells how he maneuvered her into sex with Ferrand-Sénéschal and watched it through a curtain until her French lover "croaked in bed" unexpectedly (TK, 261). Last of all, she discloses not only the details of Widmerpool's spying but also his method for saving his skin: the betrayal of the dead man's secrets, both sexual and treasonous (TK, 262–63). As the scene explodes into ultimate commotion, Glober punches Widmerpool (TK, 263–65), and departing Pamela announces "that none of us would see her again" (TK, 266). Although this constitutes the climax of volume eleven's plot, we see it all as if through the wrong end of a telescope—*tēle* plus *skopos* meaning watcher at a distance—or what Joyce might have called a *tell-a-scope*.

Chapter six's laconic and indirect telling of Pamela's lurid death opens up an even more complete sense of distance between events and the narrating web than in any previous climax. Roughly one year after Pamela's as-yet-unmentioned suicide, a letter from Gwinnett summarized by Nick mentions Glober's car-crash death but not the death of Pamela, except for a vague comment about mortality's ubiquitousness (TK, 267–69). In effect, the only eyewitness to Pamela's self-sacrifice keeps his mouth discretely shut. Nick's own first account of this unseen event conceals all visual details and merely hints at what happened:

> He [Gwinnett] did not, of course, disclose whether he had "known" Pamela's condition before she came to the hotel. . . .
> The fact is, Gwinnett must have known. Otherwise there would have been no point in Pamela making the sacrifice of herself, to herself. . . . The sole matter for doubt, in the light of inhibitions existing, not on one side only, was whether, at such a cost, all had been achieved. One hoped so. (TK, 269)

Not only does Nick's source remain unidentified (Gwinnett, after all, has told him nothing), but Nick's own speculations are teasingly vague: "Pamela's condition" (dying from a nameless self-inflicted cause?) and "all had been achieved" (mutual orgasm?). Because the narrator's discretion almost matches Gwinnett's own, only Moreland's cross-examining of Nick reveals the final secret:

> "You really think she took the overdose, told him, then. . . ."
> "What else could have happened?"
> "Literally dying for love."
> "Death happened to be the price. The sole price." (TK, 270; the ellipses appear in the original text)

Within a volume of multiple voyeurisms, no one, not even the reader with all his special privileges, spies on "the primal scene" between Pamela and Gwinnett. Although we finally know what happened, we never see it happen but learn it merely through indirect hints. Here we have the acme of the reverse-telescope principle: the more emotionally intense and significant a scene, the further that it slips from direct narrating view. In this most extreme of actions, this catastrophe of catastrophes, the visibility of events drops to almost zero.

Just as in volume ten, volume eleven's well-made plot exists side by side with a much larger pattern—one that cuts across time and the isolated sequence and requires awareness of *A Dance* as a whole. Within *Temporary Kings* itself, in fact, this cross-volume pattern builds to a powerful climax at the very same time that the plot approaches its own dramatic climax. Thus, in chapter four, right after Pamela's nude exhibition, Nick attends an army reunion and, in a very emotional scene, hears the details of Stringham's wartime death, a nostalgic reminder of a long-lost friend (TK, 201, 204–9). If its pathos matches the excitement of Pamela's misadventures, the reunion scene depends for its ultimate effect on the reader's firm recall of vanished days and years after nearly three thousand pages.

As the fifth chapter sweeps towards its climax—Pamela's revelation of her husband's misdeeds—the tale's reinsertion of long-absent characters itself approaches an emotional crescendo. A whole troop of figures come back from the past at the Stevenses' fateful party: from volume five, androgenous Norman Chandler (TK, 226, 237, 239, 247–48); from volume three, the very odd couple of Stripling and Mrs. Erdleigh (TK, 241–46, 253–54, 256, 259–61); and most importantly of all, from volume five and elsewhere, Nick's old best friend, Moreland, and a ring of acquaintances from Moreland's own past. His mistress-companion, Audrey, escorts him, but they both feel unease at the unexpected presence of Moreland's ex-wife, Matilda, whom he really still loves (TK, 227–29). And Moreland and Audrey too, though not the serene Matilda, wince at the sudden reappearance of a man named Carolo (TK, 238–41): back in volume five, he had run off with Audrey and caused her husband's suicide (CCR, 203, 216–17), yet in an even earlier time not directly described in *A Dance*, Carolo had been married to Matilda (CCR, 157–59). Amid these many echoes from very distant years, Moreland alludes enigmatically to an unforgettable character from perhaps *A Dance*'s finest comic scene: "I remember, years ago, a man who kept on quoting Omar at that party of Mrs. Foxe's, after my Symphony" (TK, 249). The unnamed "man" was Stringham, although in that scene at the end of volume five, he quoted from the "Rubáiyát" just a single time and, in fact, out of Moreland's earshot (CCR, 168). Only a reader with almost total recall can appreciate this glimpse of a long-vanished moment. Moreland himself feels so overcome by all this rich nostalgia that he coughs apoplectically and ruefully foretells the headline of his own obituary:

"MUSICIAN DIES OF NOSTALGIA" (TK, 230). Yet at the chapter's end, this connoisseur of "auld lang syne" becomes a chief eyewitness of Pamela's big scene. As a result, the cross-volume pattern from the past and the self-contained plot of the present converge with a sudden click.

In the final chapter as well, a last twist of plot mingles and blends with a moving reenactment of a long-vanished friendship. The story of Pamela's suicide appears within the context of Nick's revived closeness to a now dying Moreland (TK, 269–77). The past is recaptured as the present rolls on. Throughout *Temporary Kings*, the climaxes of plot combine with subtle interweavings of persons and events from many distant volumes, so that this single sequence cannot be read alone without much loss of poignancy.

Like many of *A Dance*'s other enigmatic titles, *Temporary Kings* withholds some of its significance until the volume's end. The words first appear in Nick's amused comment on the claim that he will "live like a king" in Venice: "One of those temporary kings in *The Golden Bough*, everything at their disposal for a year or a month or a day— then execution?" (TK, 7). Of course, Nick's joke applies to the later-described painting of *Candaules and Gyges*, for Gyges kills the king in the midst of all his pleasures, his entrancement with his wife. As Moreland notes towards the volume's last pages, Pamela's humiliation of Lord, if not King, Widmerpool (TK, 38–40) serves as the equivalent of killing the king (TK, 269–70). And Pamela, as Moreland adds, "was the Queen all right" (TK, 269). One of her lovers, Louis Glober, has a kinglike manner and appearance: "those of a . . . 'Byzantine emperor. . . .'"; (TK, 66), "a ruler with a touch of exoticism in his behaviour and tastes" (TK, 79). As the almost royal Pamela and the almost royal Glober stretch out on adjoining "console seats" to better view the painting, the narrator hints slyly at their subsequent fates:

> At first sight, the pair seemed to have fainted away; alternatively, met not long before with sudden death in the vicinity, its abruptness requiring they should be laid out in that place as a kind of emergency mortuary, just to get the bodies out of the way pending final removal. (TK, 76)

By the end of the volume, they will both be dead—poignant reminders of love's mortality—unlike the story of the painting where only the man dies. A symmetrical reversal of *Candaules and Gyges* occurs in the case of Pamela and Gwinnett. Here the woman dies at once while the man lives on. Love itself endures for a mere flickering moment till Pamela's overdose snuffs out her life. Behind the often splendid comedy of volume eleven lies a basic melancholy, a fundamental sadness about the brevity of eros and of human existence as a whole. In this broader sense of the title, we are all, at best, temporary kings.

Hearing Secret Harmonies

As the story line moves closer and closer to its end, the narrator's emotional distance from all that he relates grows more pronounced. This man who came of age in the 1920s now describes the late 1960s and early 1970s, a psychedelic world no longer his own, filled with rioting college students and bizarre hippie cults in beads, robes, or sometimes just their skins. Nick becomes further distanced from the plot by his quite restricted role as a member of the audience instead of a performer in the volume's eerie doings. Many climactic scenes derive still greater distance through tellings within tellings and, in one particular case, through Nick's remote viewing of televised events. And just as in the two preceding volumes, a well-structured plot coexists here with a series of complex recalls or fictional reinsertions from earlier parts of A Dance. Yet in spite of these complicated obstacles of distance, the narrative wisdom of Nick's old age allows him to find a highly dramatic story in the actions that take place beyond his line of vision.

In chapter one Nick gets a firsthand glimpse of the menacing Scorpio Murtlock—Widmerpool's later adversary—and also of Murtlock's hippie cult. Because Fiona Cutts, the Jenkinses' niece, has joined this ragged band, Nick and his wife allow its caravan to stop overnight on their property (HSH, 7–11). As Murtlock talks with them, Nick detects something "dubious, if not actively criminal," in this would-be hippie messiah (HSH, 4)—an uneasy suspicion increased by a very wide gap between two generations. Extraordinarily enough, Nick never again speaks a single word to Murtlock, a central figure in the plot.

In chapter two, Nick's first look at Widmerpool after "nearly ten years" occurs through the twentieth century's ultimate contrivance for long-distance viewing: ubiquitous TV (HSH, 41, 44). While the Jenkinses watch their set, a ceremony installing Widmerpool as the chancellor of a "newish" university appears on the evening news (HSH, 40–41, 43). The rapid-fire action so blurs on the screen that Nick at first mistakes what he sees: the just-appointed chancellor in a "crocodile" procession, two human beings "of indeterminate sex" emerging from the crowd, "some sort of a scuffle," one or two "objects" flipping through the air, "a flimsy poster . . . with illegible

words," "the sound of singing or chanting," and the sudden disap-
pearance of Widmerpool himself (HSH, 44–45). It takes Nick several
moments to sort out all this muddle as "some sort of . . . demonstra-
tion" (HSH, 44–45). When Widmerpool appears again on the screen
with bloodlike "stains" "dripping from" seemingly "appalling"
"wounds" on his "head," "face," "shoulder," and apparently
"mangled" "hands," Nick believes him "the victim of . . . atrocious
assault" (HSH, 45). Only when the televised chancellor congratulates
the two "on being such excellent shots with the paint" does Nick
understand his mistake (HSH, 46): paint rather than blood and
clownish humiliation instead of physical gashes (ironically, though,
Widmerpool will die at the end in circumstances every bit as
clownish). The rest of the chancellor's on-camera statement becomes
too garbled for Nick to report—"barely intelligible owing to" Widmerpool's "excitement" (HSH, 46). On top of all this distancing and
blurring of events, Nick hears a later account of the program from a
literary acquaintance with only one eye: "Salvidge . . . had a glass
eye—always impossible to tell which" (HSH, 48). He nevertheless
supplements his less-than-perfect vision with another person's story of
just what occurred: J. G. Quiggin has identified the paint-throwing
students as his own twin daughters, Amanda and Belinda (HSH, 48).
Not only does this episode reach Nick and the reader over faraway air
waves as a rather jumbled image from a quite remote location—an
image also complicated by a one-eyed observer and a secondhand
report—but the broadcast tape itself presents a greatly delayed scene.
When Nick and the others see it, it has already vanished into the past
and become the evening news, distanced from the viewers by both
time and space.

Two other important things happen in this chapter. Nick tells of his
role as a judge for the Magnus Donners literary award (HSH, 49–58,
65–70) at which, after many years, he will later see Widmerpool in the
flesh again rather than just as a TV apparition. And the chapter
introduces a significant turn in the plot that nevertheless remains on
the edges of the text: another judge for the Donners prize, Gibson
Delavacquerie, describes his son's former love for Fiona Cutts,
Murtlock's pretty disciple (HSH, 78–80), but not till long afterwards
does this judge reveal his own erotic interest in his son's ex-girlfriend
(HSH, 174–85). Oddly enough, given the importance of this genera-
tional tangle, Nick never once sees his niece and Delavacquerie together. An account of their elusive semiromance drifts across to Nick
through complex secondhand tellings.

In chapter three's fine comic scene at the Donners Prize dinner,
Nick watches Widmerpool's eerie performance from an uninvolved

vantage point as a member of the audience. Yet, as a Donners Prize judge and also as an old acquaintance of Widmerpool's, Nick does possess inside information that helps him understand Widmerpool's crazy antics. Nick knows that the Donners Prize nomination of Gwinnett's Trapnel biography, *Death's-Head Swordsman*, worried all the judges about the possible objections of Widmerpool himself, a Donners fund trustee, to the treatment of the Trapnel-Pamela affair by a writer who later became Pamela's last lover as well as the cause of her self-inflicted death (HSH, 70–75, 86–87). Here, in a curious way, Nick has unique privileges of knowledge, for in volumes ten and eleven, he recounted the same events that appear in the prize biography: a strange example of mirror-image narratives, one imaginary and one that we have read. Yet even as a privileged spectator, Nick remains completely unprepared for Widmerpool's bizarre carryings on. Lord Widmerpool has agreed to Gwinnett's getting the prize on the simple condition that Widmerpool himself attend the award along with a pair of very surprising guests, the paint-throwing Quiggin twins. (HSH, 87–90). With absolute astonishment, Jenkins observes Lord Widmerpool's surreal behavior: an uninvited after dinner speech proclaiming himself ecstatically as Pamela's cuckolded husband. (HSH, 107–12).

In spite of everything that Jenkins does know, he remains merely a spectator on the edge of all these grotesque events. Indeed, he spends the greater part of his time identifying performers for an uninformed other member of the audience (HSH, 102–8). Widmerpool sits "at the far end of the dinning-room" (HSH, 107), so that Nick has a view of the comic denouement from a playgoer's equivalent of the very last row. In fact, the Quiggin girls' climactic explosion of a stink bomb in the midst of Widmerpool's speech underscores Nick's physical distance from the action, for "a dark cloud" envelops Widmerpool immediately, but only "some" smoke reaches Nick's own table, although the "awful smell" drifts across to him as it permeates the entire hall (HSH, 112). Even at the chapter's end, when he does draw close to Widmerpool, Nick still plays essentially a passive spectator role. He stands nearby as the crazed Lord Widmerpool invites Professor Gwinnett to visit a hippie commune that Widmerpool has founded in his own country home, but neither Nick nor Widmerpool speaks a word to one another in spite of their ancient acquaintanceship (HSH, 114–16). Like a playgoer who has chanced to wander onto the stage, Nick stands apart from the actual performers.

In observing chapter four's new twist of the plot, Nick remains again just a spectator—literally, here, a member of a very large audience at the Royal Academy banquet (HSH, 119–20). After a fellow audience member, one Canon Paul Fenneau, reveals a long acquaintanceship with Murtlock (HSH, 129–34)—Windmerpool's future nemesis—Lord Widmerpool himself approaches and asks Fenneau to help him get in touch with this hippie messiah (HSH, 135–40). Throughout this whole episode, Widmerpool speaks to Nick just once and only indirectly—"Nick Jenkins here will vouch for my credentials" (HSH, 135)—and Nick does not utter anything to Widmerpool. In spite of Jenkins's presence at this rather crucial scene, he nevertheless remains on the outside of things.

Although chapter five contains a dramatic account of a strange new turn in the Widmerpool story, it reaches the reader through a distancing network of tellings within tellings. To begin with, Nick's acquaintance from wartime, former aide-de-camp Greening, reveals he has learned from a nameless third observer that a fresh "lot" of "odds and sods" has arrived at Widmerpool's commune (HSH, 142–43). But Nick fails to interpret these hints correctly until he hears thirdhand specifics, transmitted this time from Widmerpool through Gwinnett through Delavacquerie and then to Nick himself, who at last tells the reader. Murtlock, it turns out, has united his group with Widmerpool's hippie commune in order to take it over, and Gwinnett has joined them as a scholarly observer of Neo-Jacobean behavior (HSH, 146–48). Further reports drift across to Nick, and the strange grows even stranger. At an outdoor rally protesting the threatened desecration by industrial interests of a prehistoric sepulchre called The Devil's Fingers, Nick hears farmer Gauntlett's amused retelling of farmer Dunch's terrified account of the previous night's incomprehensible events alongside these ancient ruins. Dunch saw four horned "devils" dancing stark naked between the two stone pillars. From each distinct layer of telling, three quite different versions merge: Dunch feels sure that he has seen evil spirits, Gauntlett keeps an open mind but finds Dunch's cowardice "excessively funny," and Nick thinks it all a practical joke (HSH, 156–59). Yet a few pages later, a secondhand narrating act supplements this thirdhand telling as Nick hears from Gwinnett what he actually saw. He reveals that Widmerpool, Murtlock, Fiona, and the others performed a stag-mask dance around The Devil's Fingers in the nude and that, no matter what their sex, each tried to copulate with each—a grotesque parody of Poussin's great painting of *A Dance*. But the "ritual" use of a knife "got out of hand" as Murtlock slashed Widmerpool (HSH, 161–69). Although the cult invokes the spirit of the long-dead Trelawney from previous volumes (HSH, 167), the shocking events at The Devil's Fingers seem worlds away from Nick and all the other volumes—an almost galactic distance achieved, in part, by the indirect telling but also by a sense of absolute strangeness.

Not until some three months later does Nick get a final secondhand account completing the stag-dance episode. Delavacquerie reveals that Murtlock contacted Gwinnett with Delavacquerie's own help—help yielded up at a very special price: the release of Fiona from the cult, so that she might live with him at least for a while (HSH, 178–84). This important complication remains so thoroughly distanced that it almost seems to float beyond the margins of the text.

In the dramatic sixth chapter, Nick once again observes events as a member of the audience, this time as a wedding guest. Oddly enough, the two characters who wed—Clare Akworth and Sebastian Cutts (HSA, 187)—never appear directly anywhere in *A Dance*, not even in the description of their very own wedding. And a much more surprising and significant marriage, that of Gwinnett with Fiona, happens on the day before in a void between the chapters, unseen by Nick himself or by any other character (HSH, 196–98). At the Cutts-Akworth wedding, amid very many guests from earlier in *A Dance*, Nick appears almost more concerned about the past than involved in present happenings. Indeed, he came to the wedding mainly to visit Stourwater Castle, the scene where it takes place but also, of course, a highly important setting in volumes two and six (HSH, 187). Nevertheless, when the hippie cult comes jogging past Stourwater itself led by Lord Widmerpool (HSH, 210–12), he and Nick do engage in their only extended talk in all of volume twelve (HSH, 213–18, 221–25). But the embarrassed Nick longs to slip away quickly, so that other respectable guests will not link him in their minds with Widmerpool's appalling derangement (HSH, 220, 221). In fact, Fiona's invitation to the whole hippie crew to join the wedding party so dismays Nick that he feels great relief when Widmerpool hurries away into the crowded hall ahead of Nick himself (HSH, 219–20, 225). He has very good reasons for shunning Lord Widmerpool who has just confessed in tears about a certain unnamed "penance" (homosexual acts?) forced on him by Murtlock with the group's special ward, the grotesque old Bithel, a drunken homosexual hounded from the army many years before by Widmerpool's maliciousness (HSH, 216–18). Indeed, Widmerpool enters the wedding celebration in order to perform an alarming new penance, for he has just learned from Nick that grandfather Akworth, one Sir Bertram, is the very same person from public school days whom Widmerpool got expelled for a homosexual flirtation (HSH, 221–25). Like a viewer at the theater with nothing to do except to watch the show, Nick refrains from raising even his little finger to avert a catastrophe that he clearly sees ahead. Although he stands right next to Akworth for quite some time before Widmerpool's actual approach, Nick gives his host no warning (HSH, 227–28). For example, Nick does not exclaim, "Watch out, Sir Bertram! Crazy Kenneth Widmerpool has crashed your party and aims to embarrass you in some appalling way." Neither when Widmerpool addresses Sir Bertram in "an almost beseeching voice" nor when the weird penitent falls abruptly on his hands and knees in front of Akworth nor even when Flavia Wisebite tumbles virtually "on top of" Widmerpool's "crouching body" does Nick do anything but watch (HSH, 228–31). In the chaos that follows—the disturbing arrival of Murtlock, his enraged rebuke to Widmerpool, and Murtlock's stern refusal to let Widmerpool leave the cult—Nick says not a word but merely looks on, though he knows some details that might mitigate the blame (HSH, 233–38). In the midst of this frenzied climax, the detached Nick Jenkins seems almost like an observer from outermost space.

The last chapter's dramatic conclusion reaches Nick and the reader secondhand through extended conversation with *A Dance*'s most inarticulate eyewitness: a drunken and horrified Bithel. Before his fumbling narrating act, Nick learns the full background of the Murtlock-Widmerpool conflict through questions and answers with a dropout from the cult, Barnabas Henderson. Henderson notes the real "turning point" in this struggle of would-be messiahs: the arrival in the group of Bithel and Widmerpool's humiliating penance with this withered old drunkard whom he absolutely loathes—an event that breaks even Widmerpool's stubborn will (HSH, 257–62). With a certain ironic appropriateness, the unintentional cause of Widmerpool's own downfall—pathetic old Bithel—mumbles out our only account of the ultimate catastrophe. On the morning of the day now ending (HSH, 267, 271), Murtlock forced a badly ailing Widmerpool to join all the others in a naked jog. Widmerpool struggled insanely to lead the entire pack and collapsed and died in his efforts—a reductio ad absurdum of his lifelong drive for power. (HSH, 265–69). Yet this horrendous climax, this appalling reenactment of clumsy schoolboy jogging from Widmerpool's first appearance on *A Dance*'s opening pages (QU, 3–4), remains oddly distanced by Bithel's incoherence. This supremely ineffective teller keeps "muttering to himself, his voice at times entirely dying away" (HSH, 266), and he even slips once into a drunken stupor until prodded to continue (HSH, 266–67). To increase the indirection of this indirect account, one of those interrogating Bithel, Henderson, has much less interest in Widmerpool himself than in confirming the legality of Bithel's possession of a Modigliani drawing once owned by Pamela Widmerpool that Henderson now appropriates (HSH, 263–64, 270). Along with everything else, this digressive line of questioning removes the sense of presence from this episode of culminating strangeness and death.

As we noted early in our study, *Hearing Secret Harmonies*—volume twelve's title—serves as a mystic's euphemism for death (see the final paragraph of this study's second chapter). Nick specifically recalls Myra Erdleigh's saying, back in volume eleven, from "the alchemist, Thomas Vaughan," that a "soul" departed from life "ascends" to the heights, "hearing secret harmonies" (HSH, 36; TK, 246). Delavacquerie later identifies a fundamental tenet of Murtlock's "cult": "that Harmony, Power, Death, are all more or less synonymous" (HSH, 147). Furthermore, its members wear "T-shirts" "inscribed with the single word *HARMONY*" (HSH, 6). In his own pathetic struggles to attain that state (HSH, 267), Widmerpool finds its synonym of death, but his last moments hardly seem harmonious.

If *harmony* means death, *Hearing Secret Harmonies* itself contains an intermittent roll call of frequent obituaries—brief secondhand accounts of dying and death. To get the full effect of this relentless mortality, one must have read all of the previous volumes and have known the many characters who now slip away. The first mention of a decease comes almost at the beginning: the homosexual Hugo Tolland, last seen in volume ten (BDFR, 83–85), has now become "rather a sad figure after the death of his partner, Sam" (HSH, 8). Three pages later, we learn that Eleanor Walpole-Wilson has died (HSH, 10–11)—Norah Tolland's former roommate, not seen since volume four (LM, 90–97). And with "a more than usually acute consciousness of human mortality," the narrator adds two other names to the list: the military attachés from volume nine, Bobrowski and Philidor, both killed in car accidents (HSH, 19–20). The deaths grow still more insistent within the second chapter: the same clairvoyant who first equated *harmony* with death, Myra Erdleigh herself (HSH, 35–36); the old don, Sillery, just short of a hundred (HSH, 49), a character going back all the way to volume one (QU, 175); Prince Theodoric (HSH, 49), who goes back to volume two (BM, 122); Jacky Bragadin from volume eleven (HSH, 57; TK, 112, 114–15); the old survivor, Jeavons (HSH, 60–61), introduced in volume four (LM, 21–22); Jimmy Stripling from volume one and later (HSH, 81–83; QU, 79–81); and Geraldine "Tuffy" Weedon Farebrother (HSH, 83), who cropped up here and there since *A Dance*'s first volume (QU, 57–59). Not a single chapter passes without at least one death, usually more than one, and most often in allusions to printed obituaries. In the third chapter, we hear of the sudden death of Gypsy Jones Craggs (HSH, 104)—back in the second volume, a figure of importance—and of Baby Wentworth too (HSH, 104–5), introduced also in that early volume (BM, 125–26). Chapter four tells us that Bagshaw's wife has died (HSH, 122)—a woman whom he married offstage in volume ten (BDFR, 37)—and, in addition, that Gwatkin has succumbed (HSH, 134), Nick's army commander in volume seven. Chapter five reports the assassination of Colonel Flores, the second husband of Jean (MP, 233–34)—Nick's old love—and also the death of Gauntlett's dog, Daisy (HSH, 153), who played a role in the plot at the start of volume twelve (HSH, 20–22). In chapter six, the news of one particular loss touches Nick most deeply: the death of Matilda Donners (HSH, 189–90), the former wife of Nick's best friend, the long-vanished Moreland. And the very last chapter reserves to itself death's most grotesque encroachments: Quentin Shuckerly—author of "the best queer novel since" such and such (TK, 8)—"battered to death" in New York's Greenwich Village (HSH, 244), and Widmerpool himself in his fatal naked run (HSH, 265–69). Indeed, this aged would-be hippie's indirectly presented death is the volume's last obituary and death's last tolling in *A Dance*.

This mortality-haunted volume contains some significant literary allusions to death, both from actual books and from those invented by the text: Ariosto's "waters of Oblivion" in *Orlando Furioso*'s valley of lost things (HSH, 32–33); the late St. John Clark's imaginary novel, *Dust Thou Art* (HSH, 39); Gwinnett's imaginary Trapnel biography, *Death's-Head Swordsman*, as well as Gwinnett's projected second work, *The Gothic Symbolism of Mortality in the Texture of Jacobean Stagecraft* (HSH, 70, 99); and Bertram Akworth's reading from First Corinthians—"For now we see through a glass, darkly; but then face to face" (HSH, 193). Shifting to the realm of painting, the volume's final sentence transforms the image of Poussin's *A Dance* from some three thousand pages earlier—" . . . The Seasons, hand in hand and facing outward, tread in rhythm" (QU, 2) into an ultimate canvas of death: "Even the formal measure of the Seasons seemed suspended in the wintry silence" (HSH, 272). By its very title, *Hearing Secret Harmonies* whimsically supports or perhaps gently mocks the assertions of life after death in the sayings of St. Paul and also of unsaintly Myra Erdleigh. Yet the web of allusions hints as well at a somewhat less mystical hope: retrieval and survival through art. As the narrator reminds us, "well disposed swans" in *Orlando Furioso* pluck up vanished name "tablets" from "the waters of Oblivion" and fly them on "to the Temple of Fame" (HSH, 33). The dust-thou-art author, the late St. John Clarke, gets resurrected through the miracle of a TV documentary, but its organizer-promoter makes an antitheological epigram out of a liturgical "resurrection of the body and life everlasting": "the television of the body brings the sales everlasting" (HSH, 38). "By a process" that Nick considers "every bit as magical as any mutations on the astral plane" (HSH, 86), Gwinnett's *Death's Head Swordsman* resuscitates Trapnel from the waters of literary oblivion.

Gwinnett sees his study of death-filled Jacobeans as a means of making them new by showing their connection with twentieth century writers such as X. Trapnel himself, the author, after all, of *Camel Ride to the Tomb* (HSH, 67). Then, too, the deader-than-dead paintings of old Mr. Deacon arise from the dust of discarded old art and take on life again (HSH, 244–51). Through a hinted-at extension of this subastral "magic," *A Dance* itself revives on its many printed pages a large group of characters, most of them long vanished, from a half-century span and more. In other words, the textual narrating of the fictional body brings reading everlasting.

In the second chapter of *Hearing Secret Harmonies*, the narrator suggests why *A Dance*'s storytelling grows more and more spectacular in its closing three volumes of middle and old age. "Growing old," he says, has "two compensations":

> [First,] a vantage point gained for acquiring embellishments to narratives that have been unfolding for years beside one's own, trimmings that can even appear to supply the conclusion of a given story. . . . [And second,] a keener perception of the authenticities of mythology, not only of the traditional sort, but . . . the latterday mythologies of poetry and the novel. (HSH, 30)

This aging narrator-character has observed or heard of the final pratfalls, catastrophes, and deaths of most of those in *A Dance*, unlike the young Jenkins who was ignorant of their ends. Just as significantly, Nick has come to see how the stories in old and recent mythologies resemble those of the Stringhams, Morelands, Pamelas, Trapnels, and Widmerpools of the world. Jenkins has, accordingly, filled the last three volumes with a dense web of mythological reference and allusion. He has learned, in effect, that every good new story resembles an old good one, a kind of literary eternal recurrence. At the end of *A Dance*, Nick has become a supreme storyteller—not only a hearer of "secret" harmonies but also of those "harmonies" that ring out loud and clear in big climactic scenes. In this sense, *A Dance to the Music of Time* forms a narrative about how to form such a narrative from the bits and pieces of life as well as art.

Once we have finished all twelve volumes, we can at last clearly see how the marvelous overall title hints at the complex riches of the work itself. Through a paradox that applies to fictional titles in general, *A Dance of the Music of Time* refers to the world of the text but also to the text as text itself—a dual signification with special importance here. In the realm of the sequence's imaginary universe, the metaphor of the title applies to intersecting lives—those of Nick's friends and acquaintances as they move in and out of their various social orbits in patterns of repetition or thematic variation. The metaphor of *A Dance* also refers to the verbal work itself, a time-consuming pattern of words across twelve volumes. The reader's "dance" consists of the slow accumulation of connections and meanings, as the eye moves across some three thousand pages of linear prose. The writer's own "dance" takes a very different form: the twenty-five-year creation of the words on those pages and the slow tracing out of intricate repetitions, complex variations, and surprising turns of plot in a vast open-ended structure. Both "dances" require large amounts of time. Early in volume twelve, the narrator amusingly contrasts "a painter's Time" (Poussin's)—"in a sufficiently unhurried frame of mind to be sitting down"—with "a writer's Time" (Ariosto's): "appallingly restless" and engaged "in an eternally breathless scramble with himself" (HSH, 33). This whimsical contrast recalls Gotthold Lessing's famous distinction between painting as a space art of rest and single instants and literature as a time art of "signs which succeed each other" and convey successive actions.[7] Powell's overall title itself contains the space art of painting and two nonliterary temporal ones, dance and music, both of which can unfold only within time. Although Powell's title comes from painting's spatial realm (specifically, Poussin's great canvas), neither painting, dance, nor music has any true existence within the text itself except within its language. And more than most examples of written art, Powell's *Dance* depends on a huge expanse of time—one that envelops all the characters; the author himself; and also, of course, the reader. Powell's long task of writing has in turn left his readers with the virtually endless pleasures of exploring and reexploring some one million words of a complex literary masterpiece, a fascinating choreography of language.

Notes

Chapter 1. An Introduction to Anthony Powell

1. As the narrating act begins, Henchman has disappeared for "two or three years," and a later reference to Henry Kissinger's *White House Years* marks the earliest possible story-line date as 1979 (FK, 7–8, 50).

Chapter 2. Narrative Open-Endedness and Closure

1. See Henry R. Harrington, "Anthony Powell, Nicolas Poussin, and the Structure of Time," *Contemporary Literature* 24, no. 4 (Winter 1983): 433–34; Rudolf Bader, *Anthony Powell's "Music of Time" as a Cyclic Novel of Generations* (Bern: Francke, 1980), 14.

2. One must not confuse the instance of narrating with the various moments of the story or story line (the moments of the *diegesis* in Gérard Genette's term). We can, for example, locate the episode of the auction at roughly 1945 and the episode of the Deacon Centenary Exhibition at 1971, but the narrating that describes them we can locate only imperfectly by a very broad span: the *A Buyer's Market* voice, between 1945 or so and late 1971, and the *Hearing Secret Harmonies* voice, no earlier than the close of autumn 1971 and perhaps much later. On these concepts and terms, see Gérard Genette, *Narrative Discourse: An Essay in Method*, trans. Jane E. Lewin (Ithaca: Cornell University Press, 1980), 215–27.

3. Harrington *does* assume a unitemporal voice throughout all of *A Dance* except the last three paragraphs that follow the second street-workmen scene and conclude the novel: "Two thousand nine hundred and forty-seven pages later the reader learns that at the narrative's beginning [the first street-repair scene] Nick has just stepped from Henderson's art gallery in the neighborhood of Berkeley Square [the locale of the second street-repair scene]. . . . To the extent that Nick begins his narrative where he ends it, the movement of the novel is the reader's illusion."—Harrington, "Anthony Powell, Nicholas Poussin," 433. And Bader comes to the same assumption about a unitemporal voice: ". . . Towards the end of the 'Music of Time,' Nick manages to marry his little flash-backs with the one big flash-back that comprises the whole sequence novel. . . . All of a sudden we have the impression that Nick does no longer start his flash-back from the time level of his narrative, but from the time when he sits at his desk writing the last volume of Anthony Powell's sequence novel."—Bader, *Anthony Powell's "Music of Time,"* 53.

4. Marcel Proust, *Remembrance of Things Past*, trans. C. K. Scott Moncrieff and Andreas Mayor (New York: Random House, 1970), 2: 1001 and 1002, quoted by Genette, *Narrative Discourse*, 223.

5. Cf. Genette, *Narrative Discourse*, 220.

6. Neil Brennan, *Anthony Powell*, Twayne's English Authors Series no. 158 (New York: Twayne, 1974), 132.

7. Letter of Anthony Powell to Robert L. Selig, 2 July 1986.

8. This self-restriction about rewriting a previously published volume or, in fact, a whole work already published is not self-evident in the general game of writing. One might cite at random F. Scott Fitzgerald's complex revision of his already published novel *Tender is the Night* or James Joyce's elaboration of the "Aeolus" episode of *Ulysses* from the *Little Review* version. See Arthur Mizner, *The Far Side of Paradise: A Biography of F. Scott Fitzgerald* (Boston: Houghton Mifflin, 1949), 240; Michael Groden, *"Ulysses" in Progress* (Princeton: Princeton University Press, 1977), 98–114.

9. I must thank Anthony Powell himself for calling attention to this British-American divergence in his note to me of 2 July 1986.

10. On Dickens's serialization habits, see John Butt, *Pope, Dickens, and Others: Essays and Addresses* (Edinburgh: Edinburgh University Press, 1969). For Anthony Trollope's rather different serialization habits, see Mary Hames, *Writing by Numbers: Trollope's Serial Fiction* (Cambridge: Cambridge University Press, 1987). See also J. Don Vann, *Victorian Novels in Serial* (New York: Modern Language Association of America, 1985).

11. See chapter three of this study.

12. The one article explicitly concerned with *A Dance* as a "sequence novel" ignores Powell's method of building upon already published episodes. See Dan McLeod, "Anthony Powell: Some Notes on the Art of the Sequence Novel," *Studies in the Novel* 3, no. 1 (Spring 1971): 44–63. Some critics, incidentally, prefer the French term *roman-fleuve* to *sequence novel*.

13. The most dismissive comment comes from James Tucker: "I do not think very much can be learned from putting ADTTMOT alongside Proust's *A la recherche du temps perdu*."—James Tucker, *The Novels of Anthony Powell* (New York: Columbia University Press, 1976), 4.

14. On *iterative* and *pseudo-iterative* narrative, see Genette, *Narrative Discourse*, 116, 121–23. For a detailed examination of the *iterative* and *pseudo-iterative* in *A Dance*, see chapter three of this study.

15. On this simultaneous composition of *A la recherche*'s beginning and end, see Paul Ricoeur, *Time and Narrative*, vol. 2, trans. Kathleen McLaughlin and David Pellauer (Chicago: Universty of Chicago Press, 1985), 134. Except for his all-important prewritten ending, Proust did, of course, value those novelistic patterns achieved by a patchwork of creative afterthoughts. See Genette, 148–49.

16. Letter of Anthony Powell to Robert L. Selig, 2 July 1986.

17. See, for example, Tucker, *Novels of Anthony Powell*, 188: "After HSH there can be no doubt that ADTTMOT is primarily about Widmerpool. Simply, he is the only character of any sizeable development left alive." In spite of Tucker's overstatement here, he does make a valid point about Widmerpool's importance. Yet similar reasoning could suggest that Flaubert's *Madame Bovary* is mainly about Charles—a highly unconvincing critical conclusion from Charles's mere survival beyond the heroine's death.

18. On these tendencies of the *Bildungsroman* genre, see F. K. Stanzel, *A Theory of Narrative*, trans. Charlotte Goedsche (Cambridge: Cambridge University Press, 1984), 81–82.

19. *Hearing Secret Harmonies* echoes this passage in other places besides its title: see, particularly, pp. 36 and 134. The Vaughan alluded to its Thomas Vaughan (pen name: Eugenius Philalethes) (1621–66)—an alchemist and hermetic philosopher.

Chapter 3. Frequency, Analogy, and Eternal Recurrences

1. See Genette, *Narrative Discourse*, 116–21.
2. See Randolph Quirk et al., *A Comprehensive Grammar of the English Language* (London: Longman, 1985), 140, 228, 541–50.
3. Marcel Proust, *Volume Two: The Guermantes Way; Cities of the Plain*, trans. C. K. Scott Moncrieff and Terence Kilmartin (New York: Random House, 1981), 455–501.
4. Lewis Carroll, *Alice in Wonderland: Authoritative Texts of Alice's Adventures in Wonderland, Through the Looking-Glass, The Hunting of the Snark, Backgrounds, Essays in Criticism*, ed. Donald J. Gray (New York: W. W. Norton, 1971), 58.
5. On the *pseudo-iterative* see Genette, *Narrative Discourse*, 116–17, 121–23.
6. Ibid., 122.
7. Friedrich Nietzsche, *The Will to Power*, trans. Walter Kaufmann and R. J. Hollingdale, ed. Walter Kaufmann (New York: Random House, 1967), 549.
8. For a relevant but somewhat different discussion of Nietzsche's eternal recurrence, see J. Hillis Miller, *Fiction and Repetition: Seven English Novels* (Cambridge: Harvard University Press, 1982), 5–6. See also the important French work cited by Miller: Gilles Deleuze, *Logique du sens* (Paris: Les Editions de Minuit, 1969), 302.
9. Nietzsche, *Will to Power*, 548. Walter Kaufmann points out that Nietzsche considers this life-accepting "consolation" from eternal repetition as one that most human beings would reject in horror. See Walter Kaufmann, Translator's Introduction, *The Gay Science: With a Prelude in Rhymes and an Appendix of Songs*, by Friedrich Nietzsche, trans. with commentary by Walter Kaufmann (New York: Vintage, 1974), 14.
10. See, for example, *Encyclopaedia Britannica*, 14th ed., s.v. "Metempsychosis."
11. In his four-volume *Memoirs*, Powell himself touches upon many of these resemblances.
12. Anthony Powell, introd., *Invitation to the Dance: A Guide to Anthony Powell's Dance to the Music of Time*, by Hilary Spurling (Boston: Little, Brown, 1978), p. vii.

Chapter 4. Departures from Chronological Order

1. See "Instance of Narrating and Time of the Story Line" in chapter two of this study.
2. Cf. Powell's own not entirely favorable comment about his fifth published novel, *What's Become of Waring* (1939): "an almost railway time-table approach to chronology" (FMT, 75).
3. The narrator accurately calls this topic "fashionable" at about this period. Cf., for example, Charles Mauron, "On Reading Einstein," trans. T. S. Eliot, *The Criterion* 10 (1930–31): 23–31.
4. On the relative infrequency of flash-forwards as compared to flashbacks in Western narrative literature, see Genette, 67. He uses the terms *analepses* and *prolepses* for flashbacks and flash-forwards respectively.
5. On the frequent use of this type of flashback in Proust, see Genette, *Narrative Discourse*, 57–58.
6. On the relationship of literature's quasi-eternities to St. Thomas Aquinas's concept of *aevum*—a realm of neither time nor eternity yet participating in both—see Frank Kermode, *The Sense of an Ending: Studies in the Theory of Fiction* (London: Oxford University Press, 1966), 69–74. For other examples in *A Dance* of verbatim or

near-verbatum flashbacks, see BM, 146—CCR, 172; BM, 201—KO, 115; KO, 193—VB, 114; LM, 19—SA, 166; SA, 78—SA, 169; QU, 75—SA, 196; MP, 211—TK, 102; KO, 112—HSH, 45; QU, 87—HSH, 83. On Proust's use of this device, see Genette, *Narrative Discourse*, 55–56.

7. For a less complicated example of an *iterative* flash-forward, see SA, 17.

8. For various other flash-forwards with traditional narrative uses, see KO, 72; MP, 65; MP, 71–72; HSH, 32.

9. For a forerunner of Myra Erdleigh and her true fortune-telling in a very early novel of Powell's, cf. Baroness Puckler in *Venusberg* (V, 23–25).

10. The ironic ambiguity in *A Dance*'s treatment of the planchette episode has some resemblance to the half-ironic depiction of a séance in another time novel—Thomas Mann, *The Magic Mountain (Der Zauberberg)*, trans. H. T. Lowe-Porter (New York: Alfred A. Knopf, 1939), 822–57.

11. Bader, for one, falls into precisely this confusion: ". . . Nick . . . sits at his desk writing the last volume of Anthony Powell's sequence novel."—Bader, *Anthony Powell's "Music of Time,"* 53.

12. Tucker, *Novels of Anthony Powell*, 110.

13. For Powell's own willingness to subject psychic predictions to an empirical test, see MD, 190–91.

Chapter 5. Youth

1. Genette, *Narrative Discourse*, 94–95.

2. Sigmund Freud, "Creative Writers and Day-Dreaming," *Jensen's "Gradiva" and Other Works*, vol. 9 (1906–08) of *The Standard Edition of the Complete Psychological Works of Sigmund Freud*, trans. under the general editorship of James Strachey in collaboration with Anna Freud, assisted by Alix Strachey and Alan Tyson (London: Hogarth Press and the Institute of Psycho-Analysis, 1959), 150–51 and see also 143–50.

3. Marcel Proust, *Volume Two: The Guermantes Way; Cities of the Plain*, trans. C. K. Scott Moncrieff and Terence Kilmartin (New York: Random House, 1981), 432–568; *Volume Three: The Captive; The Fugitive; Time Regained*, trans. C. K. Scott Moncrieff, Terence Kilmartin, and Andreas Mayor (New York: Random House, 1981), 957–1107.

4. For an amusing account by Powell of how he thought of the title, see FMT, 38.

5. On Powell's "men of will" and "men of sensibility," see Arthur Mizner, "A Dance to the Music of Time: The Novels of Anthony Powell," *Kenyon Review* 22 (Winter 1960): 79–92.

Chapter 6. Maturity

1. Carroll, *Alice in Wonderland*, 63–65. Tenniel's illustration on page 64 of the two odd-looking footmen has special relevance here.

2. Mrs. Simpson was divorced from her husband on 27 November 1936, and the question of whether King Edward VIII would be allowed to marry a divorcée and also keep his throne occupied the Cabinet, Parliament, and the press until the King's announced abdication on 10 December 1936. Pages 135–66 of *Casanova's Chinese Restaurant* cover the period of the Abdication crisis.

3. Powell shares Moreland's interest in Giacomo Casanova. In a 1961 review of a new Casanova biography, Powell mentions his own "complete re-reading within the

last year" of the "million" or so words of the Great Lover's *Memoirs:* a remark that indicates his previous acquaintance with the whole long work. See Anthony Powell, "Casanova Told the Truth," review of *Casanova: A Biography Based on New Documents,* by J. Rives Childs, the *Daily Telegraph and Morning Post,* 30 June 1961, p. 18. And he reasserts admiration for Casanova's *Memoirs* in the closing volume of his own (SAAG, 86–89).

4. See "Analogy and Eternal Recurrences" in chapter three of this study.

5. M. M. Bakhtin, "Forms of Time and of the Chronotope in the Novel: Notes toward a Historical Poetics," *The Dialogic Imagination: Four Essays,* ed. Michael Holquist, trans. Caryl Emerson and Michael Holquist (Austin: University of Texas Press, 1981), 95.

6. Ibid., 243–46.

7. Henry Fielding, *The History of Tom Jones,* ed. R. P. C. Mutter (Harmondsworth, Middlesex, England: Penguin, 1966), 444–61, 469–93.

8. The description of Albert's hotel as a seagoing ship echoes volume three's comparison of Giles's old hotel, the Ufford, to "a large vessel moored in the street,"— AW, 1.

Chapter 7. Wartime

1. For Powell's own general admiration of Kipling, see Anthony Powell, "The Genius of Rudyard Kipling," *Daily Telegraph and Morning Post,* 30 December 1965, p. 10—an encomium run on the editorial page in honor of Kipling's centenary.

2. Rudyard Kipling, *Puck of Pook's Hill,* in *Kipling: A Selection of His Stories and Poems,* ed. John Beecroft (Garden City, N.Y.: Doubleday, 1956), I: 460–97.

3. Allusions to female homosexuality also appear in *A Dance,* though not quite as often as the masculine kind: e.g., the Norah Tolland and Eleanor Walpole-Wilson ménage (LM, 32–33, 90–91); a lesbian nightclub entertainer, Heather Hopkins (LM, 94–97, 183, 185–86); and the possibly bisexual Ada Quiggin (TK, 91–92).

4. In Powell's own *Memoirs,* he extends this little joke by a label that he puts on a photograph of himself and other attachés posing with Montgomery: "Montgomery puts the Military Attachés in the picture," here a self-reflexive pun as well as a cliché (FMT, photograph opposite 167).

5. As another sly little touch, volume nine does include one army bureaucrat who is actually a semiprofessional metaphysician; head liaison officer David Pennistone is writing a book on Descartes or Gassendi (MP, 6).

Chapter 8. Middle and Old Age

1. As Powell informs us in his memoirs, he modeled Trapnel on Julian Maclaren-Ross—the author of *Love and Hunger* and *The Weeping and the Laughter* (see SAAG, 5–13, and the photograph of Maclaren-Ross opposite 22).

2. On the impossibility of pinning down precisely the one major narrating lag within *A Dance,* see the opening pages of this study's second chapter.

3. See chapter two of this study. For a cogent discussion of *A Dance's* use of painting, see John Bayley, "The Ikon and the Music," in *The Album of Anthony Powell's Dance to the Music of Time,* ed. Violet Powell, with Preface by Anthony Powell ([London:] Thames and Hudson, 1987), 9–22. Bayley's essay introduces an "album" of paintings, illustrations, and photographs on *A Dance's* pictorial themes.

4. Genette, *Narrative Discourse*, 235–36. Genette, of course, refers to the fiction of Alain Robbe-Grillet—prominent in the French "New Novel" of the 1950s and 60s.

5. From a reference to the secret trial "earlier in the year" of Imre Nagy in Hungary (executed on 16 June 1958), we can date the year of the story line as 1958 (TK, 188). And we can place Trapnel's death at 1952 or 1953, for Nick last saw the novelist some ten years earlier than the Venice conference—in about 1948—and Nick dates this last Trapnel encounter at "four or five years before" Trapnel's death (TK, 24). We can also calculate that he died five or six years after Pamela left him—a rather long slide toward ruin and collapse.

6. The specific version of the myth utilized by Powell comes from Herodotus. See *The History of Herodotus*, trans. George Rawlinson, in *Great Books of the Western World*, ed. Robert Maynard Hutchins et al. (Chicago: Encyclopaedia Britannica, 1952), 6:2–3. Another form of the myth, one without any voyeurism, appears in Book 2 of Plato's *The Republic*. See Plato, *The Republic*, trans. Benjamin Jowett, in *Great Books* 7: 311–12. When Powell wrote *Temporary Kings*, he thought, mistakenly, that no important artist had depicted *Candaules and Gyges*, although he later learned that several had, including the Flemish painter Jacob Jordaens (1593–1678). See Powell's own Preface to *The Album*, and the photograph of the Jordaens on p. 135.

7. Gotthold Lessing, *Laocoön or the Limits of Painting and Poetry: With Incidental Illustrations on Various Points in the History of Ancient Art*, in Lessing's *Laocoön, Nathan the Wise, Minna Von Barnhelm*, trans. and ed. William A. Steel (London: J. M. Dent, 1930), 55. Lessing's *Laokoon* was first published in German in 1766.

Bibliographical Afterword

In view of Anthony Powell's very great achievement, one should like to supplement a study such as this with a richly rewarding bibliography, especially on *A Dance*. Yet not many full-length studies on Powell exist in or out of print. If numerous reviewers and critics have noted his high distinction, few have explored his works in detail. In this postmodern era, when academic critics often prefer literary theory instead of analysis of any specific work, they have tended to ignore *A Dance*'s complexities and even its challenges to narrative theory.

One very helpful book has, nevertheless, appeared: Hilary Spurling, *Handbook to Anthony Powell's Music of Time* (London: Heinemann, 1977), published in the United States as *Invitation to the Dance: A Guide to Anthony Powell's Dance to the Music of Time* (Boston: Little, Brown, 1978). Essentially a dictionary or alphabetized account of *A Dance*'s many characters, this painstaking reference work lists, in addition, allusions to the various arts in *A Dance*, to its various places, and also provides a synopsis as well as a chronology of all twelve volumes. A quite recent book on Powell's masterpiece, Violet Powell, ed., *The Album of Anthony Powell's Dance to the Music of Time*, Preface by Anthony Powell, Introduction by John Bayley ([London]: Thames and Hudson, 1987), is a collection of pictures illustrating the themes of all twelve volumes—a delightful memento for those who have already read them, though not a guide for beginners. Bernard Bergonzi, *Anthony Powell*, rev. and enl. Ian Scott-Kilvert, Writers and their Work, no. 221 (Essex: Longman, 1971), is a very perceptive study, yet even its revised edition appeared four years earlier than *A Dance*'s own completion and so, necessarily, lacks full perspective on Powell's finest work. Neil Brennan, *Anthony Powell*, Twayne's English Authors Series no. 158 (New York: Twayne, 1974), serves up many useful gleanings from Powell's own book reviews, but Brennan leans too heavily on an autobiographical reading of *A Dance*, and through no fault of his own, must exclude the final volume, which had not yet come out. John Russell, *Anthony Powell: A Quintet, Sextet, and War* (Bloomington: Indiana University Press, 1970), offers some insights of value but remains a preliminary view, as *A Dance*'s final three volumes had not yet seen the light. Robert K. Morris, *The Novels of Anthony Powell*, Critical Essays in Modern Literature (Pittsburgh: University of Pittsburgh Press, 1968)—also unavoidably incomplete on *A Dance*—dismissively exaggerates its "classical" approach to time's vast complexities. James Tucker, *The Novels of Anthony Powell* (New York: Columbia University Press, 1976), does take in *A Dance*'s closing volume, though only very briefly, but this unsympathetic study attempts, injudiciously, to measure Powell's achievement by a rough-and-ready yardstick of naturalism and realism. Most notably, Tucker frowns on all uses of coincidence—a fundamental premise of the novel itself. Rudolph Bader, *Anthony Powell's "Music of Time" as a Cyclic Novel of Generations* (Bern: Francke, 1980), is a clumsily written, pedantic, and often banal study with the highly dubious thesis that *A Dance* consists of a cycle of generations.

As for the many articles gradually accumulating in yearly dribs and drabs since the mid-1950s, much of this work is peripheral and scrappy. Still, one should like to single out a few of these articles as having special merit. John Bayley provides one of the first insightful looks at Powell's completed sequence: "A Family and its Fiction" [review of HSH], *Times Literary Supplement*, 12 September 1975, pp. 1010–12. Frederick R. Karl eloquently asserts the greatness of *A Dance:* "Sisyphus Descending: Mythical Patterns in the Novels of Anthony Powell," *Mosaic: A Journal for the Comparative Study of Literature and Ideas* 4, no. 3 (1971): 13–22. And T. P. Wiseman skillfully explores *A Dance*'s pattern of allusions to "antiquity": "The Centaur's Hoof: Anthony Powell and the Ancient World," *Classical and Modern Literature: A Quarterly* 2, no. 1 (1981): 80–92. Yet in spite of such high spots as these, the body of critical work on Anthony Powell remains, on the whole, disappointing. In view of the greatness of *A Dance* itself, one might well echo the wartime Churchill, a figure, of course, alluded to in the World-War-II volumes (VB, 179, 239; MP, 193–95): Never in recent literary history has so much great fiction by any one author evoked such a scanty response.

Select Bibliography

Primary Sources

An asterisk following the publication date indicates an edition used in this study. Within this bibliography, only the first British and American editions of Powell's works are listed except in two important groups. First, in the case of Powell's five earliest novels, Heinemann's new editions are also included, because they are used in this study. Second, in the case of *A Dance to the Music of Time* itself, Little, Brown's first editions of its four *Dance* trilogies are also included, because of their importance in Powell's publishing history. One should further note the availability, at the time of this study's publication, of all twelve volumes of *A Dance* in both British and American paperback editions: London: Fontana, 1968–83; New York: Popular Library, 1985–86.

1. Novels Prior to *A Dance to the Music of Time* (listed chronologically)

Afternoon Men. London: Duckworth, 1931; London: Heinemann, 1952*; Boston: Little, Brown, 1963.

Venusberg. London: Duckworth, 1932. *Two Novels: Venusberg, Agents & Patients*. New York; Periscope-Holliday, 1952. *Venusberg*. London: Heinemann, 1955*.

From a View to a Death. London: Duckworth, 1933. *Mr. Zouch: Superman; From a View to a Death*. New York: Vanguard, 1934. *From a View to a Death*. London: Heinemann, 1945*.

Agents and Patients. London: Duckworth, 1936. *Two Novels: Venusberg, Agents & Patients*. New York: Periscope-Holliday, 1952. *Agents and Patients*. London: Heinemann, 1955*.

What's Become of Waring. London: Cassell, 1939; London: William Heinemann, 1953*; Boston: Little, Brown, 1963.

2. Individual Volumes of *A Dance to the Music of Time* (listed chronologically)

A Question of Upbringing: A Novel. London: Heinemann, 1951*; New York: Charles Scribner's, 1951. *A Dance to the Music of Time: A Question of Upbringing, A Buyer's Market, The Acceptance World*. Boston: Little, Brown, 1955.

A Buyer's Market: A Novel. London: Heinemann, 1952*; New York: Scribner's Sons, 1953. *A Dance to the Music of Time: A Question of Upbringing, A Buyer's Market, The Acceptance World*. Boston: Little, Brown, 1955.

The Acceptance World: A Novel. London: Heinemann, 1955*; New York: Farrar, Straus & Cudahy, 1955. *A Dance to the Music of Time: A Question of Upbringing, A Buyer's Market, The Acceptance World*. Boston: Little, Brown, 1955.

At Lady Molly's: A Novel. London: Heinemann, 1957*; Boston: Little, Brown, 1957. *A Dance to the Music of Time: Second Movement; At Lady Molly's, Casanova's Chinese*

Restaurant, The Kindly Ones. Boston: Little, Brown, 1962.

Casanova's Chinese Restaurant: A Novel. London: Heinemann, 1960*; Boston: Little, Brown, 1960. *A Dance to the Music of Time: Second Movement; At Lady Molly's, Casanova's Chinese Restaurant, The Kindly Ones*. Boston: Little, Brown, 1962.

The Kindly Ones: A Novel. London: Heinemann, 1962*; Boston: Little, Brown, 1962. *A Dance to the Music of Time: Second Movement; At Lady Molly's, Casanova's Chinese Restaurant, The Kindly Ones*. Boston: Little, Brown, 1962.

The Valley of Bones: A Novel. London: Heinemann, 1964*. *The Valley of Bones*. Boston: Little, Brown, 1964. *A Dance to the Music of Time: Third Movement; The Valley of Bones, The Soldier's Art, The Military Philosophers*. Boston, Little, Brown, 1968.

The Soldier's Art: A Novel. London: Heinemann, 1966*. *The Soldier's Art*. Boston: Little, Brown, 1966. *A Dance to the Music of Time: Third Movement; The Valley of Bones, The Soldier's Art, The Military Philosophers*. Boston: Little, Brown, 1968.

The Military Philosophers: A Novel. London: Heinemann, 1968*. *A Dance to the Music of Time: Third Movement; The Valley of Bones, The Soldier's Art, The Military Philosophers*. Boston: Little, Brown, 1968. *The Military Philosophers*. Boston: Little, Brown, 1969.

Books Do Furnish a Room: A Novel. London: Heinemann, 1971*; Boston: Little, Brown, 1971. *A Dance to the Music of Time: Fourth Movement; Books Do Furnish a Room, Temporary Kings, Hearing Secret Harmonies*. Boston: Little, Brown, 1976.

Temporary Kings: A Novel. London: Heinemann, 1973*. *Temporary Kings*. Boston: Little, Brown, 1973. *A Dance to the Music of Time: Fourth Movement; Books Do Furnish a Room, Temporary Kings, Hearing Secret Harmonies*. Boston: Little, Brown, 1976.

Hearing Secret Harmonies: A Novel. London: Heinemann, 1975*. Boston: Little, Brown, 1975. *A Dance to the Music of Time: Fourth Movement; Books do Furnish a Room, Temporary Kings, Hearing Secret Harmonies*. Boston: Little, Brown, 1976.

3. Novels Subsequent to *A Dance to the Music of Time* (listed chronologically)

O, How the Wheel Becomes It!: A Novel. London: Heinemann, 1983*; New York: Holt, Rinehart & Winston, 1983.

The Fisher King: A Novel. London: Heinemann, 1986; New York: W. W. Norton, 1986*.

4. Memoirs (listed chronologically)

Infants of the Spring. Vol. 1 of *To Keep the Ball Rolling: The Memoirs of Anthony Powell*. London: Heinemann, 1976*. *Infants of the Spring*. Vol. 1 of *The Memoirs of Anthony Powell*. New York: Holt, Rinehart and Winston, 1977.

Messengers of Day. Vol. 2 of *To Keep the Ball Rolling: The Memoirs of Anthony Powell*. London: Heinemann, 1978*. *Messengers of Day*. Vol. 2 of *The Memoirs of Anthony Powell*. New York: Holt, Rinehart and Winston, 1978.

Faces in My Time. Vol. 3 of *To Keep the Ball Rolling: The Memoirs of Anthony Powell*. London: Heinemann, 1980*. *Faces in My Time*. Vol. 3 of *The Memoirs of Anthony Powell*. New York: Holt, Rinehart and Winston, 1980.

The Strangers All Are Gone. Vol. 4 of *To Keep the Ball Rolling: The Memoirs of Anthony Powell*. London: Heinemann, 1982*. *The Strangers All Are Gone*. Vol. 4 of *The Memoirs of Anthony Powell*. New York: Holt, Rinehart and Winston, 1983.

5. Other Books (listed chronologically)

John Aubrey and His Friends. London: Eyre & Spottiswoode, 1948; New York: Charles Scribner's Sons, 1948.

Two Plays: The Garden God, The Rest I'll Whistle. London: Heinemann, 1971; Boston: Little, Brown, 1971.

6. Articles and Parts of Books (listed chronologically)

Although Powell wrote regular book reviews for the *Daily Telegraph* (1936, 1956–) and occasional ones for the *Spectator* (1937–39, 1946) and for *Punch* (1953–58), the following section includes, from these, only one book review and a newspaper literary editorial—both directly cited in this study.

Introduction to *Bernard Letters, 1778–1824*, by Sir Thomas Andrew Francis Bernard, Thomas Barnard (Bishop of Limerick), Lady Anne Barnard Lindsay; edited by Anthony Powell, 9–16. London: Duckworth, 1928.

"The Wat'ry Glade." In *The Old School: Essays by Diverse Hands*, edited by Graham Greene, 147–62. London: Jonathan Cape, 1934.

Introduction to *Novels of High Society from the Victorian Age*, selected by Anthony Powell, pp. vii–xv. London: Pilot Press, 1947.

Introduction and Notes to *Brief Lives: And Other Selected Writings*, by John Aubrey, edited by Anthony Powell, pp. ix–xxii, xxiii–xxx, 387–97. London: Cresset Library, 1949; New York: Scribner's, 1949.

"Leaves from Notable New Diaries—Kingsley Amis." In *The Pick of Punch: An Annual Selection*, edited by Nicholas Bentley, 22. London: Deutsch, 1957; New York: Dutton, 1957.

"Casanova Told the Truth." Review of *Casanova: A Biography Based on New Documents*, by J. Rives Childs. *Daily Telegraph and Morning Post*, 30 June 1961, p. 18.

Preface to *The Complete Ronald Firbank*. London: Duckworth, 1961. *The Complete Ronald Firbank*, 5–16. Norfolk, Conn.: New Directions, 1961.

"Some Questions Answered." *The Anglo-Welsh Review* 14 (1964): 77–79.

"Reflections on the Landed Gentry." In *Burke's Genealogical and Heraldic History of the Landed Gentry*, pp. xxv–xxviii. London: Burke's Peerage, 1965.

"Proust as a Soldier." In *Marcel Proust: A Centennial Volume*, edited by Peter Quennell, 149–64. New York: Simon and Schuster, 1971.

Introduction to *Handbook to Anthony Powell's Music of Time*, by Hilary Spurling. London: Heinemann, 1977. *Invitation to the Dance: A Guide to Anthony Powell's Dance to the Music of Time*, pp. vii–viii. Boston: Little, Brown, 1978*.

Preface to *The Album of Anthony Powell's Dance to the Music of Time*, edited by Violet Powell, introduction by John Bayley, 7–8. [London]: Thames and Hudson, 1987.

Secondary Sources

1. Books, Articles, and Parts of Books on Powell (listed alphabetically)

Atkins, John. "Widening Sympathies: Reflections on the Work of Anthony Powell." *Kwartalnik Neofilologiczny* (Warsaw) 22 (1975): 191–205.

Bader, Rudolf. *Anthony Powell's "Music of Time" as a Cyclic Novel of Generations.* Bern: Francke, 1980.

Bayley, John. "A Family and Its Fictions." Review of HSH. The *Times Literary Supplement,* 12 September 1975, 1010–12.

Bergonzi, Bernard. *Anthony Powell.* Revised and enlarged by Ian Scott-Kolvert. *Writers and Their Work* no. 221. Essex: Longman, 1971.

――――. "Anthony Powell." *L. P. Hartley* [and] *Anthony Powell.* By Paul Bloomfield and Bernard Bergonzi, respectively. Writers and Their Work no. 144. London: Longmans, Green, 1962.

――――. "Anthony Powell: 9/12." *Critical Quarterly* 11 (1969): 76–86.

Birns, Margaret Boe. "Anthony Powell's Secret Harmonies: Music in a Jungian Key." *Literary Review: An International Journal of Contemporary Writing* 25, no. 1 (1981): 80–92.

Boston, Richard. "A Talk with Anthony Powell." *New York Times Book Review,* 8 March 1969, 2, 36.

Brennan, Neil. *Anthony Powell.* Twayne's English Authors Series no. 158. New York: Twayne, 1974.

Brooke, Jocelyn. "From Wauchop to Widmerpool." *London Magazine* 7 (September 1960): 60–65.

David, Douglas M. "An Interview with Anthony Powell, Frome, England, June 1962." *College English* 24 (1963): 533–36.

Davis, Robert M. "Contributions to *Night and Day* by Elizabeth Bowen, Graham Greene, and Anthony Powell." *Studies in the Novel* 3 (1971): 401–4.

Ellis, G. U. *Twilight on Parnassus: A Survey of Post-War Fiction and Pre-War Criticism,* 183, 184, 195, 332, 375–94. London: Michael Joseph, 1939.

Flory, Evelyn A. "The Imagery of Anthony Powell's *A Dance to the Music of Time.*" *Ball State University Forum* 17, no. 2 (1976): 51–59.

Glazebrook, Mark. "The Art of Horace Isbister, E. Bosworth Deacon and Ralph Barnby." *London Magazine* 7 (November 1967): 76–82.

Gutierrez, Donald. "The Discrimination of Elegance: Anthony Powell's *A Dance to the Music of Time.*" *Malahat Review* 34 (1975): 126–41.

――――. "The Doubleness of Anthony Powell: Point of View in *A Dance to the Music of Time.*" *University of Dayton Review* 14, no. 2 (1980): 15–27.

――――. "Exemplary Punishment: Anthony Powell's *Dance* as Comedy." *Greyfiar: Siena Studies in Literature* 22 (1981). 27–44.

――――. "Power in *A Dance to the Music of Time.*" *Connecticut Review* 6, no. 2 (1973): 50–60.

Gutwillig, Robert, "A Walk Around London with Anthony Powell." *New York Times Book Review,* 30 September 1962, 5, 30.

Hall, James. "The Uses of Polite Surprise: Anthony Powell." *Essays in Criticism* 22 (1962): 167–83.

Harrington, Henry R. "Anthony Powell, Nicolas Poussin, and the Structure of Time." *Contemporary Literature* 24, no. 4 (1983): 431–48.

Herring, H. D. "Anthony Powell: A Reaction against Determinism." *Ball State University Forum* 9, no. 1 (1968): 17–21.

Jones, Richard. "Anthony Powell's Music: Swansong of the Metropolitan Romance." *Virginia Quarterly Review* 52 (1976): 353–69.

Karl, Frederick R. "Sisyphus Descending: Mythical Patterns in the Novels of Anthony Powell." *Mosaic: A Journal for the Comparative Study of Literature and Ideas* 4, no. 3 (1971): 13–22.

———. "The Still Comic Music of Humanity: The Novels of Anthony Powell, Angus Wilson, and Nigel Dennis." Chapter 13 in *A Reader's Guide to the Contemporary English Novel*. New York: Farrar, Straus, and Cudahy, 1962.

Kermode, Frank. "The Interpretation of the Time: Isherwood and Powell." *Puzzles and Epiphanies: Essays and Reviews 1958–61*, 121–30. London: Routledge and Kegan Paul, 1962.

Leclaire, Lucien A. "Anthony Powell: Biographie Spirituelle d'une Génération." *Etudes Anglaises* 9 (1956): 23–27.

Lindemann, M. D. "Nicholas Jenkins's Bonfire." *English Studies in Africa: A Journal of the Humanities* 26, no. 1 (1983): 27–37.

McCall, Raymond G. "Anthony Powell's Gallery." *College English* 27 (1965): 227–32.

McLeod, Dan. "Anthony Powell: Some Notes on the Art of the Sequence Novel." *Studies in the Novel* 3, no. 1 (1971): 44–63.

McSweeney, Kerry. "The End of *A Dance to the Music of Time*." *South Atlantic Quarterly* 76 (1977): 44–57.

Martin, W. R. "Style as Achievement in Anthony Powell's *The Music of Time*." *English Studies in Africa* 14 (1971): 73–86.

Mizener, Arthur. "A Dance to the Music of Time: The Novels of Anthony Powell." *Kenyon Review* 22 (1960): 79–92.

———. "The Novel and Nature in the Twentieth Century: Anthony Powell and James Gould Cozzens." Chapter 8 in *The Sense of Life in the Modern Novel*. Boston: Houghton, Mifflin, 1964.

Morris, Robert K. *The Novels of Anthony Powell*. Critical Essays in Modern Literature. [Pittsburgh]: University of Pittsburgh Press, 1968.

Piper, William Bowman. "The Accomodation of the Present in Novels by Murdoch and Powell." *Studies in the Novel* 11 (1979): 178–93.

Powell, Violet, ed. *The Album of Anthony Powell's Dance to the Music of Time*. Preface by Anthony Powell. Introduction by John Bayley. [London]: Thames and Hudson, 1987.

Pritchard, William H. "Anthony Powell's Gift." The *Hudson Review* 37, no. 3 (1984): 360–70.

———. "Anthony Powell's Serious Comedy." *Massachusetts Review* 10 (1969): 812–19.

Quesenbery, W. D., Jr. "Anthony Powell: The Anatomy of Decay." *Critique: Studies in Modern Fiction* 7 (1964): 5–26.

Radner, Sanford. "Powell's Early Novels: A Study in Point of View." *Renascence* 26 (1964): 194–200.

———. "The World of Anthony Powell." *Claremont Quarterly* 10, no. 2 (1963): 41–57.

Raymond, John. "Isherwood and Powell." *Listener* 12 (1954): 1067.

Riley, John J. "Gentlemen at Arms: The Generative Process of Evelyn Waugh and Anthony Powell before World War II." *Modern Fiction Studies* 22 (1976): 165–81.

Roudy, Pierre. "Anthony Powell et l'Angleterre Proustienne." *Europe* 49 (1971): 167–73.

Ruoff, Gene W. "Social Mobility and the Artist in *Manhattan Transfer* and *The Music of Time*." *Wisconsin Studies in Contemporary Literature* 5 (1964): 64–76.

Russell, John. *Anthony Powell: A Quintet, Sextet, and War*. Bloomington: Indiana University Press, 1970.

———. "Quintet from the 30s: Anthony Powell." *Kenyon Review* 27 (1965): 698–726.

———. "The War Trilogies of Anthony Powell and Evelyn Waugh." *Modern Age* 16 (1972): 289–300.

Schäfer, Jürgen. "Anthony Powell, *Books Do Furnish a Room*." In *Englische Literatur der Gegenwart, 1971–1975*, edited by Rainer Lengeler, 24–46. Düsseldorf: Bagel, 1977.

Seymour-Smith, Martin. *The New Guide to Modern World Literature*, 295–97. New York: Peter Bedrick Books, 1985.

Spurling, Hilary. *Handbook to Anthony Powell's Music of Time*. London: Heinemann, 1977. *Invitation to the Dance: A Guide to Anthony Powell's Dance to the Music of Time*. Boston: Little, Brown, 1978.

Stone, William B. "Dialogue in Powell's Second Movement." *Modern British Literature* 2 (1977): 85–88.

Swinden, Patrick. *The English Novel of History and Society, 1940–1980: Richard Hughes, Henry Green, Anthony Powell, Angus Wilson, Kingsley Amis, V. S. Naipaul*. New York: St. Martin's, 1984.

———. "Powell's 'Hearing Secret Harmonies.'" *Critical Quarterly* 18, no. 4 (1976): 51–60.

Tapscott, Stephen J. "The Epistemology of Gossip: Anthony Powell's 'Dance to the Music of Time.'" *Texas Quarterly* 21, no. 1 (1978): 104–16.

Tucker, James. *The Novels of Anthony Powell*. New York: Columbia University Press, 1976.

Vinson, James. "Anthony Powell's *Music of Time*." *Perspective* 20 (1958): 146–52.

Voorhees, Richard J. "Anthony Powell: The First Phase." *Prairie Schooner* 28 (1958): 237–44.

———. "*The Music of Time*: Themes and Variations." *Dalhousie Review* 42 (1962): 313–21.

Wilcox, Thomas W. "Anthony Powell and the Illusion of Possibility." *Contemporary Literature* 17 (1976): 223–39.

Wilson, Keith. "Pattern and Process: The Narrative Strategies of Anthony Powell's *A Dance to the Music of Time*." *English Studies in Canada* 11, no. 2 (1985): 214–22.

Wiseman, T. P. "The Centaur's Hoof: Anthony Powell and the Ancient World." *Classical and Modern Literature: A Quarterly* 2, no. 1 (1981): 80–92.

Woodward, A. G. "The Novels of Anthony Powell." *English Studies in Africa* 10 (1967): 117–28.

Zigerell, James J. "Anthony Powell's *Music of Time*: Chronicle of a Declining Establishment." *Twentieth Century Literature* 12 (1966): 138–46.

2. Articles, Books, and Parts of Books on Time and on Time and Narrative (listed alphabetically)

Bakhtin, M. M. "Forms of Time and of the Chronotope in the Novel: Notes toward a Historical Poetics." In *The Dialogic Imagination: Four Essays*, edited by Michael

Holquist, translated by Caryl Emerson and Michael Holquist, 84–258. Austin: University of Texas Press, 1981.

Beneveniste, Emile. "The Correlations of Tense in the French Verb." "The Nature of Pronouns." In *Problems in General Linguistics*, translated by Mary Elizabeth Meek, Miami Linguistics Series no. 8, 205–15, 217–22. Coral Gables, Fla.: University of Miami Press, 1971.

Genette, Gérard. *Narrative Discourse: An Essay in Method*. Translated by Jane E. Lewin. Foreword by Jonathan Culler. Ithaca: Cornell University Press, 1980.

————. *Narrative Discourse Revisited*. Translated by Jane E. Lewin. Ithaca: Cornell University Press, 1988.

Kermode, Frank. *The Sense of an Ending: Studies in the Theory of Fiction*. London: Oxford University Press, 1966.

Mauron, Charles. "On Reading Einstein." Translated by T. S. Eliot. The *Criterion* 10 (1930–31): 22–31.

Mendilow, A. A. *Time and the Novel*. Introduction by J. Isaacs. London: Peter Nevill, 1952.

Meyerhoff, Hans. *Time in Literature*. Berkeley and Los Angeles: University of California Press, 1960.

Miller, J. Hillis. *The Form of Victorian Fiction: Thackeray, Dickens, Trollope, George Eliot, Meredith, and Hardy*. Cleveland, Ohio: Arete Press, Case Western Reserve University, 1979.

Poulet, Georges. *Studies in Human Time*. Translated by Elliot Coleman. Westport, Conn.: Greenwood, 179.

Ricoeur, Paul. *Time and Narrative*. Vols. 1 and 2. Translated by Kathleen McLaughlin and David Pellauer. Vol. 3. Translated by Kathleen Blamey and David Pellauer. 3 vols. Chicago: University of Chicago Press, 1984–88.

3. Miscellaneous Books, Articles, and Parts of Books Utilized in this Study (listed alphabetically)

Butt, John. *Pope, Dickens and Others: Essays and Addresses*. Edinburgh: Edinburgh University, 1969.

Carroll, Lewis. *Alice In Wonderland: Authoritative Texts of Alice's Adventures in Wonderland, Through the Looking Glass, The Hunting of the Snark, Backgrounds, Essays in Criticism*. Edited by Donald J. Gray. New York: W. W. Norton, 1971.

Deleuze, Gilles. *Logique du sens*. Paris: Les Editions de Minuit, 1969.

Fielding, Henry. *The History of Tom Jones*. Edited by R. P. C. Mutter. Harmondsworth, Middlesex, England: Penguin, 1966.

Freud, Sigmund. "Creative Writers and Day-Dreaming." *In Jensen's "Gradiva" and Other Works*, 143–53. Vol. 9 (1906–1908) of *The Standard Edition of the Complete Psychological Works of Sigmund Freud*. Translated under the general editorship of James Strachey in collaboration with Anna Freud, assisted by Alix Strachey and Alan Tyson. London: Hogarth Press and the Institute for Psycho-Analysis, 1959.

Groden, Michael. *"Ulysses" in Progress*, 98–114. Princeton: Princeton University Press, 1977.

Hames, Mary. *Writing by Numbers: Trollope's Serial Fiction*. Cambridge University Press, 1987.

Herodotus. *The History of Herodotus*. Translated by George Rawlinson. In *The History of Herodotus; The History of the Peloponnesian War*. By Thucydides. Vol. 6 of *Great Books of the Western World*. Edited by Robert Maynard Hutchins et al. Chicago: Encyclopaedia Britannica, 1952.

Kipling, Rudyard. *Puck of Pook's Hill*. In vol. 1 of *A Selection of His Stories and Poems*, edited by John Beecroft, 401–531. Garden City, N.Y.: Doubleday, 1956.

Lessing, Gotthold. *Laocoön, or the Limits of Painting and Poetry: With Incidental Illustrations on Various Points in the History of Ancient Art*, 1–110. In *Laocoön, Nathan the Wise, Minnha Von Barhheim*, translated and edited by William A. Steel. London: J. M. Dent, 1930.

Mann, Thomas. *The Magic Mountain* [*Der Zauberberg*]. Translated by H. T. Lowe-Porter. New York: Alfred A. Knopf, 1939.

Mizner, Arthur. *The Far Side of Paradise: A Biography of F. Scott Fitzgerald*, 240. Boston: Houghton Mifflin, 1949.

Nietzsche, Friedrich. *The Will to Power*. Translated by Walter Kaufmann and R. J. Hollingdale. Edited by Walter Kaufmann. New York: Random House, 1967.

Plato. *The Republic*. Translated by Benjamin Jowett. In *The Dialogues of Plato, The Seventh Letter*, translated by Benjamin Jowett and J. Harward, respectively. Vol. 7 of *Great Books of the Western World*. Edited by Robert Maynard Hutchins et al. Chicago: Encyclopaedia Britannica, 1952.

Proust, Marcel. *Remembrance of Things Past*. Translated by C. K. Scott Moncrieff, Terence Kilmartin, and Andreas Mayor. 3 vols. New York: Random House, 1981.

———. *Remembrance of Things Past*. Translated by C. K. Scott Moncrieff and Andreas Mayor. 2 vols. New York: Random House, 1970.

Quirk, Randolph, et al. *A Comprehensive Grammar of the English Language*. London: Longman, 1985.

Stanzel, F. K. *A Theory of Narrative*. Translated by Charlotte Goedsche. Preface by Paul Hernadi. Cambridge University Press, 1984.

Vann, J. Don. *Victorian Novels in Serial*. New York: Modern Language Association of America, 1985.

Index